Teaching and Learning in History

Teaching and Learning in History

Edited by

Gaea Leinhardt
Isabel L. Beck
Catherine Stainton
University of Pittsburgh

LEA LAWRENCE ERLBAUM ASSOCIATES, PUBLISHERS
1994   Hillsdale, New Jersey   Hove, UK

Lawrence Erlbaum Associates, Inc., Publishers
365 Broadway
Hillsdale, New Jersey 07642

Library of Congress Cataloging-in-Publication Data

Teaching and learning in history / edited by Gaea Leinhardt, Isabel
L. Beck, and Catherine Stainton
    p. cm.
  Includes bibliographical references and index.
  ISBN 0-8058-1245-8
  1. History – Study and teaching (Elementary) – United States.
  2. History – Study and teaching (Secondary) – United States.
  3. History – Study and teaching (Higher) – United States.
    I. Leinhardt, Gaea. II. Beck, Isabel L. III. Stainton, Catherine
LB1582.U6T43 1994
907 – dc20   93-34901
                                          CIP

Books published by Lawrence Erlbaum Associates are printed on acid-free paper, and their
bindings are chosen for strength and durability.

Printed in the United States of America
10 9 8 7 6 5 4 3 2 1

To Robert Glaser, whose expansive vision of scientific inquiry in education encouraged the kind of intellectual exploration of a new field—teaching and learning in history—that led to this book.

Contents

Preface

Research on history instruction and learning is emerging as an exciting new field of inquiry and is at an important moment in its development. Several significant studies have been published, special issues of journals have appeared, and conferences devoted to the study of history teaching and learning have been held. Thus, we undertook this volume because the field is at a stage where there is research of sufficient depth and breadth to warrant a collection of representative pieces.

The field of research on history teaching and learning connects both with traditional research on social studies and with recent cognitive analyses of domains such as mathematics and physics. However, the newer research goes beyond these activities as well. Where traditional research approaches to social studies instruction and learning have focused on curriculum, they have avoided the study of purely disciplinary features, the textual components of history and the concomitant demands, and the nature of various learners. Where recent cognitive analyses of mathematics and physics have dealt with misconceptions and knowledge construction, they have avoided topics such as perspective-taking, interpretation, and rhetorical layerings. The new work, by contrast, has been concerned with these issues as well as the careful analyses of the nature of historical tasks (e.g., document interpretation) and the nature of disciplinary and instructional explanations.

The lines of research presented here are both compelling and diverse. The diversity reflected in the chapters extends across topic, setting, and grain size. The range of topics includes questions such as: What affects the quality of teaching? How are historical documents interpreted in the writing of history? How is history explained? What are the classroom demands on an elementary school social studies teacher? What does text accomplish or fail to accomplish in educational settings? How do teachers think about particular topics for history teaching? The settings for the research range from early elementary school through college. The grain sizes of the research range from the paragraph level to complete volumes, and from an hour to several months of classroom instruction. Although much of the research reflects a grounding in, or the influence of, cognitive psychology, not all of it derives from that tradition. Traditions of rhetoric, curriculum analysis, and developmental psychology are also woven throughout the chapters.

We see the volume as a contribution to educational research in a subject matter and as a tool for practitioners concerned with the improvement of instruction in history. We also anticipate that it will contribute to cognitive science. For the most part, cognitive science has limited itself to examining problems of learning that are relatively "clean"—notions of ill-structured domains notwithstanding—acquiring the knowledge of computer programs, solving pulley problems in physics, reasoning in terms of formal logic. These domains do not pose the kind of challenges that multilayered, self-reflective, interpretive, dialectical disciplines such as history and literary interpretation do. Because we view this volume as opening a door, we are not suggesting in any sense that we have provided formal presentations, but we have posed questions that both the cognitive science and educational communities should find engaging.

We chose to arrange the seven chapters in this volume by considering the people who served as the focus of the study. In the first chapter, McKeown and Beck examine text treatment and young people's learning of several core ideas in U.S. history. In their research, they successfully manipulated textual presentations of central historical events to enhance the limited understandings of students. They conclude that students come out of the experience of history with confused ideas about even the simplest of historical notions. Halldén, like McKeown and Beck, also focuses on the issue of understanding and learning, but for older students at the high school level. Halldén's chapter explores the ideas of shared reasoning and the development of understanding in the context of alternative frameworks.

The next two chapters focus on how college-aged students and historians respond to, interpret, and make use of historical documents. They differ from the first two in that their studies focus on deliberately demanding historical texts, not on teaching situations. In chapter 3, Britt et al. look particularly at students' construction of historical causality as they interpret and mentally model both the specific events and the argument itself. Wineburg, in the fourth chapter, continues his existing line of research on different levels of expertise and its impact on the understanding and interpretation of texts. His research, like McKeown and Beck's, is grounded in and builds on theories of reading and textual interpretation.

Greene's chapter also focuses on college-aged learners and continues the ideas of textual response. However, Greene examines how students respond to textual cues in their own production of historical text. Given the realization that history is both multilayered *and* multivoiced, his findings that students include or exclude their own interpretive voice, depending on the cues present in the *request* for text, is suggestive.

In the final two chapters of the volume, Evans and Leinhardt examine history teaching from the perspective of historians' sense of history and teachers' interpretation of it. In chapter 6, Evans considers a typology of historical perspectives and examines teachers' beliefs and actions against these typologies. In the final chapter, Leinhardt reviews a program of research aimed at (a) understanding how the content of history is and has been defined by historians and teachers, (b) understanding how teaching and learning social systems are set up, and (c) finding out how historical phenomena are explained and reasoned about.

ACKNOWLEDGMENTS

The editors gratefully acknowledge grants from the Office of Educational Research and Improvement of the United States Department of Education, and the Mellon Foundation which enabled the production of this book. Leinhardt acknowledges support from the Spencer Foundation, which supported the book's early conceptualization. Leinhardt also wishes to thank Florencia Mallon, John D'Emilio, and the other historians who shared a wonderful year as fellows at the Center for Advanced Studies in the Behavioral Sciences for their conversations that enlightened and shaped the research. Beck would like to acknowledge the many young learners whose various and unique attempts at understanding textbook history awakened her curiosity about the learning process in this domain. Thanks are also due to Judith McQuaide for her early organizational efforts for this project.

—*Gaea Leinhardt*
—*Isabel L. Beck*
—*Catherine Stainton*

CHAPTER 1

Making Sense of Accounts of History: Why Young Students Don't and How They Might

Margaret G. McKeown
Isabel L. Beck
University of Pittsburgh

The English government put on all new taxes and taxed the colonies for stupid stuff like, uh, stamps, all documents where they had a stamp on them, tea tax, like tax on molasses, and, um, quartering tax, stuff like that. And there was breaking into people's houses and searching them and they were just treating the people real bad. And then the people would come to the, uh, North American continent to be free, have freedom of speech and all that.

This is how Lisa, an eighth grader, summarized major events of the Revolutionary period. The account is typical of her peers, average students from a middle socioeconomic status (SES) background, who have been through two rounds of instruction in American history—one in fifth grade and the second, recently completed, in eighth grade. Lisa's account is accurate and contains two themes of significance to the Revolutionary period, the issue of taxation and the desire for freedom. Yet the account shows a focus on the details of taxation without mention of the principle behind it, and the reference to freedom seems limited to a motivation for emigrating rather than a goal for founding a nation.

Although Lisa's historical account is characteristic of many of the eighth graders we interviewed, it actually represents the more knowledgeable students. More than a third of the group gave no information about the goal or outcome of the conflict between Britain and the colonies, and one fourth of the students were unable to name the agents involved.

What factors figure into students' historical knowledge at this point in their schooling? The most prominent is the social studies textbook. This is particularly true for elementary school, where most teachers are not subject-matter specialists, and therefore rely more heavily on standard resources such as commercial textbooks. But why does relying on social studies textbooks leave students' knowledge in this state?

SEEKING THE ROOTS OF PROBLEMATIC KNOWLEDGE

Because textbooks hold such a central place in the social studies curriculum, we undertook an analysis of four elementary social studies textbook series to understand the kind of learning they promote (Beck, McKeown, & Gromoll, 1989). The analysis marked the beginning of a program of research on social studies learning, which had a goal of improving instructional practice.

A foundation of our work was that to affect practice, we needed to understand current practice at a fine-grained level of detail. Our approach to generating a detailed understanding involved integrating recent cognitive theory and research into the study of instructional practice. Just as cognitive psychology is concerned with "getting inside" the process of learning rather than observing the outward manifestations of performance, our interest was with getting inside the instruction so that findings could be understood in relation to the learning process.

Backdrop for Textbook Analysis

Two areas of research served as backdrop for our work: understandings about the nature of the reading process, with emphasis on its interaction with a reader's knowledge, and characteristics of texts that promote or impede comprehension. In regard to a reader's knowledge, recent research emphasizes not only that a lack of knowledge about a topic impedes comprehension (Anderson, Spiro, & Anderson, 1978; Rumelhart & Ortony, 1977; Stein & Trabasso, 1982; Thorndyke & Yekovich, 1980), but also that the extent and depth of knowledge influence the quality of understanding derived from a text. The consequence of low knowledge, as distinguished from complete lack of knowledge, on learning was demonstrated through research by Voss and his colleagues (Chiesi, Spilich, & Voss, 1979; Spilich, Vesonder, Chiesi, & Voss, 1979) and by Pearson, Hansen, and Gordon (1979). Both sets of researchers showed that learners with high knowledge of a topic were able to create more coherent and meaningful accounts of texts about that topic, whereas students with less knowledge of the topic took only surface meaning from the texts.

An important feature of knowledge is that it is organized; knowledge of a topic is conceptualized as a schema, or framework containing slots to be filled by incoming information (Anderson et al., 1978; Minsky, 1975; Rumelhart, 1980; Schank & Abelson, 1977; Thorndyke & Yeko-vich, 1980). Schemata help a reader create expectations about the information in a text, which then allow the reader to draw relationships within the information and integrate it with what is already known in order to develop a representation of what has been read (Anderson, 1977; Kieras, 1985). Readers also have expectations about how informa-tion in particular kinds of texts is organized. Even young children know the typical structure of a story narrative; it begins with a setting, presents a problem or conflict followed by a plan to solve the problem, attempts to solve the problem, and finally its resolution (Mandler, 1978; Stein & Trabasso, 1982). Narrative structure has been shown to affect comprehension in that if an element of the structure is omitted or if elements are presented in scrambled order, comprehension suffers (Mandler, 1978; Stein & Glenn, 1978).

In addition to a reader's knowledge, the way a text is written can help a reader organize information, bring appropriate knowledge to bear, and draw relationships. Texts that assist a reader in these ways are often discussed in terms of coherence or considerateness, two closely related concepts that often overlap. Coherence refers to the extent to which the sequence of ideas or events in a text makes sense and the extent to which the text makes the nature of events and ideas and their relation-ships apparent (Beck, McKeown, Omanson, & Pople, 1984). A consid-erate text is one designed to maximize the possibility for a reader to gain information and establish relationships among concepts (Anderson & Armbruster, 1984). According to Anderson and Armbruster (1984), a considerate text is characterized by structure that conveys its purpose, logical relationships among connected ideas, unity of purpose, and audience appropriateness such that the text fits the knowledge base of the target reader.

The point of a coherent or considerate text is to present content in a way that promotes understanding of ideas rather than enabling a recitation of facts. The distinction between understanding and a more literal meaning relates to a significant focus in current research on text processing. This work proposes that readers construct a multilevel representation of a text (Johnson-Laird, 1983; Just & Carpenter, 1987; Perfetti, 1989; van Dijk & Kintsch, 1983). The first is a surface-level representation, which provides a restricted, or literal, sense of meaning. A second level calls on knowledge-based elaboration and allows a reader to go beyond literal meaning to develop an interpretation of a text. Kintsch (1986) asserted that being able to learn from a text effectively differs from being able to comprehend and remember it. In order to learn effectively, a reader needs to understand the situation described by the text.

Textbook Analysis

Drawing on the kind of research just discussed, we formulated a qualitative, content-driven approach to analyzing the texts. The focus of the analysis was the notion of a content goal and whether text was developed in service of that goal. Content goals were conceptualized as the understanding students should acquire about a particular topic. To analyze a section of text, we first determined the goal of a unit of content, which could range from a paragraph to a chapter in length. The determination of a goal involved either what the goal appeared to be upon reading the text or a goal that would be reasonably expected for the topic being presented. The text was then evaluated as to whether the goal was likely to be met for target-aged readers. This step hypothesized the understanding that seemed likely for young students based on judgments of the background knowledge that could be expected of these readers and consideration of the effects of limited background knowledge and characteristics of text that may cause the reading process to break down.

The analysis gave particular attention to explanatory material used to develop specific concepts within general topics and themes. An issue of importance in our analysis was whether concepts that support a goal were explained so that connections that would assist a reader to build a representation of a topic were made apparent. In this regard, the notion of presenting the elements of a situation, for example, the cause, event, and consequence of a chain of events, was distinguished from explaining why a caused b and why b led to c. Explaining the meaning of those elements and how they fit together are the keys to making instructional content meaningful.

We chose to analyze extensive topic sequences rather than categorize segments of text by problem type, such as ambiguous statements or confusing references, and present discrete examples of these problems isolated from the context in which they occur. Analysis of sequential text presentations allowed us to consider the learning that may develop as students move through a sequence. Examination of entire sequences also enabled us to communicate a sense of the raw material from which young students are to build a representation of a topic.

Our work with history involved examination of four fifth-grade textbooks' presentations of the American Revolutionary period, specifically the time frame from colonial development through the events at Lexington and Concord (Beck et al., 1989). Using the chronology of important events of the time as our organizing device, we looked at how each of the four programs explicated the chain of events. The result of our analysis was the identification of problems in laying out clear goals and arranging content so that the goals were met.

We found that the presentation of history content in the programs was not oriented toward developing a coherent chain of events. Two major problem areas were identified. The first was that the texts seemed to assume an unrealistic variety and depth of background knowledge from young students. For example, although the issue of "no taxation without representation" is a critical element for understanding the causes of the Revolution, the texts, in presenting that issue, merely state that the colonists had no representation in Parliament. No text attempted to explain the basic issue of what it means to be represented in a governmental body or how strong the motivation to acquire or protect that form of government can be. Rather, the texts' presentations seem to assume that students already have a full grasp of the concept of representative government.

The second major problem identified in the text analysis was that the text presentations lacked the coherence needed to enable students to draw connections between events and ideas. For example, text descriptions of the actions involved in the Boston Tea Party were portrayed quite clearly. But the cause of the event, which was rooted in the colonists' ongoing protest over Britain's taxes, was not explained. Thus, the event was not linked to the causal chain toward Revolution.

INVESTIGATING HOW WELL TEXTBOOKS
SERVE STUDENTS

Following the analysis, we investigated the extent to which our suppositions about the adequacy of the textbooks were corroborated. Toward this end, we studied both students' knowledge base about topics in history and students' understanding of the topics as portrayed in their textbooks.

What Students Know Before They Study History

The first study investigated the match between fifth graders' knowledge about a topic in American history and information assumed by the textbooks (McKeown & Beck, 1990). Fifth-grade students were interviewed about their knowledge of the Revolutionary War period just before they studied the topic. Students were asked about two important concepts related to the events of that period. Those were the role of England in the colonists' fight for independence, and the principle of representation in government.

The results showed that students' knowledge about this period was often limited to simple associations and sometimes contained confusions. Common associations were demonstrated by students who went no further than raising the issue of "freedom" in response to questions about why we celebrate the Fourth of July and what the Declaration of Independence is, and by students who merely named one or several colonies when asked to tell about the thirteen colonies. In terms of confusions, 50 percent of fifth graders named incorrect agents as combatants in the Revolutionary War.

What Students Get from Reading Their Textbooks

The results of our interviews with students confirmed our suspicions that fifth graders typically do not have the background that textbook authors assume they have. Our interest then turned to exploring the kind of representations that students would develop given impoverished background and impoverished text. To address this issue we presented fifth graders with a sequence of four textbook passages about the period leading to the Revolutionary War. The sequence covered the French and Indian War, the dispute over taxation without representation, the Boston Tea Party, and the Intolerable Acts. Students were asked to read each passage and then recall what they had read and respond to some open-ended questions. The study occurred just before the students were to study the material we presented to them, and thus they had had all the background typical of students studying the material in their regular classrooms.

Analysis of the recall and question data showed that the understanding that students were able to develop from the textbook presentation was rather shallow. A review of the information students typically gave in recall and in answers to questions demonstrates the frequent lack of the very information that provided connections among events and ideas and explained their role in the historical sequence. Students' understanding of the section about the French and Indian War typically included that there was a war, who some of the combatants were, that Britain would now control some land, and that there would be another war later. What was typically omitted, however, was any mention of the colonists and also any clear description of who was fighting against whom in the war. Without a clear concept of the colonies as an entity, or the colonists as a distinct group of people, it is very difficult to build a meaningful representation of the conflict that subsequently unfolds.

From the section on "no taxation without representation," many students understood that Britain wanted the colonists to pay taxes, that the colonists were upset about having to pay them, and that the colonists showed their disgruntlement by refusing to buy certain goods. Students missed from this section, however, that the colonists' view of the taxes was based on their desire for representative government. Instead, students seemed to believe that the colonists were driven solely by financial concerns. The belief that the conflict was simply a monetary one misses its historical significance.

The action of the Boston Tea Party—that people dressed up like Indians and threw tea into the water—was well remembered by students, as were some events leading up to it. Many students understood that a tax on tea was causing colonists some distress, that the colonists refused to buy tea, which motivated Britain to lower its price, and that the colonists remained steadfast in their refusal. The students' understanding did not include that the reason for the colonists' distress was that these were tax laws passed by Parliament, a British governmental body in which they had no voice; yet this represents the fundamental issue underlying the colonists' struggle for independence.

Regarding the final text section on the Intolerable Acts, students frequently understood that Britain was angry about the Tea Party, that they punished Boston, that British soldiers had to be housed in colonial homes, that the port was closed, and that the Bostonians contacted other colonies who feared what Britain might do next. But students did not seem to understand the severity and significance of the punishment and the escalation of the conflict that followed from the punishing laws: Britain, having closed the port and banned self-government, had taken control of Massachusetts; the harshness of these laws made the colonists cry "intolerable," and brought the other colonies to their rescue. At this point in the text, it is of little wonder that students did not develop understanding of the consequences of Britain's new laws, as they had little to connect it to. If they did not understand the significance of the conflict over taxes as it developed between Britain and the colonies, how could they be expected to grasp the significance of its consequences? A further implication is that given the kind of representation of events that students developed, they are not in a position to draw connections between the sequence up to this point and the events that follow, that is, the meeting of the Continental Congress and the skirmishes at Lexington and Concord.

On one level, considering what students typically remembered from the text passages, their performance can be described as quite poor. Yet a deeper look at the student/text interactions reveals that these young students were making active, often insightful attempts to make sense of the information they were reading. For example, students' responses to questions frequently contained ideas that, although they did not match the actual events portrayed in the text, were plausible for the general situation being queried. In this light, consider the recalls that several students gave after reading the text section entitled "No Taxation Without Representation." First, we present the text to give an idea of what the students had to work with:

> **"No taxation without representation!"** The British lawmaking body was and still is called Parliament. The colonists were not members. The British started passing laws to tax the colonies. Britain thought the colonists should pay their share of the cost of the French and Indian War. The taxes would also help pay for keeping British soldiers in America. The soldiers would serve along the borders of the colonies to protect the settlers from Indian attacks. It seemed fair to the British that the colonists share these costs too. They put taxes on legal papers and everyday items such as glass, paint, and tea.
>
> The colonists got very upset about these taxes. Their own colonial assemblies had not voted for them. They did not welcome Parliament's tax laws. Their motto became, "No taxation without representation." People would not buy anything British. Colonial assemblies would not collect the taxes. Perhaps the most excitement was caused by groups called the Sons of Liberty. They destroyed tax collectors' homes and drove some tax people out of town.
>
> Parliament and the king felt that collecting the taxes was too much trouble. In 1770 most of the hated taxes were ended. Things quieted down for a few years. (Silver Burdett, 1984, p. 106)

The students whose recalls we consider exhibit some typical patterns that we observed. The following is how Robert recalled the text section. Notice that he simply provides the first and last ideas from the text, ignoring everything in between:

> It was about Britain passing laws about, ah, about the Parliament. And then a few years later they quieted down about it and stuff.

Robert's recall is what we refer to as a very high-level summary! It is at such a high level of abstraction that it cannot be called incorrect, but it is nearly devoid of meaning. It is akin to summarizing World War II by saying that a lot of people from different countries were killing each other.

The recall of another student, Kelly, indicates some awareness of a conflict going on, but it is not between the British and the colonists. Rather, she has transformed the word *colonists* into *colonel* and has fabricated a conflict between this military leader and the troops.

> The British were making a law. Well, the colonel was making a law and the British soldiers didn't like it. So, one day they tried to end the laws and taxes and they couldn't, 'cause this colonel was too strong for them. And so the king felt that these taxes should be ended. So he ended them.

Although the agents are misrepresented, it is interesting to note that Kelly has picked up on an atmosphere of opposition to whoever is in charge and a willingness to fight against this stronger power.

The next student, Megan, has the basic sequence of events in her recall, but omits the motivations for putting taxes on and for the colonists' reactions to the taxes:

> Well the taxation of everyday items and legal papers. And the colonists were getting angry at Great Britain for putting taxes on those things. So they started to fight back and tell them they didn't want the taxes. And then they stopped buying most of the things.

Megan's recall might be considered a surface narrative. The outward markers of a narrative event sequence are present, but absent is the concept that drives the conflict—the colonists' adherence to the principle of no taxation without representation.

The recalls of Robert, Kelly, and Megan show an internal coherence. Each makes sense on its own, despite its relationship to the sequence of ideas represented in the text. The way that these students and many of their peers responded in their recalls suggests that they take from the text whatever information is most accessible and form it into a retelling.

Typical patterns of recalls from other text segments lend further support to the observation that students handle difficult text information by dispensing with much of it and creating a representation from broad inferences based largely on world knowledge or very general text circumstances. For example, many students concluded that the French and Indian War had been fought to achieve freedom for some group, a frequent motivation for war; also, when asked who closed Boston Harbor following the Tea Party, several students reasoned that the colonists closed it to keep out the British—quite plausible given the context of active colonial protests in and around the harbor.

From their accounts of what they have read, it appears that young students are not being well served by their social studies textbooks. The presentations they read are inadequate for the development of a coherent understanding of the events and ideas portrayed, and the knowledge that students bring to text is frequently insufficient to facilitate the drawing of appropriate inferences.

HELPING STUDENTS MAKE SENSE OF HISTORY

In considering the kind of assistance to provide students to facilitate their understanding of historical material, we first turned to an obvious condition of the textbooks, their lack of coherence, and created versions of textbook passages that upgraded coherence. The next stage of research involved providing assistance to students in the form of background knowledge before a text was read. Although both types of intervention helped students to some extent, we sensed a need for still more powerful enhancements to learning. This need motivated us to explore how to engage students in the process of understanding textbook accounts of history, both through further enhancements to text and through helping students develop ways to deal with text.

Revising Textbook Accounts of History

Our work with revision focused on developing revised versions of the four textbook passages about events leading to the Revolutionary War. The revisions made to the textbook passages were intended to establish textual coherence by clarifying, elaborating, explaining, and motivating important information and making relationships explicit.

A key aspect in our conception of coherence was that making information explicit should not be interpreted in too egalitarian a way. Merely making all information more explicit is not the point. What is needed is explication of the meaning of important information in a way that makes apparent its role in the event or concept being developed. The creation of coherent text means figuring out what information needs to be made explicit in order to develop an adequate explanation of an event, concept, or phenomenon.

The goal of our revisions was to create a text based on a causal sequence of events with the information presented to explain the

connections from a cause to an event and from an event to a consequence. The basis for the revisions was a mental simulation of how a
typical target-aged reader would respond to the information in the text.
Thus texts were evaluated by considering how each new piece of text
information might be handled, the kind of knowledge that the reader
would need to bring to bear, and how the developing text representation would be influenced. Points where the process might break down,
such as where requisite background information was lacking or where
an explanation seemed inadequate, were hypothesized, and ways in
which an ideal reader might repair such breaks were generated. These
potential repairs were used as the basis for the revised version of the
text. As we considered what might happen within this young learner's
comprehension process, we switched back and forth among hypothesizing what the student might be thinking, inducing what seemed to be
intended by the text, and constructing text statements that might
promote a coherent representation.

As an example of the kind of revisions made, recall the sentences
from the textbook segment presented earlier about "no taxation without
representation" that attempt to explain the colonists' distress over the
taxes:

> The colonists got very upset about these taxes. Their own colonial
> assemblies had not voted for them. They did not welcome Parliament's tax
> laws.

To understand the representation issue, students would need to
interpret these sentences to mean that the colonial assemblies, as the
colonists' elected governmental bodies, had no say in determining
British tax policy, and that therefore the colonists did not feel that they
were obligated to follow British tax laws. Because so much of this
information needs to be inferred, we judged it highly unlikely that
students would typically develop this interpretation.

In creating the revised version, we focused solely on the lack of a
voice in Parliament's decisions, because we saw it as a more direct path
to understanding what the colonists meant by "no taxation without
representation." The explanation we developed cast the notion of
representation as "having a say" in government:

> The British Parliament made the tax laws that the colonists had to follow,
> but the colonists did not have a say in deciding them. "Having a say" in
> making the laws means that you decide, by voting, for the people who
> make the laws. . . .

To determine the kind of assistance that this more coherent presentation would provide, we presented the four revised passages to a group

of target-aged students and compared their performance on recall and questions with the students who had read the original textbook version. The result was that the students reading the revised version recalled significantly more of the text and answered more questions correctly (Beck, McKeown, Sinatra, & Loxterman, 1991).

Even more important than the differences in the amount of recall and questions answered, however, was the nature of those differences. Typically, the advantage for the revised group represented exactly the concepts needed to explain the action of the text and to move the chain of events forward. For example, in recalling the French and Indian War segment, the readers of the revised text were more likely to mention the role of the colonists and to understand who fought whom in the war. For the "no taxation without representation" segment, the revised group was more likely to understand that the colonists' objection to the taxes arose from their desire for representation in government. In reading the Boston Tea Party passage, revised text readers were more likely to make the critical connection between the tea party and the tax situation. Finally, for the Intolerable Acts section, revised text readers more readily understood that it was the colonists who had labeled the new laws "intolerable," and that it was the British who had closed the Port of Boston, to punish the colonies.

Despite the advantages shown for readers of the revised text passages, the results of our study indicated that readers in both groups still had considerable difficulty understanding the texts. Lack of background knowledge suggested itself as a possible source of difficulty. Prior knowledge requirements had been addressed to some extent in the development of the revised text, in that explanations were provided and relationships made more explicit. Yet perhaps what students needed was more than could be embedded in a brief text. Certainly the evidence from our earlier study on students' background knowledge illustrated that students were operating from a slim knowledge base in terms of this period in history (McKeown & Beck, 1990).

Intervening to Provide Background

As the next step in our program of research, then, we examined students' understanding of the original and revised versions of the Revolutionary War text sequence after they received a lesson providing background for the text events. The background knowledge lesson that we designed focused on establishing and distinguishing the major agents of the Revolutionary period, the colonists and the British. This focus was selected because of the role of the information in understanding the sequence of events represented in the texts and because of evidence from our earlier work that such information was not typically part of students' repertoires.

The content of the lesson included identifying the colonies as belonging to Britain; portraying the colonists as beginning to develop an identity of their own, separate from being British; and explaining that the colonists, although under British rule, were allowed to make some of their own laws. These focal concepts were intended to provide students with an understanding of significant features of the political and social context that existed prior to the Revolution. The significance of these features is that if students fail to realize that the colonies were British, they might have little basis to understand what they might want freedom from; the emergence of a distinct American identity is an important motivation underlying the desire for independence; and some familiarity with the governmental rights of the colonies may be key to understanding the vehemence of the opposition to Parliament's taxes.

The knowledge lesson was presented to fifth-grade students in their classrooms. The students were then given either the original or the revised text sequence to read and they were then asked to recall the passages and respond to questions. The result was that the students who read the revised text were able to utilize the knowledge gained from the lesson to focus on and to remember the most important information from the text. The students who read the original text, on the other hand, seemed less able to exploit the advantage provided by the background information.

The contrast between readers of the original and revised texts was particularly evident in patterns of responses to two types of questions asked in the study. For one type, students were asked about the roles of agents in the Revolutionary conflict, such as, "Who is being asked to pay taxes?" The other type involved understanding the principle underlying the colonists' actions, such as, "Why are the colonists upset about paying taxes?" Our results showed that the knowledge lesson helped the readers of the revised text somewhat in responding to the agent questions, but provided strong advantage in responding to the principle questions. The advantage of the knowledge lesson for the original text group, however, was almost solely in response to the agent questions. Thus it seems that the enhancement provided by the knowledge lesson for readers of the original text was limited to more basic issues, such as distinguishing the two sides in the conflict. Readers of the revised text, however, seemed able to combine the advantages of enhanced knowledge with the greater coherence of the revised text to understand the more complex issues presented in the text.

The message provided by examining the contribution of enhanced background knowledge is that such knowledge can mediate problematic text, but it can not entirely compensate for textual inadequacies. Of the two interventions, enhanced knowledge and coherence, coherence proved the stronger one.

The work on the effects of text revisions and the provision of enhanced background knowledge established two directions for exploring ways to make instruction in history more effective. These two directions might be described as fiddling with text and providing readers with resources to deal with text. Subsequent work continued in both of these directions.

Promoting Student Engagement

Our subsequent work was driven by a need to get students actively engaged with text. Analyses of the recalls from our text studies illustrated that such a need existed. What we discovered in many students' recalls was that although students made valiant efforts to make sense of the information, they often did so by using only scant material from the text. The recalls presented earlier, from the "no taxation without representation" segment, illustrate this tactic. Recall that one student built a retelling by using one or two text statements and fabricating a "colonel" who was having a dispute with British soldiers; another utilized just the first and last statements from the text. Such retellings imply a very surface treatment of text information, as if students take what they can get in one swift pass through the words on a page, and then work that into a representation. This kind of cursory use of the text suggests that students resist digging in and grappling with unfamiliar or difficult content.

Our interest, therefore, became focused on exploring ways to get readers to engage with texts and to consider ideas deeply. In cognitive terms, engagement is active processing, and research suggests that little meaningful interaction with text can take place unless a reader is active.

Developing Engaging Texts. Heath (1986) wrote of the need for readers to *energize* written language in order to assign it significance. The notion of energizing written language makes contact with our concern with readers' active engagement. There seems to be consensus in the literature on textbooks that current textbooks are unlikely to engage students. Various writers have perceived this inadequacy and have characterized the prose of textbooks as "flat and voiceless" (Sewall, 1988); sounding like the "disembodied voice of HISTORY" (D. J.

Bartholomae, personal communication, October 29, 1990); demonstrating "a fairly consistent level of dullness" (FitzGerald, 1979); and exhibiting a "leaden, impersonal tone" (Ravitch, 1989).

The notion of current textbooks as voiceless makes contact with Olson's (1977, 1989) characterization of textbook prose as impersonal, separating the reader and writer and leaving the knowledge detached from identifiable human sources. This style of writing accentuates the distinction between written and oral language, creating a greater distance between the reader and the information in a text, and this distance may prevent a reader from constructing knowledge from the text.

In considering ways to help young students actively process, or engage with, expository material, we began by asking ourselves what characteristics of texts make them engaging to read. There exist a variety of descriptions of what makes texts engaging or interesting. Schank (1979) cited three rules for interestingness: an inherently interesting topic, unexpectedness, and personal relatedness. Consistent with Schank's unexpectedness and personal relatedness, Anderson, Shirey, Wilson, and Fielding (1984) established character identification and novelty as attributes of interesting text, along with a third attribute, activity level. Kintsch (1980), in writing about interestingness, distinguished emotional interest from what he calls cognitive interest. The latter includes *postdictability*—or judgment after reading a text that it seems to hang together—and relationship to a reader's background knowledge.

As thought-provoking as these descriptions are, none has been fleshed out with enough detail to support the actual development of interesting or engaging texts. Moreover, interesting or engaging properties do not necessarily translate into more comprehensible material. Some texts that have intuitive appeal have been shown to be less easy to understand than texts without those appealing features. For example, Garner, Gillingham, and White (1989) added what they call "seductive details" to texts and found that readers tend to recall these details to the detriment of their comprehension of the text's central content. Similarly, Wade and Adams (1990) and Hidi and Baird (1988) found that interestingness can overpower importance in determining what is recalled from a text.

In a related vein, three replications of a study by Graves et al. (1988) used versions of a text written by Time/Life editors, who deliberately studded the text with "nuggets"—lively anecdotes and vivid details. These texts were less successful than texts emphasizing coherence in supporting students' comprehension (Britton, Van Dusen, Gulgoz, & Glynn, 1989; Duffy et al., 1989; Graves et al., 1991). Hence it cannot be assumed that intuitively appealing features of a text will necessarily promote better learning. Our task, therefore, was to develop texts that contain engaging features but also keep the focus of engagement on the target information in the text rather than on superfluous details or nuggets.

In an effort to isolate and begin to describe qualities that might encourage active engagement with text content, we turned to some children's literature (tradebooks) on historical topics that teachers have told us their students respond to and enjoy. The prose in the tradebooks provides a strong contrast to the prose in the textbooks; the tradebooks did indeed seem to invite reader engagement. Consider, for example, the following two accounts of Britain's passing of taxes after the French and Indian War. One is from a highly regarded tradebook by Jean Fritz, *Can't You Make Them Behave, King George?* (1977). The other is from a fifth-grade textbook.

Tradebook version:

England had been fighting a long and expensive war, and when it was over, the question was how to pay the bills. Finally a government official suggested that one way to raise money was to tax Americans.

"What a good idea!" King George said. After all, the French and Indian part of the war had been fought on American soil for the benefit of Americans, so why shouldn't they help pay for it? (p. 30)

Textbook version:

The British lawmaking body was and still is called Parliament. The colonists were not members. The British started passing laws to tax the colonies. Britain thought the colonies should pay their share of the cost of the French and Indian War. (Silver Burdett, 1984, p. 106)

After examining such texts, we developed a concept that we have called *voice*. Within the concept of voice, we identified three themes: activity, orality, and connectivity. Activity includes portraying immediacy of events and active responses of agents rather than passive states; an example from the text excerpts presented would be stating that "a government official suggested" taxing Americans versus that "The British started passing laws. . . ."

Orality involves including some of the conversational tone of oral language, including colloquial expressions and emphatics, as well as explicit dialogue. The text's characterization of Britain's financial dilemma as "the question was how to pay the bills" illustrates a kind of expression typical of orality.

Connectivity involves highlighting several kinds of relationships, including making connections between the reader and the text, such as by addressing the reader directly; drawing connections between events and agents' emotional responses to events; and emphasizing interrelationships among agents within a text. The author's elaboration of King George's reaction to the tax idea is an example of connectivity, because it illustrates how the king relates to the American colonists: "After all, the French and Indian part of the war had been fought on American soil for the benefit of Americans, so why shouldn't they help pay for it?"

Toward the investigation of the effects of voiced features on students' ability to comprehend history material, we created voiced versions of the "no taxation without representation" text segment that we had used in prior studies. One voiced version was based on the original textbook passage, and a second was based on our revised version of the passage.

As an example of how we incorporated voice into the texts, consider the original textbook sentence that describes the colonists' boycott of Britain's products and the voiced version of that sentence:

Original: People would not buy anything British.
Voiced: People vowed that they would not eat anything, drink anything, or wear anything that was British.

The use of the word *vowed* illustrates connectivity. It relates emotions to actions by revealing the colonists' feelings and how they acted upon them. Adding that the colonists would not "eat anything, drink anything, or wear anything" actively portrays the situation by using wording that is explicit and thus easy to envisage. The phrasing is also more characteristic of oral language, using expressions by which a storyteller might communicate the events.

To study the impact of these features, we presented students with one of four versions of the "no taxation" text segment, that is, either the original textbook version, the original passage with voice, our revised passage, or the revised passage with voice. In this investigation we again asked the students to recall what they had read and to answer questions about the text. We found that the voiced version of the revised text showed significant advantage over all the other texts, and that the plain revised text showed advantage over both voiced and unvoiced versions of the original text in both recall and questions (Beck, McKeown, & Worthy, in preparation). The success of the revised voice text suggests that voice qualities augment the effectiveness of a coherent text, while the lack of advantage for the voiced version of the original text suggests that such qualities are not necessarily helpful to the comprehension task if embedded in a text that exhibits low coherence. Making vague, elliptical prose more active and immediate does not help communicate its message.

Encouraging More Engaged Readers. The other direction of our work with the theme of engaging students in reading focused on helping students to deal with text more productively. Productive interaction with text was promoted through an intervention aimed to keep learners' processes active by encouraging them to reflect on what they were reading. Students were simply asked to pause several times during their reading of a text and to talk about what came to mind.

The think-aloud intervention was developed for a text passage from a sixth-grade social studies book and was about the climatological phenomenon, El Niño. Thus, although the study was not done on history text, the findings seem very applicable, as the text was based on understanding a sequence of events that occur within the El Niño phenomenon and their consequences.

The study with the El Niño text involved four different reading conditions. In the first, students read the original passage taken from the textbook; in the second, students read the original text and were asked to stop and reflect along the way; in the third, students read a version of the passage that had been revised to make it more coherent; and in the fourth, students read the revised text with stopping to reflect.

The results show a clear advantage for the revised text in combination with thinking aloud. The data also suggest an advantage for each enhancement represented in the study, coherence of text and thinking aloud, given that the results fell along a continuum with the low point being the original text read silently. Of the two enhancements, coherence seems to be the stronger. The evidence for this is that thinking aloud with the original text did not produce a reliable advantage over the original text read silently, while the revised text read silently held advantage over the original text, whether read silently or with thinking aloud (Loxterman, Beck, & McKeown, in press).

Providing an opportunity to reflect was helpful for students' comprehension, depending on the type of text read. This finding suggests, as did the results with voiced text, that simple interventions that promote students' engagement with text may not be effective if the text they are reading does not present information in a coherent way.

Text Engagement in a Classroom Context

A project that we have undertaken fairly recently takes the notion of encouraging reflection a step—actually a giant step—further, into the realm of group reflection and cooperative construction of meaning in a classroom. The students read their text as a group, and are stopped by the teacher at certain intervals to reflect on and discuss what is being said in the text.

The line of thinking that brought us to this project can be traced to our observations of students' failure to grapple with text, juxtaposed to our awareness that a kind of grappling was exactly what we did with texts as we tried to revise them. From these observations we developed the idea that what we wanted to give students was a "reviser's eye." To revise a text, one must become actively engaged with its content in order to transform it into a comprehensible form. What we wanted students to do was to make texts comprehensible to themselves.

Another root of our approach to text engagement derived from an inherent obstacle of textbooks that also seemed to play a role in students' lack of grappling: that is, a textbook carries a weighty authority in the classroom. This authority comes from both the traditional role of the text as the center of the classroom curriculum, and the kind of language of textbooks, which suggests a "beyond reproach" objectivity. Having difficulty understanding a text, then, gives students the notion that the problem lies with them, not with the text. So rather than digging into what is hard, and risking failure, they opt out, disengaging from the reading process.

In the approach to textbooks that we developed, we sought to "depose" the authority of the text by telling students that what is in a textbook is just someone's ideas written down, and that sometimes authors don't write things as clearly as they intended, and that they, the readers, sometimes need to puzzle over what is written in order to figure out what is being said. In fact, we call our approach "Questioning the Author."

In a Questioning the Author lesson, the students read the text and work to construct its ideas, often with several students contributing ideas to a growing representation. Students are also encouraged to indicate when the text is not understandable and when more information is needed to determine what the author was trying to say. Reading textbooks by questioning the author provides a way to make poorly constructed texts more useful as learning vehicles.

The Questioning the Author approach to interacting with text has yielded impressive examples of text engagement and effective thinking. As a matter of course in Questioning the Author lessons, students seem to be asking sharp questions of the text, hypothesizing explanations for content that is not fully explicit, making appropriate connections, and producing excellent rephrasings that embody and clarify the content of the text.

Many of the questions students ask make evident that students are engaged with the material and monitoring the message they are building from it. For example, in a lesson about how early Polynesians established themselves in Hawaii, the text stated that they brought food with them and planted some of what they brought. One student asked why they needed to produce more food rather than eating what was available, such as coconuts. Another student offered a hypothesis of why the planting would have been necessary, saying that perhaps these early people did not know that the coconut was edible. A third student proposed that possibly there were no coconuts in Hawaii when these people arrived, and that it is because the Polynesians planted those that we now think of Hawaii as being abundant with coconuts.

Students have shown a propensity for making connections across units of study, generating a conceptual understanding from information about which the text has failed to build relationships. One such example occurred when the students were discussing the lifestyle of early Siberians, specifically that they were nomads and moved around to follow the reindeer, which were their main source for filling their needs. A student asked if the early Siberians were Eskimos, which the class had studied in an earlier unit. It was established that the Siberians were not Eskimos, but the student went on to pursue her point, that the early Eskimos lived a similar lifestyle—as nomads, following the caribou from place to place. Thus, through active grappling with the text, the student was able to construct what the text had not provided, that is, the similarity of the nomadic lifestyle of early peoples.

TOWARD A BETTER HISTORY CURRICULUM

The state of history knowledge of young students is some cause for concern, as illustrated by the opening example in this chapter. The concern is that the history curriculum is mostly text based, and the textbooks are not serving the students well. Under normal reading circumstances, we see students applying more of their ability to circumvent deep use of the text than to grapple with its content and use it to build a representation of historical sequences and concepts. Given this situation, it seems unlikely that students will readily develop the approach to historical discourse that will allow them to critically examine accounts of historical events. What young history learners are getting in their lessons does not seem to be preparing them to evaluate the content of historical material, to be aware of and make decisions about various perspectives involved, and to construct a balanced representation of what is reported.

From our studies of students, materials, and classrooms, several constructs emerge that seem to hold promise for meaningful learning in history. These are coherent presentations of historical sequences, engaging qualities of discourse, and opportunities to reflect on what is read and to construct its meaning.

By exhibiting coherence, presentations of historical sequences take advantage of the power and familiarity of narrative structure. The power of narrative structure is that it is inherently causal and explanatory in nature; a narrative is a series of events that lead from one to the other through causes and consequences. Narrative is a familiar form even to very young learners, who have experienced it in daily human interactions as well as in the stories that make up the bulk of their early contact with written text. Egan (1983) suggested that a grounding in story is the beginning of historical understanding.

The power of narrative structure can be amplified through engaging discourse. Engaging discourse can be described as giving voice to the humanity of events being portrayed and the threads that connect them to principles, motivations, and consequences. In a similar vein, Levstik (1990) observed that narrative can "encourage readers to recognize the human aspects of history and to develop a better sense of its interpretive and tentative aspects" (p. 852). Discourse that engages in this way is what we strove to create for the texts in our "voice" study.

A rich source for engaging discourse is tradebooks written to present historical events to young readers. Books such as those by Jean Fritz—mentioned earlier in conjunction with our investigation of qualities of voice—can bring history alive for young learners as well as reinforcing the motivations and principles that drove people to action. For example, consider a portrayal of the colonists' reaction to Britain's taxation as presented in Fritz's story of John Hancock (1976):

In 1765 the news was bad. England had enacted the Stamp Act, imposing taxes on Americans in 55 different ways. Americans, who had always managed their money in their own assemblies, considered the act unconstitutional. Naturally they were furious. John Hancock, too. He said there was nothing or no one on earth that could make him pay a penny of that "damned tax." He said it often and loudly. Once, at a dinner for members of Samuel Adams' Patriot Party, he said it so well that he was cheered. Huzza! Huzza! Huzza! John had never been huzzaed before and he was so pleased that he almost huzzaed himself. (p. 12)

Another source of engaging history for young learners is the Landmark Series, a set of tradebooks on American history published in the 1950s by Random House. The series was originated by Bennet Cerf, who, as the father of a young boy, found a dearth of good history books for children. The books are individually authored by distinguished writers such as Shirley Jackson, Dorothy Canfield Fisher, and Quentin Reynolds. The Landmark Series book about the American Revolution was written by Bruce Bliven, the author of a number of books as well as many articles for such outlets as *Atlantic, Harpers, Saturday Review,* and *The New York Times.* Bliven's account of the "no taxation without representation" issue as it appears in the Landmark Series is as follows:

> To make matters worse, Lord Grenville had another money-raising idea: to tax a variety of papers—legal documents, newspapers, marriage licenses, college diplomas, ships' papers and a good many others. Starting in 1765, such papers had to carry a large blue paper seal called a stamp— a revenue stamp—as proof that a tax had been paid.
>
> The stamps were expensive. Furthermore, they denied a right that Americans treasured—the right to fix their own "internal" taxes. Matters like marriage licenses and college diplomas had nothing whatever to do with the British Empire's economics. They were purely American affairs, and British interference—in the shape of that hated blue stamp—seemed obnoxious. In addition to a governor who was, in most cases, appointed by the King, each of the thirteen colonies had an Assembly, or legislature, elected by the people. These Assemblies, most Americans believed, had the right to decide on local taxes. In England, after a long fight, Parliament had won control of taxation. Americans, as British subjects living abroad, felt that their own legislatures should control American taxes. Or, as the popular rallying cry said it: "No taxation without representation!" (1958/1986, pp. 9-10)

Note that Bliven directly stated that the taxes "denied a right that Americans treasured," and then went on to explain what that right was, and how it was operationalized in the colonies in the form of the colonial assemblies. The choice of language also strengthened and enlivened the message about the colonists' reaction to the taxes; Bliven wrote that taxed items had "nothing whatever" to do with Britain's economy, and characterized the taxes as British "interference" that the colonists found "obnoxious."

The third construct for building effective history experiences for young learners is to provide opportunities to reflect upon the ideas being presented, and for students to construct their own meaning from the material. This may be the most important ingredient, for it is most in keeping with the message that research on learning has brought. That is, for learning to take place, meaning must be present, and meaning is created only when the learner has an active role in making sense of information. Our research strongly indicates that simple acts of stopping to question what one reads and being asked to frame information so as to explain it—to oneself, or to one's classmates—hold great power in the meaning-making process.

The use of coherent text, engaging discourse, and opportunities to reflect and construct meaning will likely entail certain consequences. One of the most obvious is that text that is written to be engaging and coherent is longer. Thus, dealing with such text will take up more instructional time. The requisite change in the curriculum is that, rather than covering a breadth of topics in a surface manner, fewer topics will be covered, but at greater depth. And we would strongly endorse that this is the way it should be! Often teachers faced with a choice of breadth versus depth worry about leaving topics out of the curriculum, concerned that their students will miss something. However, we submit that under the traditional curriculum, with its emphasis on cataloging facts and events with scant attention to tying them together and making them meaningful, not much is getting in. As our findings have suggested, young students often leave their study of history with limited knowledge, and often with misconceptions.

Another consequence of the suggestions we have put forth, particularly the notion of opportunities to reflect and construct, is that students will be more in control of their own learning. Given the chance to consider a text's message, students may ask questions that go well beyond the text and beyond the topic that the teacher had planned to cover. There may no longer be a straight, predictable line through curriculum content as related issues and unanswered questions arise. For example, given a textbook passage about the "no taxation" issue, some students may discover a need to know why colonists figured they were not bound to pay Britain's taxes—where this notion of a right to be represented came from. Or they may be curious as to what people in Britain thought about the Americans' refusal to pay, and whether it looked fair from the other side of the ocean.

A consequence related to taking the curriculum on the students' own path is that students may then become motivated to seek outside sources of their own to answer their questions. Of course, the teacher may take on the responsibility of supplying outside sources as well, especially if the students pepper him or her with questions beyond the teacher's own knowledge base! Just such a situation emerged in our Questioning the Author work, when one of our collaborating teachers began to spend her free time reading about the topic that her students were covering—having found that too many of her students' questions remained unanswered.

If students are provided with materials that promote their making sense of the ideas and events portrayed, and are allowed opportunities to reflect on the information and to seek answers to questions as they arise, they may come to own what they learn. This sense of ownership means understanding rather than accumulation of information, and being able to think with what has been learned.

ACKNOWLEDGMENTS

The research described in this chapter was supported by grants from the Office of Educational Research and Improvement (OERI), United States Department of Education, and the Mellon Foundation, to the Learning Research and Development Center. The opinions expressed do not necessarily reflect the position or policy of OERI or the Mellon Foundation, and no official endorsement should be inferred.

REFERENCES

Anderson, R. C. (1977). *Schema-directed processes in language comprehension* (Tech. Rep. No. 50). Urbana: University of Illinois, Center for the Study of Reading.

Anderson, R. C., Shirey, L. L., Wilson, P. T., & Fielding, L. G. (1984). *Interestingness of children's reading material* (Tech. Rep. No. 323). Urbana-Champaign: University of Illinois Center for the Study of Reading.

Anderson, R. C., Spiro, R. J., & Anderson, M. C. (1978). Schemata as scaffolding for the representation of information in connected discourse. *American Educational Research Journal, 15,* 433–440.

Anderson, T. H., & Armbruster, B. B. (1984). Content area textbooks. In R. C. Anderson, J. Osborn, & R. J. Tierney (Eds.), *Learning to read in American schools* (pp. 193–224). Hillsdale, NJ: Lawrence Erlbaum Associates.

Beck, I. L., McKeown, M. G., & Gromoll, E. W. (1989). Learning from social studies texts. *Cognition and Instruction, 6,* 99–158.

Beck, I. L., McKeown, M. G., Omanson, R. C., & Pople, M. T. (1984). Improving the comprehensibility of stories: The effects of revisions that improve coherence. *Reading Research Quarterly, 19* (3), 263–277.

Beck, I. L., McKeown, M. G., Sinatra, G. M., & Loxterman, J. A. (1991). Revising social studies text from a text-processing perspective: Evidence of improved comprehensibility. *Reading Research Quarterly, 26,* 251–276.

Beck, I. L., McKeown, M. G., & Worthy, M. J. (in preparation). *Comprehension effects of giving "voice" to textbook passages.*

Bliven, B., Jr. (1986). *The American Revolution.* New York: Random House. (Original work published 1958)

Britton, B. K., Van Dusen, L., Gulgoz, S., & Glynn, S. M. (1989). Instructional texts rewritten by five expert teams: Revisions and retention improvements. *Journal of Educational Psychology, 81,* 226–239.

Chiesi, H. L., Spilich, G. J., & Voss, J. F. (1979). Acquisition of domain-related information in relation to high and low domain knowledge. *Journal of Verbal Learning and Verbal Behavior, 18,* 275–290.

Duffy, T. M., Haugen, D., Higgins, L., McCaffrey, M., Mehlenbacher, B., Burnett, R., Cochran, C., Sloane, S., Wallace, D., Smith, S., & Hill, C. (1989). Models for the design of instructional text. *Reading Research Quarterly, 24,* 434–457.

Egan, K. (1983). Accumulating history. *History and theory: Studies in the philosophy of history* #22 (pp. 66–80). Middletown, CT: Wesleyan University Press.

FitzGerald, F. (1979). *America revised: What history textbooks have taught our children about their country, and how and why those textbooks have changed in different decades.* New York: Vintage.

Fritz, J. (1976). *Will you sign here, John Hancock?.* New York: Coward-McCann.

Fritz, J. (1977). *Can't you make them behave, King George?* New York: Coward-McCann.

Garner, R., Gillingham, M. G., & White, J. (1989). Effects of "seductive details" on macroprocessing and microprocessing in adults and children. *Cognition and Instruction 6,* 41–57.

Graves, M. F., Prenn, M. C., Earle, J., Thompson, M., Johnson, V., & Slater, W. H. (1991). Commentary: Improving instructional text: Some lessons learned. *Reading Research Quarterly, 26,* 110–122.

Graves, M. F., Slater, W. H., Roen, D. D., Redd-Boyd, T., Duin, A. H., Furniss, D. W., & Hazeltine, P. (1988). Some characteristics of memorable expository writing: Effects of revisions by writers with different backgrounds. *Research in the Teaching of English 22,* 242–265.

Heath, S. B. (1986). Literacy and language change. In D. Tannen & J. E. Alatis (Eds.), *Language and linguistics: The interdependence of theory, data, and application* (pp. 282–293). Washington, DC: Georgetown University Press.

Hidi, S., & Baird, W. (1988). Strategies for increasing text-based interest and students' recall of expository texts. *Reading Research Quarterly, 23,* 465–483.

Johnson-Laird, P. N. (1983). *Mental models.* Cambridge, MA: Harvard University Press.

Just, M. A., & Carpenter, P. A. (1987). *The psychology of reading and language comprehension.* Rockleigh, NJ: Allyn and Bacon.

Kieras, D. E. (1985). Thematic processes in the comprehension of technical prose. In B. K. Britton & J. B. Black (Eds.), *Understanding expository text: A theoretical and practical handbook for analyzing explanatory text* (pp. 89–107). Hillsdale, NJ: Lawrence Erlbaum Associates.

Kintsch, W. (1980). Learning from text, levels of comprehension, or: Why anyone would read a story anyway. *Poetics, 9,* 87–89.

Kintsch, W. (1986). Learning from text. *Cognition and Instruction, 3,* 87–108.

Levstik, L. S. (1990). Research directions: Mediating content through literary texts. *Language Arts, 67,* 848–853.

Loxterman, J. A., Beck, I. L., & McKeown, M. G. (1993). *The effects of thinking aloud during reading on students' comprehension of more or less coherent text.* Manuscript submitted for publication.

Mandler, J. M. (1978). A code in the node: The use of a story schema in retrieval. *Discourse Processes, 1,* 14–35.

McKeown, M. G., & Beck, I.L. (1990). The assessment and characterization of young learners' knowledge of a topic in history. *American Educational Research Journal, 27,* 688–726.

Minsky, M. (1975). A framework for representing knowledge. In P. H. Winston (Ed.), *The psychology of computer vision* (pp. 211–280). New York: McGraw-Hill.

Olson, D. R. (1977). From utterance to text: The bias of language in speech and writing. *Harvard Educational Review, 47*(3), 257–281.

Olson, D. R. (1989). Sources of authority in the language of the school: A response to 'Beyond Criticism.' In S. deCastell, A. Luke, & C. Luke (Eds.), *Language, authority and criticism: Readings on the school textbook* (pp. 261–262). London: Falmer Press.

Pearson, P. D., Hansen, J., & Gordon, C. (1979). The effect of background knowledge on young children's comprehension of explicit and implicit information. *Journal of Reading Behavior, 11,* 201–209.

Perfetti, C. A. (1989). There are generalized abilities and one of them is reading. In L. B. Resnick (Ed.), *Knowing, learning, and instruction: Essays in honor of Robert Glaser* (pp. 307–335). Hillsdale, NJ: Lawrence Erlbaum Associates.

Ravitch, D. (1989). The revival of history: A response. *Social Studies, 80*(3), 89–91.

Rumelhart, D. E. (1980). Schemata: The building blocks of cognition. In R. J. Spiro, B. C. Bruce, & W. F. Brewer (Eds.), *Theoretical issues in reading comprehension* (pp. 33–58). Hillsdale, NJ: Lawrence Erlbaum Associates.

Rumelhart, D. E., & Ortony, A. (1977). The representation of knowledge in memory. In R. C. Anderson, R. J. Spiro, & W. E. Montague (Eds.), *Schooling and the acquisition of knowledge* (pp. 99–135). Hillsdale, NJ: Lawrence Erlbaum Associates.

Schank, R. C. (1979). Interestingness: Controlling inferences. *Artificial Intelligence, 12,* 273–297.

Schank, R. C., & Abelson, R. P. (1977). *Scripts, plans, goals, and understanding: An inquiry into human knowledge structures.* Hillsdale, NJ: Lawrence Erlbaum Associates.

Sewall, G. T. (1988). American history textbooks: Where do we go from here? *Phi Delta Kappan, 69,* 552–558.

Silver Burdett. (1984). *The United States and its neighbors.* Morristown, NJ: Author.

Spilich, G. J., Vesonder, G. T., Chiesi, H. L., & Voss, J. F. (1979). Text processing of domain-related information for individuals with high and low domain knowledge. *Journal of Verbal Learning and Verbal Behavior, 18,* 275–290.

Stein, N. L., & Glenn, C. G. (1978). *The role of temporal organization in story comprehension* (Tech. Rep. No. 71). Urbana: University of Illinois, Center for the Study of Reading.

Stein, N. L., & Trabasso, T. (1982). What's in a story: An approach to comprehension and instruction. In R. Glaser (Ed.), *Advances in instructional psychology* (Vol. 2, pp. 213–267). Hillsdale, NJ: Lawrence Erlbaum Associates.

Thorndyke, P. W., & Yekovich, F. R. (1980). A critique of schemata as a theory of human story memory. *Poetics, 9,* 23–49.

van Dijk, T. A., & Kintsch, W. (1983). *Strategies of discourse comprehension.* New York: Academic Press.

Wade, S. E., & Adams, R. B. (1990). Effects of importance and interest on recall of biographical text. *Journal of Reading Behavior, 22,* 331–353.

CHAPTER 2

On the Paradox of Understanding History in an Educational Setting

Ola Halldén
Stockholm University

In research on teaching and learning in science, the learner's prior knowledge has been brought into focus. According to Ausubel (1968), the most important single factor influencing the learning process is what the learner already knows. Yet numerous studies examine how the already established knowledge of learners makes it difficult for them to understand concepts and reasoning within the disciplines of science (an up-to-date bibliography is to be found in Pfundt & Duit, 1991). There has been no such intensive interest for this research tradition in the research on teaching and learning in the humanities or social sciences. Research on naive conceptions held by children has focused on establishing stages or, more weakly, steps in the children's conceptualizations, with the aim of describing a path for conceptual development (e.g., Berti, 1992; Furnham, 1992; Jahoda, 1963; Torney-Purta, 1992). In this chapter, I follow the line of research used in studies on the teaching and learning in the sciences and discuss the *relationship* between the learner's naive conceptions and the subject matter taught. I also try to show how this line of research can be a fruitful approach in studies of this kind.

First, I introduce briefly the concept of *alternative frameworks* and discuss its relevance to learning history. In history, the learning task takes the form of a shared line of reasoning. I comment next on the so-called learning paradox. The remainder of the chapter consists mainly of a proposal for a practical solution to the paradox, which is demonstrated by empirical examples from instructional settings in history. Finally, the alternative frameworks of students, with respect to history, are commented upon. A starting point for introducing the concept of alternative frameworks is found in the distinctions that can be made between the teacher's assignment, the task in an educational setting, and the students' learning project or problem under study as the learners understand it.

TEACHER ASSIGNMENTS AND THE CONCEPT OF TASK

In an instructional setting, students are presented bits of information and are then asked to do something with that information, for example, to read a text and give a recapitulation of it, to execute a piece of laboratory work and give a report of the results, to discuss a problem in small groups and relate the discussion for the class, and so forth. All of this activity takes place through the medium of a linguistic intercourse, which can be described in terms of a speaker who has specific intentions, the interpreter who is the listener, and the linguistic signs that are used. In the context of teaching, we can speak of the teacher's intention as an *assignment* given to the students, the *task* as corresponding to the linguistic sign, and the student's interpretation of the task as a *problem* that is to be solved or a *project* that is to be completed. So far, the discourse in the instructional setting does not differ from ordinary situations of communication.

As in ordinary communication situations, misunderstandings arise: The intentions of the speaker may not be fully grasped, and the speaker may be mistaken in believing that his or her message has been properly received. Such misunderstandings are of interest in studies of ordinary communication, but they become of special interest in the context of instructional settings.

A student who is engaged in a learning activity is trying to learn something. For the dutiful student in a formal instructional setting, this something is his or her interpretation of the task assigned by the teacher. Now, if the student's interpretation of the task differs from the assignment as it is intended by the teacher, the student is consequently trying to learn something other than what the teacher desires. That this is not a marginal problem has been shown in a series of case studies (Halldén, 1982; Wistedt, 1987).

There are several different factors affecting the students' interpretations of a given task. There are the students' conceptions of the school, that is, what it means to learn and try to learn in school. There are the students' conceptions of the teacher, both as the intermediary agent between the school as a social institution and the work in the classroom, and as the person who imposes the norms for what counts as schoolwork and what counts as knowledge in school (cf. Becker, Geer, & Hughes, 1968; Keddie, 1971; Marton & Säljö, 1976; Miller & Parlett, 1974). But there is also another set of factors related to the students' cognitive ability with regard to interpreting the learning task; these concern the students' conceptions of the subject matter presented in the instruction and their already established conceptions of the task itself. (For a more thorough discussion of the concept of task and students' interpretations of a given task, see Halldén, 1988; cf. also Nespor, 1987.) These factors bring us to the concept of alternative framework.

ALTERNATIVE FRAMES OF REFERENCE

The term *alternative framework* was coined in studies on science teaching and is restricted in the literature to that field. In their review of the literature on concept development in adolescent science students, Rosalind Driver and Jack Easley made a distinction between *misconceptions* that are incorrect ideas resulting from a misunderstanding of formal models and theories presented to the pupils in educational settings, and *alternative frameworks* where "pupils have developed autonomous frameworks for conceptualizing their experience of the physical world" (Driver & Easley, 1978, p. 62). In a later article, Driver (1981) wrote about alternative frameworks as "the sets of beliefs or expectations they [the pupils] hold about the way natural phenomena occur" (p. 94). Osborne, Bell, and Gilbert (1983), who prefer the label *children's science*, talk about, "the views of the world and meanings for words that children tend to acquire before they are formally taught science" (p.1).

By these definitions, if a pupil gives a wrong answer, it is not necessarily a miscomprehension. The answer may be a correct statement, if it is considered within a different system for describing and explaining the world. The answer may be consistent with other beliefs, but within a different context from that presented in the instruction. This is a variation of Bruner's dictum that when pupils give wrong answers they are in fact answering other questions (Bruner, 1966).

Although the term *alternative framework* has been reserved for preconceptions in the natural and physical sciences, this may be only a formal state of affairs. It seems reasonable to suppose that individuals hold beliefs and expectations, not only about the physical world, but also about the social world as well. Here, the discussion is limited to the field of history. The question then is whether there is anything in the subject of history itself that precludes the possibility that preconceptions associated with history will have a similar effect when the pupil attempts to learn the subject.

Most studies of science teaching concentrate on learners' understandings of specific concepts or phenomena presented in the instruction (cf. Pfundt & Duit, 1991). In a series of case studies of students studying history in the upper secondary school (the Swedish *gymnasium*), it was concluded that even in the field of history, students apprehend various concepts in a manner other than that intended by the teacher (Halldén, 1986). Examples of such concepts are *estate* and *class; revolution* as distinguished from *armed struggle* and *coup d'état* and *parliament* to designate the political institution as opposed to the people serving in the institution. Another example from the study was the difficulty students had in distinguishing between the underlying meaning behind expressions such as, "Sweden regards" and "the Soviet Union wants," on the one hand, and "what all of the citizens of a country want or regard," on the other. However, as was also pointed out in the study, it is trivial to claim that students do not understand all of the words used in instruction and that some concepts are more difficult to acquire than others. This state of affairs becomes interesting only if we relate such problems to the whole structure of concepts pertaining to a subject matter taught in school, or if we can specify the difficulties in more detail.

With regard to the structure of concepts pertaining to history, it has been argued that history has an open structure, as opposed to scientific subjects and mathematics, which have a closed structure (Jurd, 1978). In history, facts and events are subject to reinterpretation in quite a different manner than is the case in science. In the light of new findings, past descriptions and explanations may lose their relevance and old facts may change in meaning (cf. von Wright, 1971). As a consequence, in history it is problematic to clearly delineate an area for investigation and thus to define relevant variables and their functions in explanations. All of this makes it difficult to identify a set of central concepts within the discipline as we can do in the case of science subjects.

THE ASSIGNMENT IN HISTORY, A SHARED LINE OF REASONING

The preceding characterization of history refers to the academic discipline of history. Its relevance to history as a subject taught in school, however, is questionable. Through instruction, students are exposed to certain descriptions and explanations; it is these that they are expected to learn. The history to be learned in school is history as it is presented by the textbook and, perhaps foremost, by the teacher. This situation will continue to be the case, whether we like it or not, for as long as the teacher has the power of evaluation. Or, as a student said to her teacher when she was advised to concentrate on the most important parts when studying for a test, "But what's important to me may not be of importance to you. After all, it's your test I am supposed to take" (Wistedt, 1987, p. 83).

In Sweden, a common method of instruction in history (Johansson, 1981) is the *classroom conversation* (but cf. also Edwards, 1986, with references). The students are presented with bits of information and the teacher tries to get them to draw conclusions about the circumstances of the event in question and what was likely to happen next. Thus, a line of reasoning is established that constitutes the description and explanation of the actual historical event. From the learner's point of view, this line of reasoning is as closed as are the descriptions and explanations occurring in the natural sciences.

We can talk about a *shared line of reasoning* established by the classroom conversation. It is shared in the sense that it is the result of a cooperation between the teacher and the students; it becomes established by means of the teacher's questions together with those of the students' answers to these questions which fit in with the line of reasoning the teacher is striving to establish. This is then what will constitute the learning task. This line of reasoning is not shared in the sense that every single student actually adopts it, but rather in the sense that it is the teacher's intention to get the students to adopt it (for a more thorough explication of the concept of shared line of reasoning, see Halldén, 1992b). The following example of a shared line of reasoning is taken from a classroom conversation about Sweden's Consolidation of Farms Reform during the 18th and 19th centuries.

The teacher's intention in this example is to arrive at a description of how Sweden evolved from a society of status into a class society. By presenting facts and encouraging the students to discuss how these could affect the situation in Sweden, the shared line of reasoning was established. A condensed and schematized illustration of some of the students' attempts at interpretation of the given facts and the interpretations accepted by the teacher as steps in the explanation is shown in Fig. 2.1. It is a problem for the learner to discover the meaning of the presented facts because their meaning is dependent on what they lead up to. It is the aim of the classroom conversation to get at this conclusion.

Another example of the shared line of reasoning is taken from the beginning of a period of classroom instruction that focused, among other things, on the democratization process in 19th and early 20th

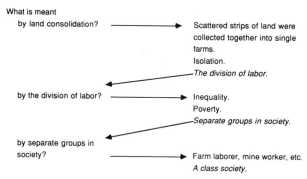

FIG. 2.1. Suggestions from the students for interpreting a given set of facts and the interpretation accepted by the teacher as leading to the desired conclusion. The example is of the Consolidation of Farms Reform. The interpretation accepted by the teacher is in italics.

century Sweden and the acceptance of parliamentarianism (for details about the study see later discussion). The excerpt comes from a lesson where the teacher was trying to establish the theme for the forthcoming lessons.

T Shortly after World War I, there was another domestic issue in Sweden that was very much in the foreground . . .

S Was it the question of a two-chamber parliament?

T Yes, it concerned the parliament, but what you're talking about came into being in the middle of the 19th century, so we've already passed that period.

S The right to vote for women.

T We're going to take that up here. But that's another question. What kind of government was there to be in Sweden?

S The form of government?

T Ummm [doubtfully]. We're talking about a form of government.

S What do you mean? Do you mean what it's supposed to represent?

T Yes, right.

S The order of succession.

T No.

S Democratization.

T No.

T The representative side of it.

T Yes, representation is when members are voted into parliament. But what's the kind of government we have?

S A parliamentary congress.

T A parliamentary government, OK, not just parliament. The break-through of parliamentarianism.

The suggestions from the students for interpreting the situation and the interpretations accepted by the teacher as the ones that form the shared line of reasoning are illustrated in Fig.2.2. As shown in Fig.2.2, the

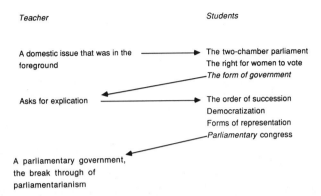

FIG. 2.2. Suggestions from the students for interpreting a situation and the interpretations accepted by the teacher as the one supporting the desired line of reasoning. The example is of parliamentarianism. The interpretation accepted by the teacher is in italics.

problem for the students was to discover what event was of central importance, a process that is dependant on students' understanding of what the event leads up to. According to Searle, "the explanatory power of a statement of the form *x* caused *y* depends on the extent to which the specifications of *x* and *y* describe them under *causally relevant aspects*" (Searle, 1983, p. 117, emphasis his). Thus, in order to understand the explanatory value of a fact, students have to find an interpretation of the fact in the context of what needs to be explained. Yet, what needs to be explained is what is intended to be stated by the presentation of these facts. Here we seem to be confronted with a paradox.

ON THE LEARNING PARADOX

In order to grasp the point of a description, a prerequisite is the understanding of what the description is intended to explain and, inter alia, in order to understand what there is to be explained, an acquaintance with the description is presupposed. This assertion echoes Collingwood's contention (1980) that, without historical knowledge, we can learn nothing from a given piece of evidence, and the more historical knowledge we have, the more we can learn. This statement is a variation of the old paradox of Plato's Menon where Menon says to Socrates that if we know what justice is we do not have to make any investigations about it and, on the other hand, if we do not know anything about justice, how do we know when we have found it. (cf. also the debate between Piaget and Chomsky in Piattelli-Palmarini, 1980, and the discussion in Bereiter, 1985).

There seems to be a genuine paradox here if we see learning as being a linear process that entails the piecemeal building up of a body of knowledge by adding separate bits of information to one another. But such bits and pieces can have no meaning if there is no body of knowledge to give them meaning. There must already be a cognitive structure into which these bits of information can be assimilated, and in order to solve the paradox we must assume that the structure is in flux. Learning anything entirely new would then require the simultaneous processing of the cognitive structure and the bits of information, with learning taking place when these two processes fit together and form a new "Gestalt." It may be so that for these two processes to fit together, an element of chance must be taken into account if we are to avoid the paradox. The important thing in this context, however, is that the learner must have a general idea about the subject matter of the instruction that can provide a framework for interpreting the information presented. This seems also to be the view of Dickinson, Gard, and Lee (1986), that "professional historians know what questions are worth asking" (p. 6) and they have "a thorough knowledge of what, in practice, might *be* evidence" (p. 8). After all, this is also in keeping with the approach taken in the Piagetian tradition for solving the paradox in its general form (Piaget, 1970).

Now, it can be assumed that before any formal instruction has taken place, students often have little or no knowledge of a wide range of historical events. A historical situation or event does not exist in the same sense as natural phenomena in the world. Even if we do not have direct acquaintance with atoms or genes, such entities nevertheless relate to the perceptible world around us in a different manner than do historical events. The historical phenomenon has to be described and, as pointed out above, the crucial point is that this description already entails parts of an explanation of what is being described.

In order to account for students' difficulties in understanding historical explanations, it would appear that we must allow for the fact that, before instruction, students already entertain ideas about the discipline of history. It is by means of such ideas that they arrive at interpretations of the information presented them in the instruction.

SOME IDEAS ON STUDENTS' CONCEPTIONS OF HISTORY

History teaching in Swedish upper secondary school aims at structural explanations. There are *interests* and *forces* within a society that make events come about. These factors may also influence the relationships between countries. In so far as "powerful men" are actors within a course of events, one attempts to see their actions as being rational when viewed from their own point of view. This is done by pointing out what interests they were serving and how they most probably understood the situation in question, that is, how they estimated different forces and the interest of actors on the historical scene. In other words, one is trying to establish a practical syllogism in von Wright's sense (von Wright, 1971).

This was the approach to history taught in the lessons observed in the case studies referred to earlier (Halldén, 1986). A general conclusion from these studies was that the students' attempts at interpretation and explanation focused on actions and on agents. A characteristic of explanations accepted by the students was that they were definable in terms of intentional actions. For the students, the object of study in history is thus people and personified phenomena (for details see Halldèn, 1986). The same finding—that pupils tend to seek explanations of historical events exclusively in the actions, reactions, and intentions of individuals or individualized phenomena—was earlier reported by von Friedeburg and Hübner (1970); it was also discussed in Søring Jensen (1978), and recently by Voss, Carretero, Kennet, and Silfies (1992). Ramsden concurred when quoting a university student who expressed the opinion that history "is just hypothesis, why did this guy do this? and so on—it's a lot less certain than physics for example" (Ramsden, 1984, p. 156).

The suggestion that "*situations* cause more problems for children than intentions," one of the results of a study by Dickinson and Lee (1986, p. 107), points in the same direction. However, Dickinson and Lee argued that this confusion is an effect of the complexity of understanding what a situation is all about. Another way of explaining this difficulty is to maintain that it is the pupils' conception of what history is actually all about which has this effect. If pupils do not see any explanatory value in situational characteristics, they will not give them any attention. Just as the professional historian "knows" that evidence can be sought in the conditions prevailing in a situation, the lay historian "knows" that evidence is to be sought in the intentions of individuals and personified organizations.

In the study mentioned earlier (Halldén, 1986), the learners' conception of history was inferred from their descriptions of historical events. The phenomenon of personification was a result of an analysis of pupils' attempts to describe a specific historical event. It is an open question whether the type of understanding they possess is an effect of personality traits, (e.g., their level of development), or if it is a consistent way of acting according to their conceptualization of the world. The latter can, of course, be an effect of the former, but it does make a difference if the learners' difficulty is an effect of their intellectual limitations or if it is an effect of their conceptual frameworks, even if these conceptual frameworks, in turn, depend on psychological factors such as developmental level. This was also the idea behind a series of interviews that were made with upper secondary students concerning their conceptions of history (Halldén, 1993). The study confirmed the personification phenomenon. With regard to the students' conceptions of cause in history, their views can be summarized in the words of one of them: "History is a series of events where every single person, even the least little worker, is at least as important as maybe King Karl the 12th. Everyone has played some small part. It's people who make up history." But this personification also leads to problems with regard to the explanation of a historical event. If each and every person can affect the historical course of events, then "There are too many things that need explaining. Different people have affected the course of events all the time." It seems as though the students subscribe to what science sometimes calls "the butterfly effect" – that is, even the least little draft from the wings of a single butterfly on the islands in the sun might affect the weather situation in, say, Scandinavia. This is also a view expressed by Tolstoy in *War and Peace*, when he spoke ironically of academic historians with an obscure common sense being carried away by the process of research and thereby disregarding the fact that there are a countless number of causes, all of which are insignificant in comparison with the immensity of the events one is trying to explain (Tolstoy, 1982).

AN EMPIRICAL EXAMPLE

In the studies mentioned earlier we derived our understanding of students' conceptions of history either from their utterances in the classroom conversation or from interview data. When derived from the students' utterances in the classroom, their concepts were examined in order to explain difficulties they had in following the line of reasoning introduced by the teacher. Because we lacked corroborating data from both the interview and the classroom interaction for each of the students, we undertook an additional study of history instruction in the upper secondary school. At the time of the study, the class was studying the historical development in Sweden during the middle of the 19th century and 1917. This period of Swedish industrialization is described in Swedish history books as the period of the Democratic Breakthrough. By 1917, parliamentarianism had become established as the system for democracy in Sweden (for terminology and a comprehensive history of Sweden, see Scott, 1988).

The teacher devoted about 5 weeks to the study of these events. At the beginning and end of this period, the students were interviewed separately about their conceptions of history and what constitutes explanations in history. In the interview carried out at the end of the instructional period, the students were also asked questions about the historical development that took place during the era under study. Throughout the 5-week period, classroom lessons were observed and at the end of each lesson the students were asked to answer the following three questions in writing: "What was the purpose of the lesson?"; "How does this lesson relate to the previous lessons?"; and, "How does this lesson relate to what happened thereafter in history?" These questions were also answered by the teacher.

The era between the middle of the 19th century and 1917 was an apt choice for the study. As history is generally taught in Swedish upper secondary schools, there is a greater emphasis on structural explanations for the developments that took place during this period in history than for other periods. The instruction that was observed during the study, for example, dealt mainly with the rise of industry, the growth of political parties, and the changes that occurred in political institutions. It seemed reasonable to assume that the students would have greater difficulty in applying their personalization approach to this period than they had when studying other periods in history.

Other major political events that took place during this period of Swedish history and were taken up in the instruction were the breaking up of the union between Sweden and Norway and the situation of the Scandinavian countries during World War I. Because several different related and interwoven themes were treated in the instruction, it was difficult to detect one single line of reasoning in the observed lessons. Thus, there were examples of what Leinhardt has called *ikat* explanations in the instruction, that is ideas that "weave in and out of the discussion" (Leinhardt, 1993, p. 48) and that are elaborated later on in the instruction. However, because the teacher treated this period as a unity, we undertook to do the same in the analysis.

The principal aim of the instruction was to present and explain the process of industrialization and democratization in Sweden. In addition, the instruction presented the other great historical events of that period. The teacher introduced the period by summarizing the developments that took place in Sweden during the first half of the 19th century. He then presented the main themes to be taken up in the next lessons: (a) industrialization (b) the labor movement, (c) political parties, (d) universal suffrage, (e) the breaking up of the union between Sweden and Norway, (f) the Scandinavian countries during World War I, and (g) the full emergence of parliamentarianism.

The seven themes were not treated independently of each other, but rather as aspects of the period as a whole. The main line of reasoning, as intended by the teacher, centered on the full emergence of parliamentarianism. In his introduction of the period under study, the teacher presented parliamentarianism as one of the themes that would be discussed in the class. The discussion then proceeded to the conditions in Sweden that led to industrialization, which included a study of the conditions of work, wages, and housing for the workers and led to a discussion of the emergence of the labor movement and to the occurrence of industrial disputes. Next, the teacher gave a brief recapitulation of the political parties that existed earlier, before introducing the establishment of modern political parties. The party system discussion promoted questions about universal suffrage and the electoral system. The principles of parliamentarianism that were in effect at that time were elucidated. The last point in this line of reasoning concerned the crisis that parliamentarianism underwent in Sweden during this time. The crisis had its origin in a disagreement about the Swedish national defence system. The dispute ended in 1914 after a cabinet crisis in which the Swedish king also played a role, thereby challenging the basic concepts of ministerial government. In 1917, the parliamentary system was reestablished. We followed the classroom instruction up to this point.

When we examined the students' written answers to our questions, the line of reasoning just described was almost totally absent. From the beginning to the end, the students wrote that the period marked "The change from an agrarian society with a nonrepresentational government to industrialization and democracy" and the development of a social welfare system. According to the teacher, the aim of the lessons was to give a description of these processes and to provide background material. But in the students' answers, the specific chain of events in the line of reasoning presented was almost wholly absent. The question of parliamentarianism was not mentioned at all. Instead, students wrote about formulations such as "the development of democracy" and, "the rise of political parties." These answers can be compared to the teacher's where parliamentarianism was mentioned as a central theme in 4 of the 11 lessons.

A similar picture emerges from the interviews carried out with the students at the end of the instructional period. Seventeen of 26 students in the class were asked to describe the development that took place in this period. The students gave rather jejune descriptions and presented mostly isolated facts and separate bits of information.

Thus, it would appear that the students had difficulty in following the teacher's line of reasoning. I argue that this difficulty is the result of the inability of the students to form meaningful syntheses of what they were confronted with in the instruction. This, in turn, can be understood as a problem of contextualization.

In the discussion of the research presented earlier in this chapter, it was concluded that students have a personalized view of history and mainly seek their explanations of historical events in the actions, reactions, and intentions of individuals or individualized phenomena. If this conclusion is correct, it is also reasonable to assume that students try to contextualize given information through their personalized concept of history. However, the historical period as presented by the teacher was described, and events explained, mostly by reasoning at the structural level. If the students try to interpret such information in a personalized concept of history, they are likely to get lost. This point is illustrated by means of two examples that show the verbal interaction in the classroom.

The first example is from the beginning of the observation, when the teacher established the themes that were to be treated in the subsequent lessons. The theme of industrialism had been established and the teacher asked what else could be related to it.

1 S1 The labor movement.
2 T Yes, right. In close connection with this, something else happened—the emergence of something that is connected to the labor movement.
3 S2 Social reforms.
4 T Yes, exactly.
5 S3 Liberalism.
6 T Yes, there is the political aspect lying behind it. But how—you said social reforms—what brought about social reforms?
7 S3 The right to vote.
8 T Yes, that's right. And what do you do when you have the right to vote? When is it used?
9 S1 In elections.
10 T That's right. But not only that. Imagine that elections are taking place. We get . . .?
11 S3 Opinions, views.
12 T Yes, you express your opinions in an election.
13 S4 You vote about things. You have these large groups which can exert a lot of pressure until there is a proposal of some kind that gets voted into effect.
14 T Uhmm [doubtfully]. You said that it gets voted into effect.
15 S4 Yeah, not directly, but indirectly.
16 T But where does it get voted on?
17 S4 It gets voted on in Parliament. The actual proposal, I mean. But Parliament itself is elected by the people.
18 T Yes, exactly. And you vote for the political party that works for what you want.

19 S4 But then there are the big pressure groups which aren't directly a part of the party. —like when LO [the Swedish Confederation of Trade Unions] puts pressure on the Social Democrats.

20 T Yes. OK. So, because of the labor movement a political party emerged, a labor party, and because of that other political parties sprung up. What we get is the emergence of the institution of political parties.

The teacher managed to bring the line of reasoning around to a successful close, by establishing the theme of the rise of the political parties.

As a whole, the excerpt can be seen as an example of how a shared line of reasoning is established. The answer, "The labor movement" (utterance 1) is quite in keeping with the shared line of reasoning the teacher is trying to establish. The answers from 3 up to 11 seem to have been interpreted by the teacher as possible steps in forming a continuous line of reasoning, with the exception of utterance number 5, "Liberalism," which the teacher rejects. But, from utterance 13 on, the teacher has a tougher job. Here, Student 4 tries to establish an idea that is different from what the teacher has in mind. In a sense, the student disregards political parties as being political agents and argues instead that it is the people behind the political parties who are of interest in understanding how events in society come about. This line of reasoning is also quite in keeping with the view of historical development expressed by this student when interviewed. He had a rather elaborated theory of how pressure exerted by the people, "It all comes down to the people," finds its way up through the hierarchies in society and how it then becomes distorted. It is questionable whether he ever accepted the political party theme as being of any interest at all.

The next example, taken from the end of the observed period, concerns the theme of the establishment of the parliamentary system. It had been stated that the Liberal Party had won the election in 1911 and the teacher asked:

1 T What did it mean for the winning party?

2 S3 It got more influence.

3 T Yes, in what way?

4 S3 Greater influence.

5 T OK, greater influence. It's a question of what you mean by that.

6 S3 Well, they got a greater voice in things.

7 T Yes, in what way?

8 S3 Yeah, they could get their own proposals adopted, or whatever. Like everyone has to be a teetotaller, or something. [Restriction on drinking alcohol was one of the points on the program of the Liberal Party.]

9 T   Right, they could push their own questions more effectively. What helped them to get a lot of their proposals passed? What happens when a particular party wins the majority in an election?

10 S3 They are the ones who decide. They get to govern.

11 T   Exactly. They get to govern the country. They form a government.

12 T   Now, what are we talking about here in Swedish politics, when the party that wins the election also gets to form a government?

13 S5 Parliamentarianism.

Again, we can see that the student taking part in the first part of this excerpt (utterances 1–11) did not engage in a discussion of the structural forms for ascendancy but talked solely about power as such. It is not until the teacher rephrases the question in the form of a definition that another student answers, "parliamentarianism." In the interview after the observed period, however, this student did not mention parliamentarianism as a topic treated in the classroom instruction. Thus, both in the introduction and in the final phase in which the topic of parliamentarianism is presented, the students appear to be still rather ignorant of the forms for exercising political power and the relation of these forms to democratic principles. They are more concerned with the exercise of power itself, in this case, with the political party as an agent and the influence of the actions performed. Thus, with regard to the types of answers given by these students to the teacher's questions, it would seem to be a rather good guess that their answers are dependent on their view of the subject of history, and that this view does not entail structural conditions and structural reorganizations, but rather deals with individuals, personalized phenomena, and the actions performed by these agents.

CONCLUDING REMARKS ON LEARNERS' UNDERSTANDING OF HISTORY AND THE CONCEPT OF ALTERNATIVE FRAMEWORKS

The verbal discourse formed a shared line of reasoning in the sense that the learning task is constituted by this verbal discourse. Of course, it is questionable whether the students ever realized that this was the learning task. It can be argued that the central concepts that formed the links in this particular line of reasoning became hidden in a pattern of questions and responses, much like that of a quiz game, but where most of the responses are wrong. The right answer is swamped by all of the rest, and the students never realize what is the central concept. We still have to contend with the difficulty students have in finding the "right" answer, and with the consistency in the pattern of their answers and in their ideas about history.

In rhetoric one speaks of the *exordium*, which, "like the prelude of the flute player hints at what is to follow, puts a main thread in our hands which guides us through the course of the speech" (Johanneson, 1983, p. 19, my translation). Then there is the *narratio*, which elaborates on the presented connecting thought, followed by the concluding speech, all of which is intended to result in convinced listeners. In the empirical example of this chapter it is doubtful whether the students realized the connecting thought in the *exordium*; it is also questionable if they followed the main thread in the *narratio*; and it is evident that they were not convinced by the concluding speech. There is little reason to simply blame the teacher for this. There was an elaborated *exordium*, and the established themes were followed up during the successive lessons. At the same time, there is little reason to blame the students either. They were serious-minded and did what could be reasonably expected of them. Instead, we have to try to uncover the pitfalls in situations like the one we have looked at above. To do this, let us retain the metaphor from the art of rhetoric for a moment.

In order for individuals to realize the connecting thought in the *exordium*, both the *exordium* and the connecting thought must already contain some meaning for them. To ascribe meaning to something is, in Ausubel's (1968) terms, to relate it to already embraced ideas in a nonarbitrary fashion. A problem in teaching and learning history is that what is indicated in the *exordium* is often identical with the material to be learned. Thus, the full realization of democracy (in terms of parliamentarianism based on universal suffrage and modern political parties) was part of the *exordium*; this realization was also what the students were supposed to learn. For students putting these topics into a context, this context can be no other than their already existing ideas of history. As was pointed out earlier, these ideas differ from ideas fostered in history as a scientific discipline. This difference holds for conceptions of specific phenomena, such as *parliament*, and in this respect we can talk about students' alternative frames of references in history as we do in the natural sciences. This type of alternative frame of reference is of less interest in history because history lacks science's fixed structure of concepts.

The students have ideas about the subject of history as a discipline, that is, ideas of what history is all about, what makes history, and what constitutes an explanation in history. This last point becomes of crucial interest if we look at the concept of parliamentarianism.

The students did not identify the concept of parliamentarianism as being of interest until prompted to do so by the teacher's assiduous piloting. In the discussion of what happens when a new political party in Parliament gains a majority, in the last excerpt given, the teacher was trying to get the students to draw a conclusion about how the government was formed, that is, in accordance with a parliamentary principle. The students' answers, however, dealt consistently with the possibilities for political parties to exercise influence and power. These answers are also to be expected if we look at them as derived from a conception of history as a description of actions and agents. If this analysis is accepted, we can claim that learners interpret the information given in the instruction by contextualizing the information into a more embracing conceptual system. Such general frameworks are discussed in the literature in terms of *conceptual ecology* (Posner, Strike, Hewson, & Gertzog, 1982), *matrix of understanding* (Niedderer, 1987), and *different levels of alternative frameworks* (Halldén, 1988, 1990, 1992a). Thus, there seems to be an alternative framework at a *meta level* that guides the students through the instruction by forming a context for interpretation of the information presented during the lessons.

If we identify an alternative frame of reference at a meta level, the students' difficulties and the consistency in their answers are actually reasonable. If such a meta level is defined as the sum total of beliefs that determine what kind of questions can be asked in the realm of a specific topic, this level constitutes a context for interpretation that makes some interpretations of data possible and others impossible. When discussing the right to vote, the students considered elections as an expression of opinions or views. The students believed that large groups could exert pressure (utterances 11 and 13 in the first excerpt), but the concept of the emergence of political parties (the teacher's utterances 18 and 20), which is a concept at a structural level, was absent. The same features also hold for the discussion in the last excerpt. When the Liberal Party won the election in 1911, this resulted in more influence, a greater voice in things, and they became the ones who decided (utterances 4, 6, and 10). These are answers to questions at an action level or within a framework characterized by a personalization of the driving forces in history. The effects in terms of the forming of a government and the establishment of a parliamentary system, which are answers to questions at a structural level, were much harder to establish. Thus, it appears that, in instruction, if we persist in presenting data intended to be interpreted within a context not realized by the student, we are bound to fail. The instructional problem, then, is how to help learners to the desired interpretations of data without having access to the context for interpretation which is required.

In a discussion of the learning paradox, Steffe (1991) said, with reference to Piaget, that it is by reflection on objects and actions performed on objects that an accommodation can occur. Related to our discussion, this means that reflection ought to be stimulated both at the level of data information and at the level of the conceptual framework. It is by the simultaneous processing of the meta level and the data that these two levels, the context for interpretation and the data level, can come to fit together. This requires simultaneous processing because it is not until they fit together that they both gain meaning. It is when they are viewed from a definite context for interpretation that data become meaningful, and it is by its explanatory power that the context appears fruitful and gains meaning.

REFERENCES

Ausubel, D. P. (1968). *Educational psychology, a cognitive view.* New York: Holt, Rinehart, and Winston.

Becker, H. S., Geer, B., & Hughes, E. C. (1968). *Making the grade: The academic side of college life.* New York: Wiley.

Bereiter, C. (1985). Toward a solution of the learning paradox. *Review of Educational Research, 55,* 201–226.

Berti, A. E. (1992, October). *Comprehension of the concept of state in the context of historical events and current affairs in 8 to 14 year old children.* Paper presented at the Seminar on Cognitive and Instructional Processes in History and Social Sciences, Madrid, Spain.

Bruner, J. S. (1966). *Toward a theory of instruction.* Cambridge, MA: Harvard University Press.

Collingwood, R. G. (1980). *The idea of history.* Oxford: Oxford University Press.

Dickinson, A. K., Gard, A., & Lee, P. J. (1986). Evidence in history and the classroom. In A. K. Dickinson & P. J. Lee (Eds.), *Historical teaching and historical understanding* (pp. 1–20). London: Heineman.

Dickinson, A. K., & Lee, P. J. (1986). Understanding and research. In A. K. Dickinson & P. J. Lee (Eds.), *Historical teaching and historical understanding* (pp. 94– 120). London: Heineman.

Driver, R. (1981). Pupils' alternative frameworks in science. *European Journal of Science Education, 3,* 93–101.

Driver, R., & Easley, J. (1978). Pupils and paradigms: A review of literature related to concept development in adolescent science studies. *Studies in Science Education, 5,* 61–84.

Edwards, A. D. (1986). The "language of history" and the communication of historical knowledge. In A. K. Dickinson & P. J. Lee (Eds.), *Historical teaching and historical understanding* (pp. 54–71). London: Heineman.

Furnham, A. (1992, October). *Young people's understanding of politics and economics.* Paper presented at the Seminar on Cognitive and Instructional Processes in History and Social Science, Madrid, Spain.

Halldén, O. (1982). *Elevernas tolkning av skoluppgiften* [Pupil interpretation of a learning task]. Department of Education, Stockholm University.

Halldén, O. (1986). Learning history. *Oxford Review of Education, 12,* 53–66.

Halldén, O. (1988). Alternative frameworks and the concept of task. Cognitive constraints in pupils' interpretations of teachers' assignments. *Scandinavian Journal of Educational Research, 32,* 123–140.

Halldén, O. (1990). Questions asked in common sense contexts and in scientific contexts. In P. L. Lijnse, P. Licht, W. de Vos, & A. J. Waarlo (Eds.), *Relating macroscopic phenomena to microscopic particles* (pp. 119–130). Utrecht: CD-B Press.

Halldén, O. (1992a). *Conceptual change, conceptual rigidity or different domains of understanding.* Paper presented at the Fourth Biannual Conference of the European Association for Research on Learning and Instruction, Turku, August 24–28, 1991. Department of Education, Stockholm University.

Halldén, O. (1992b, October). *Constructing the learning task in history instruction.* Paper presented at the Seminar on Cognitive and Instructional Processes in History and Social Sciences, Madrid, Spain.

Halldén, O. (1993). Learners' conceptions of the subject matter being taught. A case from learning history. *International Journal of Educational Research, 19*, 317–325.

Jahoda, G. (1963). The development of children's ideas about country and nationality. *British Journal of Educational Psychology, 13*, 47–60.

Johannesson, K. (1983). *Svensk retorik från Stockholms blodbad till Almedalen* [Rhetoric in Sweden from Stockholm's Bloodbath to Almedalen]. Stockholm:Norstedts.

Johanson, M. (1981). Ämnesanalys i historia och samhällskunskap för gymnasieutredningen [Subject analysis of history and social science undertaken for the survey of the Swedish Upper Secondary School]. In *Ämnesanalyser för gymnaasieutredningen* [Subject analyses for the survey of the Swedish Upper Secondary School] (Part 4, vol. 16, pp. 65–149). Stockholm: Ministry of Education and Cultural Affairs.

Jurd, M. F. (1978). Concrete and formal operational thinking in history. In J. A. Keats, K. F. Collis, & G. S. Halford (Eds.), *Cognitive development, research based on a neo-Piagetian approach* (pp. 285–314). New York: Wiley.

Keddie, N. (1971) Classroom knowledge. In F. D. Young (Ed.), *Knowledge and control* (pp. 133–160). London: Collier Macmillan.

Leinhardt, G. (1993). Weaving instructional explanations in history. *British Journal of Educational Psychology, 63*, 46–74.

Marton, F., & Säljö, R. (1976). On qualitative differences in learning—Outcome as a function of the learner's conception of the task. *British Journal of Educational Psychology, 46*, 115–127.

Miller, C. M. L., & Parlett, M. (1974). *Up to the mark: A study of the examination game.* London: Society for Research into higher Education.

Nespor, J. (1987). Academic task in a high school English class. *Curriculum Inquiry, 17*, 203–228.

Niedderer, H. (1987, July). *Alternative framework of students in mechanics and atom physics: Methods of research and results.* Paper presented at the Second International Seminar on Misconceptions and Educational Strategies in Science and Mathematics, Cornell University, Ithaca, NY.

Osborne, R. J., Bell, B. F., & Gilbert, J. K. (1983). Science teaching and children's views of the world. *European Journal of Science Education, 5*, 1–14.

Pfundt, H., & Duit, R. (1991). *Bibliography: Students' alternative frameworks and science education* 3rd ed.) Kiel: Institut für die Pädagogik der Naturwissenschaften and der Universität Kiel.

Piaget, J. (1970). *Structuralism.* New York: Basic Books.

Piattelli-Palmarini, M. (Ed.). (1980). *Language and Learning: The debate between Jean Piaget and Noam Chomsky.* London: Routledge & Kegan Paul.

Posner, G. J., Strike, K. A., Hewson, P. W., & Gertzog, W. A. (1982). Accommodation of a scientific conception: Toward a theory of conceptual change. *Science Education, 66*, 211–227.

Ramsden, P. (1984). The context of learning. In F. Marton, D. Hounsell, & E. Entwistle (Eds.), *The experience of learning* (pp. 144–164). Edinburgh: Scottish Academic Press.

Scott, D. S. (1988). *Sweden: The nation's history.* Carbondale, IL: Southern Illinois University Press.

Searle, J. (1983). *Intentionality.* London: Cambridge University Press.

Sødring Jensen, S. (1978). *Historieundervisnigsteori* [Theory of history teaching]. Kobenhavn: Christian Ejler's Forlag.

Steffe, L. P. (1991). The learning paradox: A plausible counterexample. In L. P. Steffe (Ed.), *Epistemological foundations of Mathematical Experience.* New York: Springer Verlag.

Tolstoy, L. (1982). *War and peace.* London: Penguin Books. (original work published 1869)

Torney-Purta, J. (1992, October). *Dimensions of adolescents' reasoning about political and historical issues: Ontological switches and development processes.* Paper presented at the Seminar on Cognitive and Instructional Processes in History and Social Sciences, Madrid, Spain.

von Friedeburg, L., & Hübner, P. (1970). *Das Gesichtsbild der Jugend.* Munchen: Juventa.

von Wright, G. H. (1971). *Explanation and understanding.* London: Routledge & Kegan Paul.

Voss, J. F., Carretero, M., Kennet, J., & Silfies, L. N. (1992, October). *The collapse of the Soviet Union: A case study in causal reasoning.* Paper presented at the Seminar on Cognitive and Instructional Processes in History and Social Sciences, Madrid, Spain.

Wistedt, I. (1987). *Rum för lárande* [Latitude for learning]. Department of Education, Stockholm University.

CHAPTER 3

Learning from History Texts: From Causal Analysis to Argument Models

M. Anne Britt
Jean-François Rouet
Mara C. Georgi
Charles A. Perfetti
University of Pittsburgh

Much of what students learn about history comes from reading texts. To learn from history texts, students must possess not only general reading and learning skills, but also specific knowledge about how information is organized in texts. As researchers concerned with how students learn from texts, we consider it important to develop models of how history texts are organized and to assess what effect text organization has on student learning.

The most common form of text organization that history students encounter is the narrative. In grade school, students usually read only one type of historical discourse: textbooks (Ravitch & Finn, 1987; Thorton, 1991). Textbooks present historical events in the form of simple narratives, with few references to the uncertainties and controversies that surround many history topics (Crismore, 1984). A considerable body of research has examined how information is organized in narratives (Mandler & Johnson, 1977; Omanson, 1982; Stein & Glenn, 1979; Thorndyke, 1977; Trabasso & van den Broek, 1985). We can attempt to explain how students acquire and represent information from history texts by applying models of narrative analysis to these texts. In this chapter we present such a *causal-temporal analysis* based on the work of Trabasso and van den Broek (1985). We then describe two studies that examined students' learning from real-world history texts. In one study, the text was a fifth-grade history textbook excerpt. In a second study, the texts were primarily from selected chapters in published history books. A narrative analysis enables us to describe the event organization of these history texts and to predict patterns of learning in grade school and college students.

When we move away from the textbook to consider learning from other types of historical texts, we find that students need to deal with greater complexity than that captured by narrative analysis. Historical information is conveyed through a variety of texts with highly different structures and purposes. Complex historical problems also include a significant amount of uncertainty and controversy that must be conveyed by texts. Students may have to identify biased interpretations and distinguish them from factual accounts. Moreover, many historical problems require the integration of several sources of evidence, which are presented in many discourse forms (i.e., historians' accounts, press reports, treaties, autobiographies, and private correspondence). A student learning about a historical topic from these documents must be able to do much more than represent the main events and causal relations of a text. In this chapter we endeavor to explain how students integrate multiple sources of information from different, and sometimes contradictory, sources. We present a description of a study in which college students learn from documents of various types with the task of writing an opinion essay about a controversy described in the documents. The documents in this study were excerpts from actual history texts, ranging from historians' essays to public and private letters from President Roosevelt. These texts provided basic information, evidence, or commentary on a controversial topic: the U. S. acquiring the right to build the Panama Canal. Based on our analysis of the students' written essays about historical controversies, we propose that students construct *argument models* of the relations between the documents and arguments that the student reads on a single controversial historical problem.

We suggest that both models of text organization are important to understanding how students learn from actual history texts. The causal-temporal model is a representation of the characters, events, and causes, and the argument model is a representation of the claims and the evidence used to support them.

This chapter is divided into three sections. In the first section, we describe our system of representing the narrative information in a history text. The focus of this analysis is on events and their relations.

In the second section, we use this system to describe the narrative component of students' learning from history texts by presenting the results from two recent studies. The first study we conducted (Britt, Bell, & Perfetti, 1990) compared what 31 students in fourth, fifth, and sixth grade and college learned from reading a three-page textbook passage about the building of the Panama Canal. We were interested in the type of information that they chose to include in an oral summary and how overall learning was influenced by skill. The second study (Perfetti, Britt, & Georgi, 1993) described what college students learn over time when reading about the same historical event. We had six college students read four accounts of the acquisition of the canal. These texts consisted of one or more chapters from published works representing a variety of perspectives. We examine what type of information college students acquire after the first reading and how that changes on subsequent readings.

In the third section, we suggest that in addition to representing history texts as narrative information, there is a need to describe how history texts account for complex, controversial problems. We propose argument models to represent how arguments are organized in a set of documents about a historical controversy. Then we describe a study providing preliminary evidence for such a representation (Rouet, Britt, Mason, & Perfetti, 1993). We had 24 college students study four different historical controversies about the United States gaining permission to build a canal in Panama. For each controversy, students were given a set of seven excerpts from various sources (e.g., a textbook, secondary sources, treaties). Then students were required to write a short essay expressing their opinion on the controversy. The analysis of these essays suggests that college students build a mental representation of an argument model when learning about a historical controversies.

CASUAL MODELS OF HISTORICAL EVENTS

Typical texts from middle-grade history textbooks have a narrative structure in which events are linked both temporally and causally. For instance, most textbooks tell the story of the United States' acquisition of the Panama Canal by including the following simplified state/event chain:

> The U.S. needed a faster route between the Atlantic and Pacific oceans. They wanted to build and control a canal through Panama. However, Panama was part of Colombia at that time, so the U.S. had to negotiate with Colombia. Colombia rejected the U.S. offer. Roosevelt, knowing that Panama wanted independence, provided assistance to Panama so it would revolt against Colombia. Once Panama gained independence, it agreed to let the U.S. build the canal.

A causal analysis of the information in this text is a listing of the events that make up the story and the causal and temporal relationships among those events. For example, in the text just presented, each clause represents a major event or state in the story. The clauses are arranged in temporal order, and no events occur concurrently, so each clause is temporally linked with the clause that precedes and follows it. Locating casual links is more difficult. Some causal links, like "so the U.S. had to negotiate with Colombia," are explicitly stated. Most links, however, are only implied. For instance, "the U.S. needed a faster route between . . . oceans" motivates "they wanted to build and control a canal through Panama," even though this relation is not explicitly mentioned.

Trabasso and van den Broek (1985; Trabasso, 1989; van den Broek, 1989) have argued that causal representations of text have psychological validity. They have analyzed short narratives by segmenting a text into clause units that state events and then determining which events are casually related to other events. Once all the appropriate connections are made between events, there is usually a clear causal chain from the beginning of the story to the end of the story. Using their system, Trabasso and van den Broek have been able to predict what students recall, summarize, and view as important after reading a story. For instance, Trabasso and others have found that the more causal links an event has, the higher the probability it will be recalled, included in a summary, and judged as important. They also found that dead-end events, those not on the main causal chain, are less well recalled, judged less important, and not mentioned in a summary (Trabasso, 1989; Trabasso, Secco, & van den Broek, 1984; Trabasso & van den Broek, 1985; Trabasso & Sperry, 1985; van den Broek, 1989).

Because many history texts have a narrative structure, we developed a system, influenced by the system of Trabasso and van den Broek (1985), to analyze history texts in order to predict what students learn from these type of texts. We found that several modifications were necessary to enable us to apply the typical causal analysis system to history texts.

Analyzing Events in Addition to Clauses. Because the history texts selected for the following two studies were significantly longer and more complex than the simple narratives typically subjected to causal analysis, we found it necessary to shift the grain size of analysis from the clause level to the event level. In single-paragraph narratives, each clause is a major event in the story. In the history texts we used, which ranged in length from three pages to several chapters, major events might occur only once every three to four paragraphs. With texts of this complexity, students are more likely to show learning at the larger grain size of the event rather than at the smaller one of the clause. Therefore, the unit of our casual analysis is the abstract event rather than the clause.

Analyzing Expository As Well As Narrative Information. Although history texts are primarily narratives, they also contain a significant proportion of important expository information. Authors of historical texts usually provide commentary on the motivations of characters or the causes of events. Other expository details, such as names, dates, and places, often convey important information, and there is a testing-induced emphasis on learning this information. Therefore, we found it necessary to represent the expository information as part of the causal model of a text.

Analyzing Multiple Documents. In addition to looking at what students learned from a single text, we were also interested in looking at what students learned from reading different authors' accounts of the same events. Including information from several texts in the same model enabled us to compare texts according to their coverage of the total amount of information and to compare students with respect to their learning of this information. Extending the analysis also enabled us to examine when students learned about events and relations that were common (and sometimes discrepant) among the different texts.

These modifications of causal analysis allowed us to construct idealized representations of the events and causal-temporal relations among the events to characterize learning from history texts. We next will describe in detail our causal-temporal event model.

Constructing Causal-Temporal Event Models of History Texts

We were interested in assessing grade-school students' learning from history texts. The students' task was to understand the information in the text. The students were not expected to recall verbatim the information from any text. Because understanding how students learn and use the information was our research goal, we had students summarize history texts, answer comprehension questions, and answer reasoning probes. We wanted our causal-temporal analysis to allow for the variety of ways that students could paraphrase the same information. For these reasons, we used the approach to propositionalizing texts proposed by Bovair and Kieras (1984). Bovair and Kieras adapted Kintsch's prose analysis system (van Dijk & Kintsch, 1983; Turner & Green, 1978) for the purpose of scoring summaries. They argued that propositions should be represented at a general level so it is easier to detect paraphrases.

In this section, we describe in detail our causal-temporal event models and go through two students' summaries as examples. For easier readability, we do not state individual propositions in standard predicate-first form. Instead, propositions are stated in a pseudo-sentence format.

Main Events. We analyzed the history texts used in our experiments by first selecting out the *main events*. These main events were events that are essential to the comprehension of the story. Table 3.1 shows a list of main events extracted from a series of texts about the Panama Canal. Note that some states, such as "Colombia Owned Panama," are included as main events.

Some of the texts we analyzed were very long (between 1700 and 13, 110 words). To account for the more complex hierarchy of information in such texts, it was necessary to introduce a further distinction concerning the type of main events available in the texts. Events were distinguished in terms of each event's importance to a core story. *Core events* were those events that must be mentioned to tell a complete but shortened story, while *noncore events* were those events that could be left out of a shortened story without affecting the story's coherence. Core and noncore events were determined by having two of the researchers sort the events with the goal of eliminating approximately half of them while still telling a coherent story. This sorting produced 18 core events and 19 noncore events, which are shown in Table 3.1 and are represented as boxes in the causal-temporal model shown in Fig. 3.1. In one of our studies (Britt et al., 1990) core and noncore were combined to form only one category—main events. It should be noted, however, that there were very few noncore main events in the texts from this study; the texts were shorter and centered on the most significant events.

Supporting Information. Propositions that were not main events were classified as *supporting information*. Supporting information includes both supporting events and specific details. They are not shown in the network of Fig. 3.1 but are contained within the nodes. Events are classified as supporting events because they support the more general main event. Events were classified as main or supporting based on experimenter agreement after studying several texts about the same events. To illustrate the distinction, Table 3.2 contains an excerpt from a text used in one of our studies. Notice that the following propositions, although events, are considered supporting information since they support the main event "Colombia Rejected Treaty":

> Colombia demanded $15,000,000
> Colombia rejected establishment of U.S. courts
> Colombia officials believed (U.S. pay Colombia $40,000,000)

Supporting information also includes specific details such as time of occurrence (e.g., 1903), terms of treaties (e.g., Colombia was to receive $10,000,000 in payment), and locations (e.g., in Colon harbor).

TABLE 3.1
39 Core and Noncore Main Events for the Learning Study

Core Events

#1 United States interested in creating a shorter route
#3 Gold rush
#6 Early United States–Great Britain treaty—for neutral ownership
#9 French attempt to build a canal
#10 Spanish–American War
#15 Committee set up to find a place to build the canal
#16 Later United States–Great Britain treaty—for sole ownership
#22 Committee's final recommendation is to build in Panama
#24 Panama is a department of Colombia
#25 Panama not happy being ruled by Colombia
#27 United States–Colombia treaty—to build canal
#29 Colombian congress rejects treaty
#30 Panama revolts
#31 United States supports Panama in revolution
#33 Panama successfully gains independence
#34 United States recognizes Panamanian independence
#36 United States–Panamanian treaty—right to build in Panama
#39 United States builds canal

Noncore Events

#2 United States–Colombia treaty—gave United States right of way
#4 Great Britain involved in region
#5 United States build railroad
#7 Present routes
#8 French–Colombia treaty to let French build
#11 United States expands trade
#12 United States wants sole control
#13 United States gains new territories
#14 United States–Great Britain renegotiate
#17 Committee recommends building in Nicaragua
#18 U.S. Congress debates about where to build canal
#19 French Company offers to sell rights and property to United States
#20 Lobbyists try to persuade United States to build in Panama
#21 United States passes law to build in Panama
#23 French Company lowers price for canal property
#26 United States negotiates with Colombia
#28 Colombia busy with internal problems
#32 Colombian military force present in Panama
#35 United States negotiates with Panama
#37 Panamanians unhappy with deal
#38 Panamanian Congress ratifies treaty

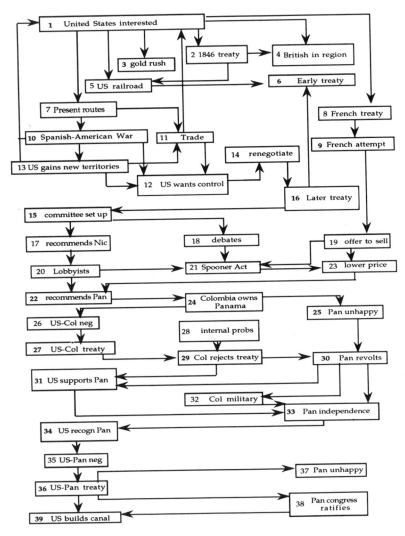

FIG. 3.1. Streamlined representation of the history of the acquisition of a U.S. Canal.

It is important to point out that although we refer to some information (main events) as more central than other information (supporting information: details and supporting events), it is not our claim that this information is less important. The distinction we are making is one of grain size; main events relate the central story, and supporting information elaborates on the central story. This distinction comes from a belief that an important component of skill in reading history texts is the

TABLE 3.2
Excerpt from a Text in the Learning Study

President Theodore Roosevelt's Secretary of State John Hay called upon Bogota to confer. The result was the Hay–Herran Treaty of 1903, which gave the U.S. government the right to acquire the holdings of the French canal company and proceed with construction of a canal neutral and open to all the world. It granted the United States. . . . The U.S. Senate approved the treaty on March 17, 1903, but the Colombian congress denounced Herran and the terms he had signed. They demanded $15,000,000 and rejected establishment of U.S. courts in the zone. Some Colombian leaders believed that they might collect the entire $40,000,000, which the United States would otherwise have to pay the French. . . . Historians still dispute what role the United States played in the revolution, but the arrival of the U.S.S. Nashville in Colon harbor on the evening of November 2, 1903, and the refusal of U.S. officials of the Panama Railroad Company to transport Colombian troops across the isthmus, leaves little doubt that the United States favored the independence of Panama. On November 3, 1903, the revolution took place and Panamanian independence from Colombia was declared. Three days later, on November 6, the United States recognized the sovereign nation of Panama. And, on November 18, 1903, the United States signed a treaty in Washington with the Frenchman, Bunau-Varilla, who diplomatically represented the new nation.

ability to organize information into a main story and qualifications or elaborations.

Our causal-temporal analysis resulted in four types of information shown in Table 3.1: core main events (e.g., #34: the U.S. recognized Panama's independence), noncore main events (e.g., #14: U.S. and Great Britain renegotiate), core supporting information (e.g., contained within #34: the recognition occurred on Nov. 6, 1903), and noncore supporting information (e.g., contained within #14: the British were busy in a war in South Africa).

Connectors. In addition to categorizing the propositions in a text, we also specified the connections among main events. Figure 3.1 shows a network representing the connections between the main events of the Panama Canal story listed in Table 3.1. Although the links in Fig. 3.1 are not labeled, we distinguished several types of relations, such as *Enable, Result, Motive,* and *Temporal.* In some cases, the connections are explicit in the text. For instance, the connection

#26: U.S. Negotiates Colombia → enables → #27: Treaty gave U.S. right to build

is identified by the phrase "The result [of the negotiation] was the Hay-Herran treaty of 1903, which gave the U.S. government the right . . ." in the example passage of Table 3.2. In other cases, identifying a connection required making an inference. For example, the United States' motivation for backing the Panamanian revolution is the link:

> #29: Colombian congress rejects treaty → motivates → #31: U.S. supports
> Panama

The text does not explicitly state this connection, but the reader must make an inference that the treaty rejection somehow spurs United States support for the passage to be coherent. Connectors can also be temporal rather than causal. For example, main event #33 (Panama gains independence) is related temporally by the phrase, "Three days later, on November 6," to main event #34 (U.S. recognized Panamanian independence). Just as the analysis of events in a historical narrative can be more or less fine-grained, the categorization of connectors can be more or less detailed. For one experiment (Britt et al, 1990) we were able to carry out a more complete and detailed analysis of connectors than described previously. In this analysis, we included referential connectors (e.g., manner, location, qualifiers, instance). Conversely, different categories of connectors can be collapsed for more coarse grained analysis purposes.

Our coding of several history texts into main events, supporting information, and connectors provided us with an idealized causal model of the Panama Canal story. This model was used to evaluate what each student learned from reading texts and to identify confusions that students held after particular readings. It also provided us with a description of the type of information that students initially learn from a text and what new information they acquire with subsequent readings.

Examples from Subject Summaries. To illustrate how our scoring system was actually used, we show in Table 3.3 a detailed analysis of two grade-school students' summaries. These were oral summaries following one reading of a short text, and the students were not pretrained in summarizing. Each box contains information about a main event, and the links represent connectors between main events. Within a box, both the main event information and the supporting information are represented.

The first student example, LB, was a fifth grader. The first two sentences convey two main events: that the United States encountered disease that was killing the workers (event 1, and E1) and that the United States was building a canal (E2). This student initially links the two main events using the word *when* as a temporal connector. She then elaborates on the first main event by stating two supporting events (supporting information 1; S1 and S3) and one supporting detail (S2). She concludes her summary by linking the solving of the problem of disease as an enabling relation to the United States building the canal. After a prompt for more information, the student mentioned two more main events. She stated that the United States asked for permission to build (E3). She was given credit for this proposition even though she made the extremely common error of saying that the United States asked Panama and not Colombia. This main event was connected by the student to the final main event (E4) through a result connector. In her summary, LB mentioned only a few main events but elaborated these events with supporting information.

The second student, BE, was a fourth grader. She mentioned seven different main events with many connections. As with many of the protocols, the connectors were classified according to the relationship, rather than the particular words used by the student to convey the relationship. Students very rarely stated the connection explicitly as *result motivate,* or *enable.* The students' most common connector was "and they." In this respect BE was typical, stating three of her links in terms of "and (they)." We classified them each according to the relationship mentioned in the text (motivate, result, enable). Only in her final sentence did she make an strong connection between two events (E6 and E7). Note that unlike LB, BE did not elaborate much on any of the main events she mentioned.

In the next sections we present two studies in which we used the causal-temporal event model to analyze students' summaries and answers to comprehension questions about history texts. We discuss what these experiments tell us about the nature of learning from reading history texts.

Learning About Narrative Structure and Details

Schools generally use historical texts that are in narrative form. These texts focus on characters and events and their causes. To understand these causes, students must be capable of constructing a representation of the narrative structure of the text that captures the causal-temporal relations among events. In addition to such relationships, students must memorize detailed information about the events (i.e., individuals, dates, etc.). Although the main story can frequently be understood without remembering names and dates, the students must be able to judge which facts and supporting details to include when building a representation of the text.

TABLE 3.3
Two Student Summaries Propositionalized

Grade 5 (LB): They had disease when they were trying to build it. It kept on killing the workers. They had two doctors come down and see what was causing it. Then they had people come down and spray it with insecticide for germs so they could keep them working. Ships sailed through and the first ship that sailed through was August 15.
(PROMPT) DO YOU REMEMBER ANYTHING ELSE?
That they asked Panamanians if they could build the canal through there and they said no. They were going to give them 10 milion dollars if they's [sic] let them build the canal.

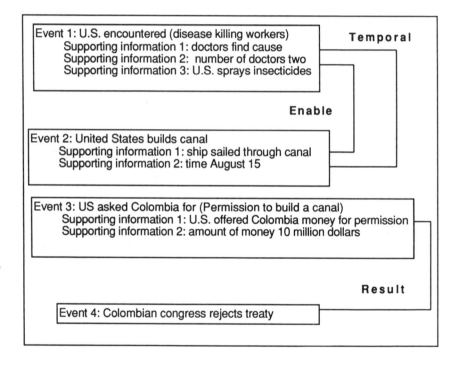

(Continued)

In this section we describe how well students of varying grades and abilities learn information about the Panama Canal story. First, we describe how grade-school students' ability to summarize the main events of a history text is influenced by their skill at reading a complex narrative. Second, we examine how the event structure and supporting information of a complex history text are learned by students at different grade levels. Finally, we look at how students improve their recall of the story following multiple exposures to the same information. Overall,

TABLE 3.3 *(Continued)*

Grade 4 (BE): The first ships to sail through the Panama Canal was in 1914, August 15. Panama was run by the Colombian government and wanted to be free. The United States asked the Panamanian government if they could build a canal through there and offered them ten million dollars and something else, and they said no. Panama wanted to fight against the Colombian government. And they won the war because they asked for help from the United States.
(PROMPT) DO YOU REMEMBER ANYTHING ELSE?
No.

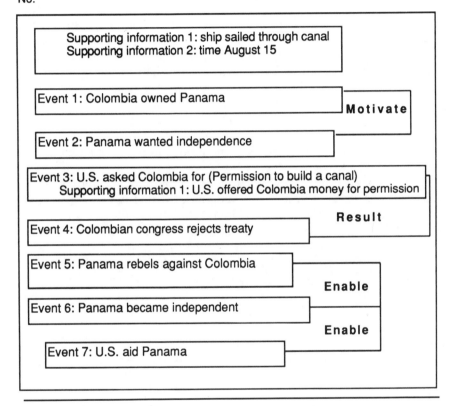

these two studies suggest that learning from history texts depends on a student's skill at organizing complex narrative information.

Student Summaries

A student's ability to summarize a history text should depend on the student's recognition of the narrative organization of the text and the skill with which he or she uses this organization to construct a text representation. Thus, one might expect that students with greater reading skill would produce better summaries of the text. In the Britt et al. (1990) study, we had grade-school students (nine fourth graders, eight fifth graders, seven sixth graders) and college students (seven undergraduates) read about the building of the Panama Canal.[1] Prior to reading, students were given an oral pretest devised to tap both general history knowledge and specific knowledge relevant to the Panama Canal. In addition to the knowledge questions, the history pretest also included a short geography test. After completing the pretest, students were given a three-page passage from a fifth-grade textbook (1986, Macmillan Publishing) to read, silently. After reading the text, students were asked to give an oral summary of the events leading up to the building of the Panama Canal. They were then asked a series of open-ended questions designed to tap specific structural elements from the causal-temporal event model of the text. We begin our discussion of the results by examining student summaries. Examples of these summaries are given in Table 3.4. Then we discuss results for combined learning, which includes knowledge mentioned in the summaries and in answer to the specific comprehension questions.

We identified three types of summaries. The most common type of summary was a *list of facts*. These summaries would not be considered coherent discourse, but rather a simple listing of details or events with no storyline. For example, as Table 3.4 shows, both JB and BS mention concepts without connecting them. The second type of summary was one in which the student told a coherent story, but a *substory* rather than the main story of the text. Every example of this type was a summary of how the problem of workers contracting diseases was overcome. The text described how the French attempt to build a canal was hampered by tropical diseases. The students who made a substory summary mentioned that a problem with disease existed and how it was solved. Although this substory accounted for a significant portion of the text (20%), it was only one of two major obstacles to the canal that was described. The other obstacle, the need to obtain permission from Colombia, accounted for a similar portion of the text (24%), but was not mentioned by students telling a disease story. The summaries by students LB and SW are examples of this type of substory. The final type of summary was the *main story* of the text—the United States acquiring permission to build a canal. These summaries told the main events in a connected discourse. Students BE and MN in Table 3.4 gave examples of

---

[1]For a more detailed account of the method please see Britt et al. (1990). In this study we also compared learning from the history text with learning from a science text, but these results are not discussed here.

TABLE 3.4
Examples of Three Types of Students' Summaries from the
Elementary–College Study

List Summary

Grade 4 (JB): The article tells you that all the history of North America and the
Panama Canal and about all the rivers. It tells you how they got yellow fever and
built the canal and all kinds of things.
[PROMPT] DO YOU REMEMBER ANYTHING ELSE?
No.

Grade 4 (BS): There was a war. [pause] Something was killing the workers. It talked
about Cuba . . . and ships. Something about a war.
[PROMPT] DO YOU REMEMBER ANYTHING ELSE?
No.

Substory

Grade 5 (SW): When they first built the canal it was in the 1900s and they had to
build it [pause] it was because Panama . . . They had yellow fever and everyone got
infected from the mosquitoes so Dr. Gorgas came and sprayed stuff so they wouldn't
be infected. The first ship that sailed through there was August 15, 1914.
[PROMPT] DO YOU REMEMBER ANYTHING ELSE?
No.

Grade 5 (LB): They had disease when they were trying to build it. It kept on killing
the workers. They had two doctors come down and see what was causing it. Then
they had people come down and spray it with insecticide for germs so they could
keep them working. Ships sailed through and the first ship that sailed through was
August 15.
[PROMPT] DO YOU REMEMBER ANYTHING ELSE?
That they asked Panamanians if they could build the canal through there and they
said no. They were going to give them 10 million dollars if they's [sic] let them
build the canal.

Main Story

Grade 4 (BE): The first ships to sail through the Panama Canal was in 1914, August
15. Panama was run by the Colombian government and wanted to be free. The
United States asked the Panamanian government if they could build a canal through
there and offered them ten million dollars and something else, and they said no.
Panama wanted to fight against the Colombian government. And they won the war
because they asked for help from the United States.
[PROMPT] DO YOU REMEMBER ANYTHING ELSE?
No.

Grade 6 (MN): The Spanish people and the Americans were having a battle and were
having all sorts of problems because the ships had to always travel around South
America to get to North America. So the Americans asked permission from the
people who owned Panama to dig a canal. And they said yes and the United States
offered them money. Then the people began to go against them and the Americans
decided to help the people that were rebelling because they wouldn't let them build
the canal. They won and got to build the canal.
[PROMPT] DO YOU REMEMBER ANYTHING ELSE?
No.

(Continued)

TABLE 3.4 *(Continued)*

Main Story *(continued)*

College student (RH): It starts off by saying that the United States and Spain were two leading world powers that wanted to take over countries that didn't have a stable government yet. And that was the main reason for the Spanish-American War because Spain and the United States wanted more power. The United States wanted to find a way—to fight them they had to bring supplies from the Pacific to the Atlantic and they had to go all the way around South America so they had to make a canal through Panama to cut through a short cut. At that time Colombia owned—was in control of Panama. Roosevelt asked if he could build a canal through there but he offered to pay them 10 million dollars and rent every year but they said no. And the people in Panama at the time wanted to throw out Colombia so they revolted and the U.S. stuck up for them. They won the war so after that they let them build the Panama Canal through but they had to get rid of malaria and yellow fever. So a doctor that studied those diseases in Cuba found that it was because of mosquitoes so he went there and found it was the same thing there. So they got the army to spray insecticides over and they got rid of the disease. It took ten years for them to build it because they had to go through mountains and swamps and all kind of other stuff but now it's done.

this type of summary. The majority of the summaries were easily classified as only one type. Those summaries composed of more than one type were classified based on the majority of the summary prior to the experimenter probing for more information.

The quality of the grade-school students' summaries improved with grade level. As shown in Table 3.5, the majority of fourth graders were list-of-facts summarizers: 78% listed facts, 11% told the disease substory, and 11% told the main story. Although the fifth-grade summaries also included many list of fact summaries, more were of the substory type: 38% listed facts, 50% told a substory, and 12% told the main story. The sixth graders were most often main-story summarizers (57%), although there were a fair number of list-of-facts summaries (43%). As expected, all the college students were main-story summaries. An example of a college student summary (RH) is given in Table 3.4. Thus, with increasing grade level, students' summaries were more narrative (22%, 62%, 57%, and 100% for each of the four grade levels), and the summaries reflected more the information given in the text (11%, 12%, 57%, and 100% for each of the four grade levels).

The three types of summaries were associated with differing amounts of total learning for the grade-school students. Learning scores are the proportion of summary and interview information relative to the information available in the text. The three types of summarizers learned different amounts of the main story, which included that the United States wanted a canal, why they wanted it, and how they got permission to build it. The main story information was learned least well by the

TABLE 3.5
Proportion of Students in Each Grade Providing Each Type of
Summary from Elementary–College Study

Grade	Type of Summary			Total
	List of Facts	Substory	Main Story	
Fourth	78 (7)	11 (1)	11 (1)	9
Fifth	38 (3)	50 (4)	12 (1)	8
Sixth	43 (3)	0 (0)	57 (4)	7
College	0 (0)	0 (0)	100 (7)	7

list-of-facts summarizers (12%) and the substory summarizers (18%), and learned best by the main-story summarizers (56%). Thus, the students whose summaries best reflected the information in the text were also the students who learned the most from the whole text. On the other hand, learning of the substory distinguished the substory summarizers from the list-of-fact summarizers. The substory summarizers, although not learning as much about the whole story, did learn a significant portion of the substory (i.e., the problem of disease). Those students who gave a list-of-facts summary learned less of the disease information (25%) than the other two groups (44% for the substory summarizers and 37% for the main-story summarizers). These numbers suggest that the students' learning of the story may have been affected by their representation of the narrative organization of the text. An alternative explanation of these results is that students who learned more about the text produced better summaries.

In fact, prior knowledge and reading ability were both associated with the types of summaries grade-school students gave. We calculated mean grade, mean reading grade equivalent, and mean score on a history knowledge test[2] taken before reading the text. Table 3.6 shows these values for fourth, fifth, and sixth graders. Grade and reading grade equivalent are approximately the same for list-of-facts summarizers and substory summarizers, but prior knowledge is greater for substory summarizers. In contrast, prior knowledge is equivalent for substory and main-story summarizers, but grade and reading skill are greater for main-story summarizers. From the trends found in the data, we tentatively suggest that substory summarizers were better able than list-of-facts summarizers to use their prior knowledge to learn more from the text and organize this information into a story about the problem of disease. Main-story summarizers, however, appeared to use their greater reading ability to build a better representation of the text's

---

[2]The maximum score on the history test was 60. Table 3.6 reports mean scores.

TABLE 3.6
Reading Ability and Prior Knowledge for Each Summary Type
from Elementary–College Study

	Type of Summary		
	List of Facts	Substory	Main Story
Grade	4.6	4.8	5.5
Reading grade equivalent	4.5	4.8	6.7
Prior history knowledge	14.6	19.8	18.3

narrative structure and used this structure to organize what they read for later recall on the summary task. It should be noted, however, that these tentative interpretations are largely adhoc, and we did not attempt to assess the statistical significance of the observed trends.

Skill Differences in Learning Text Structure

If history learning depends on a reader's ability to organize a complex narrative, then one might expect different types of information to be learned at different levels of skill. To look at overall learning, we combined the information that students gave in their summaries with information they gave to a posttest interview. This latter interview was specifically designed to elicit knowledge that students might not have included in their summary. The proportions of main events, supporting information statements, and connectors that students mentioned on both summary and question-answering tasks (as compared to the number possible from the text analysis) are shown in Table 3.7. College students scored higher than grade-school students.[3] The grade-school students did not significantly differ from each other in overall learning (sixth graders mentioned 31%, fifth graders 24%, and fourth graders 19%). They did, however, show a difference for type of information. Main events were mentioned proportionally more often than the other information types.[4] Fourth and fifth graders mentioned significantly more main events than supporting information (see Table 3.7). Sixth graders and college students also mentioned a greater proportion of causal connectors than supporting information.[5] Thus, across several

---

[3]According to the analysis of variance on these proportions, there was a significant main effect of grade, $F(3,26)=29.6$, $p < .01$. Differences between means are significant with Tukey's test at $p < .05$.

[4]There was a significant main effect of the type of proposition, $F(3,78) = 36.5$, p, $< .01$. Differences between means are significant with Tukey's test at $p < .05$.

[5]There was a significant grade × type of proposition interaction, $F(9,78)=4.7$, $p < .01$. Differences between means were significant based on a Tukey's test with $p < .05$.

TABLE 3.7
Proportion of Information Recalled from Elementary–College Study

	Grade			
Type of Information	Fourth	Fifth	Sixth	College
Event	.29	.34	.44	.82
Supporting information	.11	.15	.16	.40
Causal connectors	.18	.22	.37	.78

grade levels (fourth, fifth, sixth, and college), students' learning of main events is superior to their learning of supporting information. It is not the case that students learned the details and elaborations as well as the significant events from the history text. Even the fourth graders focused on learning main events. The younger students, however, did differ from the older students in terms of stating the connections among the main events. Younger students (fourth and fifth graders) do not appear to learn as much about the connections among events as the older students (sixth and college students).

The students' increasing ability to connect events into causal chains is apparent from their statements. Most of the fourth graders were able to mention discrete events, for example, that the canal was built, that disease was an obstacle, and that disease was caused by infected mosquitos. In addition to discrete events, some of the fifth graders could state the function of the event in the story. For example, they knew that the purpose of the canal was to create a shorter route, and that the United States needed to get permission from Colombia to build the canal. By the sixth grade, students were able to reliably connect events. For example, two connections sixth graders made were between the United States asking Colombia for permission and Colombia refusing, and between the swamps being sprayed and the problem of infected mosquitoes. College students, of course, could relate the entire causal chain. They were able to say that the canal was built so ships could have a shorter route and move more quickly, and that it was the Spanish-American War that made the United States recognize the need for a canal. Also, all the college students were able to recall that disease was a difficulty in building the canal and that the United States needed to ask Colombia for permission but Colombia refused.

These results suggest that fourth and fifth-grade students are less prepared to learn from history texts than older students. Although the text read by all students was a simplified version of a fifth-grade textbook story, only sixth-grade and older students were able to go beyond learning discrete events or short connected chains of events. These older students appeared to have the reading skill required to organize the events of the main story according to the story's causal connections.

Learning Text Structure with Multiple Exposures

In the previous two sections we argued that students' skill at reading complex narratives will affect their learning of a history story. One result was that college students, who are presumably skilled at reading, learn not only more of the main events and causal connections, but more supporting information as well. In this section we look at how college student readers acquire information about a specific story over multiple readings.

In our learning study (Perfetti et al., 1993) we had six college students read four different authors' accounts of the acquisition of the canal. These texts consisted of one or more chapters (between 1700 and 13,110 words long) from published works representing a variety of perspectives. One text was a more complex version of the neutral text used in the previously described study. In an effort to study how students learn history in a more ecologically valid way, the students were given the final three texts as "homework assignments" over a 3-week period.[6] Each of the three texts presented an argument about the events: One was written to aid U.S. policy decisions (Center for Strategic Studies, 1967), another argued the United States was justified in its actions (Crane, 1978), and the last provided a more Panamanian perspective (LaFeber, 1978). After each text, students were asked to write a long summary (24 lines) followed by a short summary (8 lines) of the "events leading up to the building of the canal." They were then asked six comprehension questions followed by various probes for more detail (e.g., What was the main purpose of the Hay-Pauncefote treaty? Probes: What countries signed the treaty? What was happening in Great Britain at the time that enabled this new treaty?).

We discuss what students selected to include in their short summaries and what they learned from the text as measured by combining anything mentioned in either of their summaries and in answer to comprehension questions. The amount learned after the first reading was computed in the same way as the previous experiment. In order to assess students' learning after the first text, we computed the proportion of textual information correctly stated. For the following readings, however, the length of the texts (several thousand words) prohibited the use of this method (percentages would be too low to be meaningful.)

---

[6]The study actually involved eight sessions covering both the acquisition period and the later 1978 treaty negotiations to turn control of the canal over to Panama. For purposes of comparison, only results concerning the acquisition period are discussed here.

For this reason, we present proportions only for the first reading, and then for comparisons across reading we present the data in raw scores.

Expert Readers Recognize Core Information.   Learning from history texts requires the ability to distinguish the central story of the text from supporting events and anecdotes that may be present in the text. As discussed earlier, young readers may fail at this task and get caught up in a substory. One of the things we looked at in our learning study was how well college students identified the core story from several very long complex texts (between 1700 and 13,110 words).

College students learned the central story very quickly. In fact, they learned it after reading the first text. When broken down by information type, students' overall learning reflects a preference for learning the main events of the story. Figure 3.2 shows the proportion of core and noncore information recalled after the first reading (information mentioned after comprehension questions and two summaries). Students were able to mention approximately 75% of the core main events, 50% of the noncore events, and 50% of the connections among the core events. In contrast, students did not learn many of the supporting details and events. Thus, after an initial reading of a history text, college students focused on learning the central story, rather than on learning the details or elaborative events.

An analysis of the short (eight-line) summary task suggests that the college students actively distinguished between the core story and other supporting information and events. As Fig. 3.3 shows, the students summarized the core events and noncore events and included connections between these events. They mentioned only a small proportion of the possible supporting information. It is worth noting that we found a similar pattern in the Britt et al. (1990) study for the older students (sixth graders, college students). Students are able to select out the main

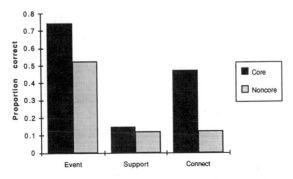

FIG. 3.2.   Proportion of each type of statement college students mentioned following the first reading assignment.

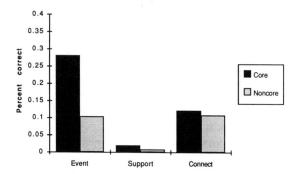

FIG. 3.3. Proportion of each type of statement in the college students' summaries following the first reading assignment.

events from the supporting events and details. In addition, every student mentioned more core events in their summary than noncore events. Even after an initial reading of a short history text, students were able to recognize core information and include it in their summaries. This is an interesting finding, given that the students knew considerably more information of each type than they provided on the constrained short summary task. In their summaries, the students selected only information they considered to be important to the storyline.

Over the course of the study, the pattern of mentioning more core information in college students' summaries remained stable. As the raw scores in Fig. 3.4 indicate, after the first reading, core events and supporting information were mentioned at a higher frequency than noncore information. This preference for mentioning more core information appears after each subsequent reading. On the average, 75% of each student's summary was composed of core events or supporting information, and this preference did not increase with additional reading assignments (75%, 74%, 75%, 80% after each reading). Because the comprehension task informs us that the students were gaining knowledge of supporting information, we must conclude that the students chose not to include supporting information because of the constraints of the short summary task.

The increase in students' use of core events did not arise from their adopting a simple story and merely adding more information to it. Rather, the students' summaries were highly influenced by their most recent reading assignment. Students showed a tendency to reflect the emphasis of the author of the most recent text, despite experimenter instructions requesting a summary of the overall story rather than any particular text. Thus, the students' increased use of core events reflects a change in sensitivity to information required to comprehend the basic story rather than just memory of "the story thus far."

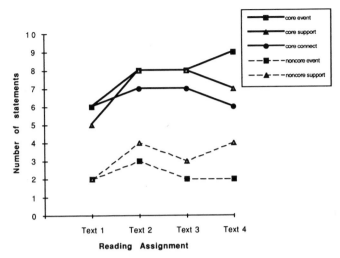

FIG. 3.4. Number of correct statements of each type in the college students' summaries following the each reading assignment.

Supporting Information Is Acquired Gradually. As one might expect, the students learned more of the story with each reading assignment. After their first reading assignment, the students mentioned an average of 19 of the core and noncore events and supporting information. Following the second and third assignments the students provided an average of 28 and 33 of these information types, respectively. By the fourth reading the students mentioned an average of 36 of the core and noncore events and supporting information. Thus, the students continued to increase the amount of the story they used in answering the comprehension questions after each successive reading.

As Fig. 3.2 shows, there was superior learning of the core events following the first reading. Fig. 3.5 shows that supporting information, both core and noncore, increased over subsequent readings, whereas main events and connections remain relatively stable. When broken down by information type, students' overall learning reflects a preference for initially learning the core events of the story, followed by a more gradual learning of the supporting information. The use of core supporting information increased rapidly from its initial mentioning of 42 after the first reading to 65 after the second reading and then increased more slowly to 82 and 80 after the third and fourth readings, respectively. Similarly, appearance of noncore supporting information increased from 22 after the first reading and continued to increase to 37, 52, and 70, after the final three readings, respectively. In contrast, students reported about 16 of the 18 core events and 11 of the 21

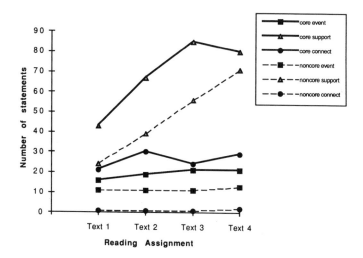

FIG. 3.5. Number of correct statements of each type mentioned in the college students interviews following each reading assignment.

noncore events. Thus, students appeared to learn the basic story (i.e., the core events) by the first or second reading while acquiring more elaborative information (i.e., core and noncore supporting information) upon each rereading of the story.

Summary

In this section we have seen how students' differing levels of skill at reading narrative texts affects their learning of a history story. Young students, who have reading experience only with simple narrative structures, appear to have difficulty identifying the main story of a text and are limited in their ability to connect events into causal chains. Older students can successfully construct more complex structures that they can use to organize more of the text information. This difference in reading ability appears to produce a difference in learning. Students whose summaries indicated a good grasp of a text's narrative structure learned more of the information in the text than did students whose summaries indicated they had difficulty with the text's structure. College students who are expert readers appear to have the further ability to quickly identify a core story in several texts with a complex structure and more gradually acquire a fair amount of the supporting information in texts.

ARGUMENT MODELS OF HISTORICAL CONTROVERSIES

In the first part of this chapter we showed how historical texts can be analyzed in terms of causal-temporal structures. We found that this representation is consistent with grade-school and college students' patterns of learning from history texts. Thus, a history text can be seen as a complex form of narrative. In learning from history texts, readers apply the skills and knowledge they possess about narratives.

Causal-temporal structures are probably most valid for representing simple, noncontroversial accounts of historical events, such as the ones elementary and secondary school students are accustomed to finding in textbooks. However, the noncontroversial narratives presented in textbooks are simplified and somewhat distorted views of history problems (Crismore, 1984). Textbook accounts typically fail to represent two important features of most history problems: (a) uncertainty, the fact that the story told is partly unknown and partly reconstructed from indirect sources, and (b) controversy, the fact that different versions of the same story may exist and may be discrepant or even contradictory.

Although textbooks are the main support of historical knowledge acquisition in high school and even in college (Wineburg, 1991b), students may be fruitfully introduced to some of the uncertainty and controversy that surrounds our understanding of historical events (Wineburg & Wilson, 1991). Students may be confronted with materials that reflect a particular author's perspective. Moreover, students may be asked to consider several sources of information when learning about historical events. Even textbooks frequently contain "documents" aimed at promoting a better grasp of historical events. It is important for students to understand the role documents play, and how they enhance the description of historical events. Therefore, we suggest that learning from multiple documents involves more than the understanding of causal-temporal relationships between events. First, in learning from a document, students must consider the conditions in which they were produced (by whom, when, for what audience). Thus, students have to be aware of the *source* information provided with documents, in addition to their content. Second, when acquiring information from more than one text, students must frequently deal with multiple and sometimes contradictory accounts or interpretations of a story. These accounts may be based on different claims and different evidence statements. Organizing such information requires the student to construct separate representations of what each author stated and what the texts agree and disagree about. Third, history documents often relate to each other in various ways. For instance, second-hand accounts may refer to primary documents as evidence. Information from several documents cannot be simply added in a cumulative fashion. Instead, learning from documents involves representing a network, with information sources as the nodes and relations between sources as oriented and labeled arcs.

In this section we argue that, in addition to the causal-event model representation described in the first part of this chapter, readers must be skilled at constructing a second high level of representation when learning from history texts. This representation includes the various sources of information, the arguments they bring, and how these arguments relate to each other and to sources of evidence. In short, we assume that readers of history documents build an *argument model*, or a mental representation of the organization of arguments and evidence. Whereas the causal-event model is a representation of the characters, events, and causal relations involved in a story, the argument model is a representation of the various interpretations in the available documents and how they relate to each other and to pieces of evidence.

Following is a tentative and somewhat idealized description of historical argument models as we envision them. The purpose of this description is to provide a set of hypotheses on the psychological processes involved in using historical documents. Next, we present a set of empirical findings supporting our notion that argument models may have some relevance in explaining how students learn and reason about historical controversies.

A Profile of Historical Argument Models

We propose that argument models operate at two levels. At a *local level*, each document is represented as a series of arguments supporting a claim. Arguments are connected to pieces of evidence, such as facts or other documents. At a *global level*, the model represents relationships between the different documents available in the context of the problem. This level represents information both across and within documents and may also account for a reader's assessment of the relative support for one interpretation of events over another interpretation.

Representing Arguments at a Local Level. A naive view of history texts assumes that they present objective, trustworthy accounts of past events. Several studies report that such a conception is frequent among high-school and even college students (see Wineburg, 1991b, pp. 511–512). In contrast, historians adopt a more suspicious attitude toward textbooks and other secondary accounts. More generally, historians devote much attention to the source of a document and use source information to represent the conceptions, biases and purposes of the author, what Wineburg (1991b) describes as the *subtext* of a document.

Authors of history texts manage to offer convincing interpretations of historical events by presenting a delicate blend of facts and evidence, along with their own claims and arguments. Skilled reading of such texts involves identifying the claim(s) made, the arguments brought to support this claim, and the evidence attached to the arguments.

Consider the passage presented in Table 3.8. This passage presents an opinionated interpretation of the U.S. intervention in the 1903 Panamanian revolt against Colombia[7]. The author's main claim is that the U.S. intervention was not justified. Three main arguments are proposed to support this claim: that the United States was prepared to intervene before the actual uprising; that the so-called revolution was a setup aimed at giving the United States control over Colombian territory; that there was no legal justification for the intervention. Two of these arguments draw upon primary documents for support: correspondence between military leaders and the 1846 United States–Colombia Bidlack Treaty.

Understanding this type of text involves building a *local argument model*: The reader has to identity the author's claim and arguments; in addition, the reader must remember the links between arguments and pieces of evidence (i.e., other documents). Figure 3.6 presents an idealized local argument representation for the passage presented in Table 3.8.

The local argument representation includes *source information* (e.g., Professor J. Norman's book *America and the Canal Title*, 1986, p. 192), the author's main *claim* (U.S. military intervention was not justified), the *arguments* mentioned by the author (e.g., Military orders were sent before revolution), and the *evidence* that supports the arguments (e.g., November 2–3 correspondence between U.S. officials and military leaders).

In summary, the local argument model may be seen as an interface between the causal-temporal model and the global argument model. On one hand, the individual arguments clearly belong to a description of the situation: facts (e.g., orders were sent), characters' motivations (e.g., the United States wanted to control the Canal Zone), and evaluations e.g., the United States violated the treaty). On the other hand, learning

---

[7]This passage, like all the texts used in this section, is drawn from an actual historical essay. The original texts were slightly edited for readability and all references were removed. The sources, including the author's name, were modified for experimental purposes. Original references are available upon request to the authors.

TABLE 3.8
One of the Secondary Documents Used in the Multiple
Document Study

Excerpt from Prof. J. Norman's book "America and the Canal Title" (1986, p. 192). The author argues that the U.S. military intervention in the Panamanian revolution was not justified.

If Commander Hubbard of the Nashville had had the telegram sent him on November 2, the troops and administrative officers on the Cartagena would not have been allowed to land. In short, Colombia would have been prevented from landing troops on a part of her territory when there was no disturbance whatsoever. And that is called protecting the transit and maintaining order! It is the only interruption of the transit and of the peace there was.

As already stated, there was no revolution, there was no uprising. Certain interested persons merely volunteered to organize a civil government in the Province of Panama, independent of that of Colombia, if assured of protection by the United States. The protection was assured and was given. The purpose was to enable the one to grant and the other to receive title to the Canal Zone. Colombia was to be barred from interfering by the display of overwhelming force.

That is what was planned, and that is what eventuated.

The military forces of Colombia arrived at Colon in fulfillment of her obligations under the Treaty of 1846 and in the performance of the most elementary duty of a sovereign state. Those of the United States were there to interrupt in its most sacred use. It was the sovereign right of Colombia to secure transit from Colon to Panama for her troops, and the duty of the Railroad, under its charter, to supply it. The United Stated did interfere without a scintilla of right and in violation of the Treaty of 1846.

---

these events only makes sense in the context of the author's global claim (i.e., the U.S. intervention was not justified), which also belongs to the global argument model.

Representing Arguments at a Global Level. Studying the document of Table 3.8 in isolation is probably of little value for understanding the controversy surrounding the Panama revolution. Is the author's interpretation shared by other historians? Are the arguments valid? Do these arguments make proper use of primary evidence? Answering these questions is an essential part of understanding the controversy. This understanding can be achieved through reading several documents, including more storylike accounts of the events, contradictory points of views, and the relevant primary documents. The result of these activities is a mental representation in which each document contributes to the issue by providing either a factual background, an opinionated interpretation, or the evidence to support or confirm these interpretations. We define this document-based representation as a *global argument model*.

The global argument model includes noting the controversial aspects of a story, the claims being made, and the connections between the

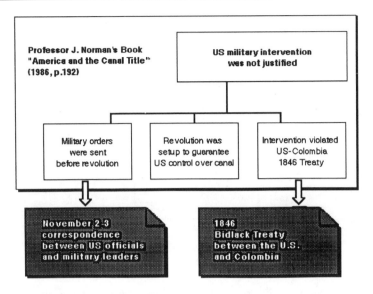

FIG. 3.6. Local argument structure for Norman's document (shaded documents are used to support arguments).

claims and the specific evidence used to support them. Information from every document that a student reads about a topic may be included in this representation. For example, in reading several accounts of the U.S. acquisition of a canal one quickly realizes that there is disagreement over the extent of U.S. involvement in the Panamanian revolution. Some authors argue that the 1846 Bidlack Treaty gave the United States the right to prevent the Colombian troops from suppressing a revolution in Panama. Others argue that the treaty allowed the United States only the right to protect transit, not to interfere in Colombian sovereignty (see Table 3.8, for an example). The ensemble of potentially available documents, their contribution to the issue, and the relationships among them define the global level of an argument model. Figure 3.7 shows the global argument model of a set of seven documents addressing the issue of U.S. intervention in the 1903 Panamanian revolution (Rouet et al., 1993).

The documents presented in Fig. 3.7 are categorized along two dimensions. The first dimension is *neutrality/bias*, or the position taken on the issue. Documents in the central column (textbook, correspondence, treaty) may be considered *neutral* in that they do not contain any conclusion regarding the issue. Documents located on each side (historians and witness accounts) are *opinionated*—that is, they present evaluations and conclusions on the issue. A second dimension is *primariness*, or the temporal/situational relation between a document and the events

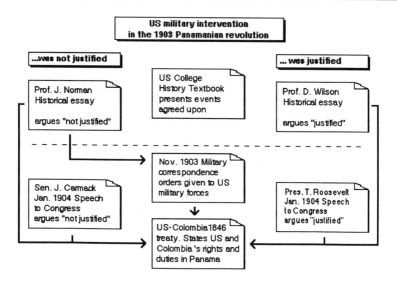

FIG. 3.7. Global argument structure for the problem *"Was the US military intervention in the Panamanian revolution justified?"* (arrows indicate references between documents).

it depicts. This characteristic is represented by the vertical arrangement of documents in Fig. 3.7. Documents below the dotted line may be considered primary; documents above this line may be considered secondary. Primary documents tend to be "closer" to the events: They were written before or by the time of the events, by persons taking part in the events. Some primary documents, like military correspondence, even play an active role in the events. Secondary documents are usually written after the events by people who did not participate (e.g., historians). Notice, however, that the primary/secondary distinction— although commonly accepted—cannot be established using a single characteristic of the documents. In addition, the two dimensions represented in Fig. 3.7 account for some, but not all, of the features of historical documents. Other characteristics (e.g., are the documents official or private) may also serve as distinctive features.[8]

The documents of Fig. 3.7 are related to each other in many ways. *Explicit references* are the most salient trace of a relationship between two documents. Norman's historical essay, for instance, refers to the military correspondence and to the Treaty of 1846 (see Table 3.8). Norman actually uses these documents to support the claim that the U.S.

---

[8]So far, there seems to be very little empirical evidence of how historians represent features of historical documents, and what role these features play in expert historical reasoning (but see Wineburg, 1991a).

intervention was not justified. Notice that Norman's arguments may be based on source information, such as when the military orders were issued, as opposed to content information, that is, *what* the orders were.

Less visible relations between documents also play an important role in understanding a controversy. For example, Norman and Wilson's accounts are related in that they present opposite views on the same issue; Carmack's speech is contextually related to Roosevelt's (both took place in the same session of the U.S. Congress, in January 1904).

A student learning about a complex historical problem, such as the one described in Fig. 3.7, must identify the sources of information, how they contribute to the problem, and the relationships between sources. In other terms, the student will have to build up a representation of the global organization of the argument model.

Students' Representation of Argument Models

Constructing an argument model from history texts undoubtedly requires specific skills (e.g., knowing what makes a reliable source and what is acceptable evidence; processing different texts simultaneously). It may be questioned whether students without any expertise in history possess these skills. Indeed, the study by Wineburg (1991a) illustrates the gap that exists between historians and high school students when studying a historical problem. Only historians were able to apply several important study heuristics, such as skipping the text to read the source first, comparing information across documents, or placing the information given in a broader context.

Despite those earlier findings, we believe that students may be able to build up argument models from history documents, under appropriate study conditions. For instance, students may be able to transfer useful heuristics from everyday life situations. When listening to a report of an event, most students have learned to take into account who is giving the information (e.g., what are their motives) and to judge how they know the information (e.g., was the person a firsthand witness). When given the opportunity to hear more than one side, students have learned to compare different versions of a story and note discrepancies.

It is also our assumption that learning from different sources may promote an awareness of the uncertainty that surrounds historical problems. That certain assertions made in a document are one-sided opinions rather than unchallenged truths becomes clear only when one confronts a second document taking a different stance on the same point. Similarly, accessing primary evidence may contribute to a better understanding of the issue. Opposite points of views often rely on different interpretations of the same piece of evidence. For example, in Fig. 3.7, the 1846 Treaty is referred to in four other documents, and is used to support arguments on both sides of the controversy. Although the legal jargon of a treaty might be an obstacle to the average reader, reading this document allows a better evaluation of contradictory claims. In return, reading discussions of the treaty may help a reader understand the significance of certain clauses and their consequences.

An experiment conducted with college students allowed us to observe the building and use of argument models (Rouet et al., 1993). In this study, we wanted to assess students' use of different types of documents when reasoning about historical controversies. More specifically, we wanted to study the role of primary documents in students' representation of the controversy. We gave 24 college students the task of studying four controversies about the Panama Canal story (e.g., To what extent was the U.S. intervention in the Panamanian Revolution justified?). For each controversy, students read seven different documents presented with a simple hypertext interface. Then, they were asked to write a short essay expressing their opinion, and to evaluate the sources. For half of the subjects, the document set was a textbook excerpt, two secondary documents (historians' accounts), two intermediate documents (accounts written by participants), and two primary documents (e.g. treaties); for the other half, the two primary documents were replaced with additional secondary documents.

It was not the primary purpose of the experiment to test for students' use of an argument model. We did, however, find some indications that they were representing this level of information in their essays and their evaluation of the sources.

Evidence for a Global Argument Model. One aspect of the global argument model is whether there is a trace of the relations between documents indicated through the use of references in the students' essays. In this study, we did not specifically ask students to refer to documents. We found, however, that a majority of the essays (56%) contained at least one reference to a document read. This proportion was higher in the primary group (67%) than in the secondary group (46%). Moreover, of the 77 document references found in the essays (across the four problems), 51% concerned primary documents, 28.5% concerned intermediate documents, and 21.5% concerned secondary documents. Thus, when asked to express their opinion of a historical problem, students were able to recall the source of the information they read. This finding indicates that at least part of the global argument model is learned during the study process. The larger number of references in the primary group also suggests that primary documents may enhance students' awareness of the argument model.

We hypothesize that students might make use of their argument model even though they do not quote their sources. Restating arguments from the documents is an example of the use of the global level of the argument model. Consider the essay written by AZ in response to problem 2, as shown in Table 3.9. AZ accurately repeats arguments from three different documents (though only citing the specific source of one). The three arguments that AZ recalls are (a) the 1846 treaty provided legal justification to protect the railroad, (b) because no threat to the railroad existed, the United States was not justified in interfering, and (c) no country would sign a treaty giving up their right to protect their own sovereignty. For this controversy, most of the subjects' essays (88%) contained at least one argument from an available document. Again, this suggests that college students are able to represent the global level of arguments.

A more qualitative analysis of the references showed that students were sensitive to different types of documents. Some students referred to historians' accounts explicitly to support their assertions (e.g., "As Prof. Norman wrote in his book, . . . "). They were more likely to challenge the points made in intermediate documents (e.g., President Roosevelt's autobiography) than in other types of documents. For

TABLE 3.9
Examples of Students' Essays from the Hypertext Study

The following two essays were written to answer the question: "To what extent was the U.S. military intervention in the Panama revolution justified?

(AZ): I believe that the U.S. had a right to interfere as long as there was a conflict going against the 1846 treaty. However, this doesn't seem to be the case. There was no threat to the transit system, so the U.S. really had no right to intervene as they did. I have to stand behind Senator Carmack who said that no country is going to give up their own right to land on their own soil. Most of the evidence given tends to go against the U. S. as far as the intervention being justified.

(BY): Legally, the intervention of the U. S. military forces in the Panama Revolution was totally unjustified. According to the Bidlack Treaty, the U. S. promised to recognize the sovereignty of the Colombian government over the territory and guarantee free passage to all. Prof. Norman was correct in stating that if Hubbard had received his telegram earlier, he would not have even allowed Colombian troops to land in their own nation. It is true that Shaler was instructed to deny use of the railroad to both sides, but the revolutionaries did not need the railroad, the Colombians did. Thus, U.S. actions were prejudiced against Colombia and contrary to the terms of the Bidlack Treaty.

example, after restating the points made by Roosevelt to justify U.S. intervention in the Panamanian revolution, a student humorously concluded, "Sorry, Teddy, but I don't buy it." Knowing that the author was directly involved in the events in question made his position weaker in the eyes of this student. Similarly, we found that students considered the documents in which an author defended his or her own actions to be less trustworthy than documents in which the author—although a participant—did not defend himself.

Evidence for a Local Level of Representation. The essay data also indicated that students had learned at least part of the local argument model. Partial evidence for the local level is found by examining the accuracy of explicit references in student essays. For each reference ($N=77$), we determined if the material cited was, in fact, in the document mentioned. Only seven errors were found: four errors (2×2) resulted from an exchange of sources and contents. For example, one subject attributed a statement from Norman to Wilson, and vice versa. Two subjects confused the provisions of two treaties. One subject attributed to Roosevelt a statement made in the textbook excerpt. In all other cases (91%), subjects correctly recalled the content of documents they referred to. This suggests that subjects can accurately remember the specific connection between the source and the document, at least when detailed source information is supplied when reading.

Further evidence for the local level of an argument representation comes from the justifications of trustworthiness and usefulness the students made for the sources. After writing their essays, the students were asked to rank the trustworthiness or usefulness of each source without looking back at the contents. In approximately 14% of the justifications, the students mentioned information contained in the document. For example, one student found a document useful because it "cites precedent of guarding the railroad, but not of interdicting Colombian troops." Another subject thought a document was trustworthy because "this excerpt shows how Panama benefited."

Some of these statements were not specific enough to verify that the content came from only that particular document. However, there were 110 justifications that had identifiable origins. Of these, the vast majority (92%) were found to be accurate. In addition, the majority of the students (88%) mentioned at least one verifiably correct statement of content given the source. In other words, when students justified their rankings on the basis on the content, they were correct in attributing the information to that source. When students were incorrect, they often confused one source with a similar source. In fact, most of these confusions were in the first controversy, which had three documents written by Roosevelt (two letters during the same time period, and an excerpt from his autobiography). This finding suggests that students do connect the content with the source, and that source discriminability may influence this skill.

Discussion

In this section, we argued that students construct a model of the argument that includes remembering who said what and what evidence was used to support their conclusions. We argued that building an argument model is an important component of learning from multiple documents. We found evidence of this argument representation in the Rouet et al. (1993) study. Students accurately identified the contents of a specific document in their justifications of trustworthiness and usefulness and in their essays.

Although we believe students form an argument model during incidental reading, our conclusions about students' skills were made in light of our explicit learning task (essay writing and source evaluation). There are two ways our procedures could have enhanced the construction of an argument model. First, the task was to study controversies and come to an educated opinion. We gave the students the controversial aspects of the story rather than asking them to pull the controversies out of longer documents. It may be that this task helped the students focus on the arguments. Although aiding this focus was our intent, it leaves us unsure about how readers of long texts build up a global level of the argument model.

Second, it may be that because we gave our subjects detailed source information, had them write an essay, and had them judge sources, they were more apt to build up this level of representation. In fact, Wineburg (1991a) gave high-school students and experts several documents with the source information printed last instead of first, as in our study. Wineburg found that, unlike the experts, the high-school students did not go to the source information first. Thus, reading the source of a document first may be a critical aspect of building up this type of representation.

Finally, several questions remain unanswered in the conceptualization of argument models presented here: Is the distinction between local and global components functionally valid? What exactly constitutes the units of an argument model at the local and global level? For what type of learning task is the use of an argument model relevant? Obviously, the theoretical propositions and empirical data presented here cannot address these important points. They suggest, however, that specific models must be developed to account for how people represent historical problems based on multiple documents.

SUMMARY AND CONCLUSIONS

We have described a causal-temporal event model as a method of representing the narrative structure of history text. In a series of experiments with fourth graders to college students, we have demonstrated the usefulness of this model in assessing the knowledge that students acquire from history texts and in predicting specific aspects of the text that will cause difficulty in understanding.

Using the model to score students' answers, we found that as early as fourth grade, students are able to use their experience with narratives to learn discrete events from a history story. However, only the older students were able to build a representation of the text's complex narrative structure that included both the events and their causal connections. Although early practice with reading narratives allows the young student to initially learn facts from the text, it is not until sixth grade that the relations between discrete events are routinely learned. Younger students appear to need more assistance in understanding the motivations and causes of the events. The causal-event model was also useful in studying what college students learn from lengthy texts in the course of repeated readings. We found that these students were more likely to include core events in their summaries, although they continued to learn about peripheral information.

In analyzing how history texts account for complex, controversial problems, we propose argument models to describe how arguments are organized in a set of documents about a historical controversy. An argument model involves two levels of organization. At the local level, each source is associated with its position, or claim. The position may be supported by several arguments. In turn, these arguments may be based on various pieces of evidence, including other documents or sources. At the global level, an argument model represents all the sources available and their relationship. We suggest that building a mental representation of an argument model is an important component of understanding historical controversies. The analysis of inexpert students' argumentative essays provides some evidence for the psychological validity of argument models.

ACKNOWLEDGMENTS

The research reported in this chapter was primarily supported by a grant from the Office of Educational Research and Improvement (OERI), United States Department of Education to the Center for Student Learning, Learning Research and Development Center. Additional funding was also provided by the Mellon Foundation. The opinions expressed do not necessarily reflect the position or policy of OERI or the Mellon Foundation and no official endorsement should be inferred.

REFERENCES

Bovair, S., & Kieras, D. E. (1984). A guide to propositional analysis for research on technical prose. In B. K. Britton & J. B. Black (Eds.), *Understanding expository text* (pp. 315–362). Hillsdale, NJ: Lawrence Erlbaum Associates.

Britt, M., Bell, L., & Perfetti, C. A. (1990). *Learning from middle grades science and history texts: General comprehension skills and domain specific knowledge.* Unpublished report.

Center for Strategic Studies. (1967). *Panama: Canal issues and treaty talks.* Washington, DC: Georgetown University.

Crane, P. M. (1978). *Surrender in Panama: The case against the treaty.* Ottawa, IL: Green Hill.

Crismore, A. (1984). The rhetoric of textbooks: Metadiscourse. *Journal of Curriculum Studies, 16,* 279–293.

LaFeber, W. (1978). *The Panama Canal: The crisis in historical perspective.* New York: Oxford University Press.

Macmillan. (1986). *The United States and the other Americas.* New York: Author.

Mandler, J. M., & Johnson, N. S. (1977). Remembrance of things parsed: Story structure and recall. *Cognitive Psychology, 9,* 111–151.

Omanson, R. C. (1982). The relation between centrality and story category variation. *Journal of Verbal Learning and Verbal Behavior, 21,* 326–337.

Perfetti, C. A., Britt, M. A., & Georgi, M. C. (1993). *Learning and reasoning about history.* Manuscript in preparation.

Ravitch, D. R., & Finn, C. E. (1987). *What do our 17-year-olds know? A report on the first national assessment of history and literature.* New York: Harper and Row.

Rouet, J. F., Britt, M. A., Mason, R. A., & Perfetti, C. A. (1993). *Using multiple sources of evidence to study historical controversies.* Manuscript in preparation.

Stein, N. L., & Glenn, C. G. (1979). An analysis of story comprehension in elementary school children. In R. O. Freedle (Ed.), *New directions in discourse processing* (pp. 53–120). Hillsdale, NJ: Lawrence Erlbaum Associates.

Thorndyke, P. W. (1977). Cognitive structures in comprehension and memory of narrative discourse. *Cognitive Psychology, 9,* 77–110.

Thornton, S. J. (1991). Teacher as curriculum-instructional gatekeeper in social studies. In J. P. Shaver (Ed.), *Handbook of research on social studies teaching and learning* (pp. 237–248). New York: Macmillan.

Trabasso, T., & Sperry, L. L. (1985). Causal relatedness and importance of story events. *Journal of Memory and Language, 24,* 595–611.

Trabasso, T., & van den Broek, P. (1985). Causal thinking and the representation of narrative events. *Journal of Memory and Language, 24,* 612–630.

Trabasso, T., Secco, T., & van den Broek, P. (1984). Causal cohesion and story coherence. In H. Mandl, N. L. Stein, & T. Trabasso (Eds.), *Learning and comprehension of text* (pp. 83–111). Hillsdale, NJ: Lawrence Erlbaum Associates.

Trabasso, T. (1989). Causal representation of narratives. *Reading Psychology, 10*(1), 67–83.

Turner, A., & Green, E. (1978). *Construction and use of a propositional textbase.* (from JSAS catalogue of selected documents in Psychology, 1713).

van den Broek, P. (1989). The effects of casual structure on the comprehension of narratives: Implications for education. *Reading Psychology, 10*(1), 19–44.

van Dijk, T. A., & Kintsch, W. (1983). *Strategies of discourse comprehension.* New York: Academic Press.

Wineburg, S. S. (1991a). Historical problem solving: A study of the cognitive processes used in the evaluation of documentary and pictorial evidence. *Journal of Educational Psychology, 83,* 73–87.

Wineburg, S. S. (1991b). On the reading of historical texts: Notes on the breach between school and academy. *American Educational Research Journal, 28,* 495–519.

Wineburg, S. S., & Wilson, S. M. (1991). Subject-matter knowledge in the teaching of history. *Advances in Research on Teaching, 2,* 305–347.

CHAPTER 4

The Cognitive Representation of Historical Texts

Samuel S. Wineburg
University of Washington

My purpose in this chapter is to describe how historians read historical texts. This charge seems simple enough, yet it has been curiously avoided in the explosion of research known as the "cognitive revolution" (Gardner, 1985). To be sure, there is a considerable body of work by historians on the "historical method" (e.g., Barzun & Graff, 1962; Cantor & Schneider, 1967; Gray, 1959; Shafer, 1969) and a growing body of work on the rhetorical and linguistic properties of written history (e.g., McCloskey, 1985; Struever, 1985; White, 1973). But there is no substantial empirical tradition, as we have in such fields as physics (Chi, Feltovich, & Glaser, 1981; Larkin, McDermott, Simon, & Simon, 1980) or mathematics (Schoenfeld, 1985), that investigates the "on-line" cognitions of historians as they think about issues of professional practice.

The end products of historical cognition are available for examination by studying the expansive monographic literature in history. But what about the intermediate processes of historical cognition? How is it that historians come to know what they know? What cognitive processes do they use to piece together the past when the documents they review are fragmented and internally inconsistent? What rules of thumb do they use to resolve textual contradictions and how do they get from sketchy document to comprehensive narrative? These questions, at the heart of any investigation of historical reasoning, recall an earlier set of questions about the "historic sense" raised by J. Carleton Bell (1917) in the fledgling *Journal of Educational Psychology*. Remarkably little progress has been made in addressing Bell's questions in the ensuing nine decades (cf. Wineburg, in press).

I begin this chapter by introducing readers to the theoretical framework for my work. From there, I sketch out a model of how historical texts are represented in readers' minds, drawing on a set of think-aloud protocols from eight historians. I conclude by discussing where this work fits into a larger research program, and how explorations of historical reasoning can inform educational research more generally.

THEORETICAL FRAMEWORK

Researchers who study the processing of written texts must make decisions about the appropriate level of analysis for the questions they ask and phenomena they investigate. My goal was not to understand the act of reading in all of its perceptual and cognitive complexity, but to shed light on the controlled processes (Shiffrin & Schneider, 1977) that occur when people read in the particular subject matter domain of history. But even among researchers who study controlled processes, there is a range of levels at which one can look at the reading process. At one end of the spectrum are researchers such as Kintsch and van Dijk, whose goal is nothing short of a comprehensive model embracing all forms of discourse processing. In their analyses of text processing (van Dijk & Kintsch, 1983; Kintsch, 1986) these researchers break sentences down into their smallest meaning units, called *propositions*, in order to design computer simulations to test their models. At the other end of the spectrum are a host of literary critics and reading-response theorists less concerned with the processing of single sentences than with the processing of thousands of sentences in the form of whole novels and literary works (e.g., Tompkins, 1980). Bypassing the basic psychological processes of text comprehension, these critics ask questions about the global meanings attached to literary works and the validity of these meanings as they apply to the intentions of the author (Hirsch, 1976), to one's "interpretative community" (Fish, 1980), to the world of textuality that resides within the pages of the text (Derrida, 1976), or to the material conditions in society that frame the act of reading (Barthes, 1975).

The goal of the present research was not to create a computer simulation (however useful that may be) but to describe the cognitive processes that occur when reading a series of historical texts. In view of this goal, the reduction of texts into propositions would be premature, for the amount of detail generated by such an enterprise would obscure the more global questions being asked. On the other hand, leaving texts whole would be equally intractable, given the goal of understanding the intermediate cognitive processes that contribute to the construction of meaning. Therefore, the "unit of analysis" here lies somewhere between the atom-like proposition and the unwieldy whole text. I discuss the construction of historical meaning in terms of *cognitive representations* of text. By representation, I mean, simply, the private cognitive structures that readers build in their minds as they read.

The data presented here come from a larger research program examining how historians, teachers, and high school students think about history and historical texts (e.g., Wilson & Wineburg, 1988, in press; Wineburg, 1991a, 1991b, 1992; Wineburg & Fournier, 1992a, 1992b; Wineburg & Wilson, 1991). Specifically, the data for the following presentation come from eight historians who were taught to "think aloud" (Ericsson & Simon, 1984) as they read documents about the Battle of Lexington, the opening volley of the Revolutionary War. These historians were presented with a series of documents about the battle, ranging from eyewitness accounts and recollections by contemporaries to textbook treatments and even an excerpt from a historical novel (see Appendix). As they read these documents, historians articulated their thoughts about what happened at Lexington on the morning of April 19, 1775.[1]

I purposely recruited historians with varied specialties and backgrounds because I was interested in what, if anything, united historians as a group. In particular, I wondered whether historians who knew a great deal about the time period would read documents differently from historians who knew little about Lexington or the American Revolution more generally. Some of these historians were steeped in the Colonial period, but others, such as a specialist in Japanese history and a medievalist, knew little more about the Revolution than what they remembered from high school or college survey courses. Six held a PhD and two were doctoral candidates. Four historians considered themselves to be Americanists (and had taught American history), and four did not.

Comprehending Comprehension

Asking people to articulate their thoughts as they read texts tells us much about the act of comprehension (Bereiter & Bird, 1985; Collins,

---

[1]See Wineburg (1991a) for a full explanation of the methodology used in this study.

Brown, & Larkin, 1980; Flower, 1988; cf. Norris & Phillips, 1987). Yet the dominant mode of assessing reading comprehension ignores intermediate cognitions to focus instead on their end points: students' answers on multiple choice tests (Durkin, 1978–1979). A second approach to assessing reading comprehension, used less widely than multiple choice tests, defines it as the ability to reproduce information contained in texts. In such studies, students typically read a passage and write down all they can remember. According to Graves and Slater (1986), this system is a "valid and reliable indicator of comprehension and is widely used and accepted" (p. 37).

Not all researchers agree. As Kintsch (1986) noted, the fact that people can read a text and remember what it says hardly means they have understood or learned from it. Indeed, Schmalhofer (cited in Perrig & Kintsch, 1985) showed that novice programmers could formulate the gist of passages from a computer programming manual and still have little idea how to write a program using this computer language. Similarly, Perrig and Kintsch (1985) found that subjects who read a description about a town could recognize statements from that description and summarize the text reasonably well, but still be unable to draw a map or make simple inferences based on what they read.

Such examples raise questions about whether we have confused the act of *remembering* a text with the act of *understanding* it. Certainly the ability to understand and remember the literal meaning of a text is a necessary prerequisite for comprehension. One cannot understand a passage without first understanding the words it uses, the sentences it contains, and the relationship between these words and sentences. But a literal understanding of the text, or what van Dijk and Kintsch (1983) called the *text base*, is only one aspect of comprehension. In addition to the text base model, readers must construct, according to van Dijk and Kintsch, *situation models*, or cognitive representations of the situation or event described by the text. In their words, situation models feature "all of the knowledge that is left implicit in the text or otherwise presupposed" (p. 338).

The applicability of van Dijk and Kintsch's *situation model* to historical texts makes intuitive sense. For example, primary sources that describe a battle are scarcely understandable if a reader cannot construct a representation of where the forces stood, what the battlefield looked like, and how the commander might have felt as he faced his adversary. Yet, while Kintsch has made great progress in understanding how people construct text base models, he notes that our understanding of "how situation models are formed and how they are used is still in its infancy" (Kintsch, 1986, p. 90).

It is impossible for readers of history to comprehend texts without forming situation models, or something akin to them. But the unique imperatives of historical texts may spur readers to form cognitive representations different from either text base or situation models. The act of writing history is not a process of simply recording what happened or even imagining how the participants felt as it was happening. Rather, the writing of history is itself an act that reflects human authorship and is fraught with human concern. As Alan Nevins (1962) explained:

> No greater error can be made in historical study than to regard man as primarily a rational being; he is primarily an emotional being, and even when he is most rational his thinking processes are insensibly colored by subjective feeling. Everyone recognizes the five or six principal sentiments which dominate men: racial feeling, national feeling, local feeling, political feeling, religious or sectarian feeling, class feeling, professional or vocational feeling, and the feeling of attachment to particular codes of morals. (p. 221)

When we ask how a source reflects its author's understanding of reality our appeal is not to a world of situations, events, and occurrences. Rather, we make reference to a *linguistic* world, a world composed of words. It would be a mistake to equate this "world" with the traditional province of rhetoric and its focus on authorial intent, for as Derrida has argued, texts are cultural artifacts and, once written, often eclipse and elide their authors' intentions (Derrida, 1976). But just as van Dijk and Kintsch's (1983) situation model does not address these "world making" (Goodman, 1978) aspects of text, so their text base model, a model of the literal meaning of the text, is also an inadequate snare for capturing how texts go beyond their authors' intentions. To probe such textual features, a reader must look beyond—or beneath—the words on the page.

In what follows, I present a framework for analyzing the cognitive representations formed in the minds of historians as they read a series of documents about the American Revolution. My goal is to present a terminology for discussing, analyzing, and differentiating among the representations built by historians. Whether or not the representations I describe constitute discrete levels (an unlikely prospect) or form multilevels of a single representation is a concern I leave to future investigations. My goal here is chiefly heuristic: to formulate a set of constructs that will begin the process of charting and documenting historians' cognitive activity.

FROM EVENTS TO "EVENTS AS TEXTS"

I begin with a simplified model for understanding the cognitive representations formed by the historians in this study (Fig. 4.1). The model takes as its starting point the historical event, which was recorded by someone interested in preserving its memory. This record, be it a document, a hieroglyph, or even a drawing in a prehistoric cave, is itself a representation—a selection of key features and an interpretation of the event it sets out to preserve.

The reasons for the lack of isomorphism between an event and its representation are legion. First, the act of writing history, or of translating actions, motives, and events into words, is at base a linguistic enterprise, and to casually equate words with the deeds and actions they represent poses many problems. To cite one example: Hitler's destruction of European Jewry is not equal to the thousands of words used to describe it by such historians as Lucy Davidowicz (1975) and Raul Hilberg (1967), no matter how complex and multifaceted their accounts may be. The act of writing constrains how the past can be represented by forcing historians to order events sequentially even when they may have occurred simultaneously; writing something down means putting one thing before another. Moreover, as Jerome Bruner reminded us, language can never be neutral but

imposes a point of view not only about the world to which it refers but toward the use of mind in respect of this world. Language necessarily

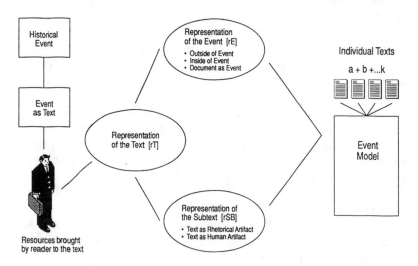

FIG. 4.1.   Model of the cognitive representation of historical texts

imposes a perspective in which things are viewed and a stance toward what we view. It is not just, in the shopworn phrase, that the medium is the message. The message itself may create the reality that the message embodies and predispose those who hear it to think about it in a particular mode. (1985, pp. 121–122).

That texts represent (as opposed to *capture, mirror,* or *fix*) events may seem obvious, living as we do in an era when the architects of deconstructionism have shaken our faith in the correspondence theory of text. But the obviousness of this assertion derives from the fact that how we think is shaped by the prevailing ideas of our time. Indeed, during much of human history, including the recent past, the historical work was seen as a true and authentic copy of past events. As Gossman noted, the 19th-century historian appeared "as a privileged reporter reconstructing what happened. The historical text is thus not presented as a model to be discussed, criticized, accepted, or repudiated by the free and inquiring intellect, but as the *inmost form of the real, binding, and inescapable*" (1978, p. 24, emphasis in original). Similarly, Lord Acton, writing at the end of the last century, expressed an unbridled faith in the objectivity of written history: "In critical places," he wrote, "we must indicate minutely the sources we follow, and must refer not only to the important books, but to articles in periodical works, and even to original documents, and to transcripts in libraries." This would be "history, original and authentic" as opposed to "antiquated" history (cited in Stern, 1972).

The relationship between historical events and the words used to represent them is a complex philosophical issue and the subject of a voluminous literature that cannot be adequately reviewed here. I might only state that my position is closest to that of Stanford (1986), who argued against extreme historical idealism by positing a past reality to which the words of history *refer* (as opposed to *correspond*). This chapter and the larger research program it represents will hardly lay to rest debates that rage within the philosophy of history. For the most part, historians are too busy writing history to even be concerned with the epistemological battles that enthrall philosophers (cf. Bailyn, 1963; but see also Novick, 1988). And philosophers, as the late Louis O. Mink (1987) was fond of saying, are more interested in the remains, than the views, of historians. Nonetheless, inquiries into the nature of the relationship among texts, events, and evidence invariably butt into issues of epistemology, and among the ranks of historians one can find epistemologists of all stripes (e.g., Barzun, 1974; Berkhofer, 1988; Degler, 1963, 1976, 1980; Harlan, 1989; Hexter, 1971, 1979; Hollinger, 1989; LaCapra, 1985). An extreme position, cited by Gossman (1978), coyly claimed that George Washington has the same epistemological status as an electron, for "each is an entity postulated for the purpose of giving coherence to our present experience, and each is unobservable by us" (p. 27). At the other end of the spectrum, and probably more representative of the bulk of working historians, are the views of the eminent Americanist Gordon Wood:

> It is precisely because ever-widening circles of our culture are casting doubt on this traditional epistemology [of nineteenth-century positivism] that historians feel more humble about what they do. Some of the most eminent working historians such as G.R. Elton and Oscar Handlin know that ultimately there can be no alternative for their craft than this old-fashioned epistemology. Historians, warns Elton, "require not the new humility preached in the wake of Heisenberg, but some return to the assurance of the nineteenth century that the work they are doing deals with reality." "The historian's vocation," writes Handlin, "depends on this minimal operational article of faith: Truth is absolute; it is absolute as the world is real." This faith may be philosophically naive, may even be philosophically absurd in this skeptical and relativist-minded age; nevertheless it is what makes history writing possible. Historians who cut loose from this faith do so at the peril of their discipline. (1982, p. 59)

Whether or not texts mirror reality or are only vague approximations of it, they are still comprehended by a reader, who brings to that text a set of *resources* (cf. Schoenfeld, 1985) for understanding it—background knowledge, meaning-making and problem-solving strategies, and beliefs about what it means to read a historical text. Using these resources, the reader of history creates various cognitive representations of the text (for more on resources see Wineburg, 1991a). Each of the representations depicted in Fig 4.1, while sufficiently distinct from one another to merit separate categories, work together in fostering historical understanding by communicating results between each other and interacting in highly-complex and unpredictable ways. The *representation of the text* (rT) and the *representation of the event* (rE) correspond to van Dijk and Kintsch's text base and situation models, respectively.[2] These representations are joined by a third, the *representation of the subtext* (rSB), which embraces readers' efforts to reconstruct authorial intentions and purposes, and to determine the guiding assumptions, biases, and convictions that frame historical texts. In the sections that follow, I describe

---

[2]The departure from van Dijk and Kintsch's terminology—the use of *event* in place of *situation*—is due to the use of the former term in the historiographic and philosophical lexicon, where it refers to the consequences of human actions, as opposed to *occurrence*, which typically refers to a nonhuman phenomenon, like earthquakes or volcanic eruptions.

each of these representations with excerpts from historians' think-aloud protocols.

Representation of the Text

If readers are to go beyond the literal meaning of the text, they must first understand it. Extensive linguistic knowledge, knowledge that is often tacit, must be marshaled to understand the meanings of words. Readers must be able to link clauses and sentences together to see the basic connections between them. They must be able to determine the correct referents for pronouns and other anaphoric references. They must be able to strip away surface features of the text to get at its kernel or main point. All of these processes occur when readers construct the representation of the text (rT).

The rT operates at both local and global levels. The local level refers to the construction of meaning at the word, phrase, or sentence level. The global level is concerned with the formation of meaning that embraces sentences, paragraphs, or whole texts. Global representations also make use of the structural aspects of text, such as story grammars (e.g., Stein & Glenn, 1979; Thorndyke, 1977) or the textual structures that characterize scientific writing (Dee-Lucas & Larkin, 1988). Inferences are a part of the rT, but only those that are necessary for establishing textual cohesion and coherence—in short, for understanding who did what to whom. Inferences that go beyond the literal meaning of the text come under the purview of the other two representations (cf. van Dijk & Kintsch, 1983).

Constructing representations of historical texts presents challenges not encountered with everyday texts. Words and phrases in historical texts often convey different meanings from their modern usage, and the lexical knowledge automatically activated in memory may turn out to be inappropriate or misleading. Consider an example in which a familiar word with an unfamiliar meaning first leads a historian to represent the subtext, but ultimately pulls her back to the more basic, but in this case less obvious, literal meaning.

The following example comes from the protocol of a specialist in Asian history who received her doctorate from Harvard. This historian (denoted by the initials MB) hesitated when she first encountered Document 1, Joseph Warren's cover letter to Parliament, which states near the beginning: "By the clearest depositions relative to this transaction, it will appear that on the night preceding the nineteenth of April instant . . . " At this point in her reading, MB made this comment: " 'it will appear,' he's trying to show objectivity, or—no no, he's not. He's saying it will be made manifest to you, that's what he means by 'appear'."

In this brief comment, MB seems to shift gears in her construction of a representation. She initially represented "it will appear" rhetorically, that is, as a linguistic device the author uses to convey a sense of evenhandedness. In this reading, the phrase is not something the author actually believed (i.e., there are no doubts in the author's mind as to what really happened) but is placed in the text to gain credence with the audience. Had this comment stopped here it would have been considered a representation of the subtext. But almost as soon as MB suggested this reading, she retreated from it. "It will appear," she suggested, simply meant that "it will be made manifest," or that in the course of reading this communication, the sequence of events will become clear to the reader. This is not the most common meaning of "appear," but historians, familiar with documents from different time periods, are generally attuned to uncommon word meanings. Familiar words are often deceptive, for words, too, have histories of change and evolution. Indeed, the *Oxford English Dictionary* (1986) supports MB's reading of this phrase: Entries from this time period show that "appear" as "made manifest" was common usage.

MB's reading is a successful and highly creative example of the rT at the local level. It is a reading that shows sensitivity to language, a knowledge of linguistic change, and a willingness to subject initial readings to further scrutiny. But a second example shows how things can go wrong, even with highly skilled and knowledgeable professionals. In this example, a flawed representation of the text necessitates a highly creative representation of the event that, though creative, still misses the mark. In reading Lister's diary (Document 8), SY, a Wisconsin trained specialist in American business history, paused after this sentence: "Major Pitcairn of the Marines, second in command, called to them to disperse, but their not seeming willing he desired us to mind our space which we did when they gave us a fire":

> but their "not seeming willing" to disperse, he, Pitcairn, "desired us to mind our space." I'm not quite sure what that means, presumably it would be—"mind our space"—okay, I suspect that probably means to space out so they could fire, because you'd fire muzzleloader in—because it takes time to reload them, you have ranks fire one at a time, so you'd space out and you'd have one group fire, then another group fire while the first was reloading. I expect that's what it means, I don't know.

SY began by identifying Pitcairn as the reference for "he." But he ran into trouble with his representation of the phrase "mind our space."

Again, the *Oxford English Dictionary* offers various definitions of "mind" that correspond to how that verb is now used in such idioms as "mind your manners" or "mind your temper." Indeed, this was how several of the other historians interpreted the phrase. However, SY, baffled by the phrase, hypothesized that it has something to do with the procedures used by the British to fire muzzleloading guns. In this instance, his extensive knowledge of colonial firearms steered him down the wrong path.

The rT is also evident when the construction of meaning breaks down, and historians, like other skilled readers, deploy various "fix-up" procedures (Brown, 1980) to regain comprehension. The antiquated syntax and vocabulary of historical documents can be the source of these problems, many of which are seen in the example presented in Table 4.1. MB makes an initial error in representing the text, wrongly attributing to the minutemen the action of "dispatching six companies." Her initial comments show that her representation of the text is at odds with what she would have predicted: The organization of men into formal companies contradicts her impression of the minutemen as a "rag-tag" group of soldiers. MB becomes aware of a comprehension problem when she encounters the phrase "to secure two bridges"; apparently it is her representation of colonists securing their own bridges that sends her back to the beginning of the document. The middle of this protocol provides further insights into the source of MB's confusion: She has created a connection between "the ringing of bells" (a signal to muster the troops) and the dispatching of companies, without realizing that it was the British who dispatched the companies. But again she runs into the same obstacle—the order to secure bridges—which sends her to the beginning of the document for the third time, at which point her initial error in representing the text finally becomes clear.

This is an example of a reader in trouble, but one who possesses a repertoire of generic comprehension monitoring skills for reestablishing comprehension. Examples such as this were relatively rare in the protocols of historians, as the representation of the text was largely fluid, straightforward, and automatic. More frequent, however, were global representations of the text, in which historians reduced strings of sentences or whole paragraphs to short formulations of gist. For example, SY turned the 94-word introduction of Document 2 into a succinct distillation of action verbs—the minutemen were *called up, alarmed, gathered,* and *dismissed.* Similar distillations of meaning were present in every historian's protocol in practically every document read.

TABLE 4.1
MB's Comments on Document 5, *London Gazette*[a]

Lieutenant Nunn, of the Navy arrived this morning at Lord Dartmouth's and brought letters from General Gage, Lord Percy, and Lieutenant-Colonel Smith containing the following particulars of what passed on the nineteenth of April last between a detachment of the King's troops in the Province of Massachusetts-Bay and several parties of rebel provincials. [+]Lieutenant-Colonel Smith finding, [+]after he had advanced some miles on his march,	
	So it was probably like 2:00 in the morning because he had already started from Boston.
that the country had been alarmed by the firing of guns and ringing of bells,	
	Yeah, that was the whole idea, with Paul Revere running through the night, galloping through the night.
dispatched six companies of light-infantry,	
	Six companies of light-infantry, I thought it was 34 guys. Well, 200 to 300.[b] Light-infantry implies more organization, too, than one is led to believe from the American accounts, which seems to be just a bunch of citizens picking up their rifles and running out into the night . . .
in order to secure two bridges on different roads beyond Concord,	
	Now who's doing this? Let's see, "finding, after he had advanced some miles, that the country had been alarmed by the firing of guns and ringing of bells, dispatched," okay, now the question is who's doing the dispatching of six companies of light-infantry? I think the implication here is that they are American and they had been alarmed by the firing of guns and ringing of bells and then gotten together

(Continued)

96

TABLE 4.1 *(Continued)*

in order to secure two bridges on different roads beyond Concord,	
	Who wants to secure? This is not a very clear thing, I'd have to spend more time on this, because I'm not really sure who's doing the securing and who's dispatching the companies of light-infantry.
[backtracking to reread the first part of the text] *Lieutenant-Colonel Smith finding, after he had advanced some miles on his march, that the*	
	It sounds like this light-infantry, now I take this back, light-infantry is being dispatched by the British.
in order to secure two bridges on different roads beyond Concord, who, upon their arrival at Lexington,	
	Because those are the six companies are arriving in Lexington so I've changed my interpretation of this sentence here.

[a]The words in italics in the left column are from the document presented to the historian. The column on the right contains the words uttered by the historian immediately after the last italicized work in the left column. Dagger denotes a place in the protocol where comments not relevant to this example were deleted. [b]The number 34 refers to the men who signed Mulliken's deposition (Document 2), and the 200–300 is the estimate of the colonial force given by Barker (Document 4).

The Representation of the Event

> The historian's picture of his subject, whether that subject be a sequence of events or a past state of things, thus appears as a web of imaginative construction stretched between certain fixed points provided by a statement of his authorities, and if these points are frequent enough and the thread spun from each to the next are constructed with due care . . . and never by merely arbitrary fancy, the whole picture is constantly verified by appeal to these data, and runs little risk of losing touch with the reality which it represents. (Collingwood, 1946, p. 242)

Without Collingwood's "web of imaginative construction" the writing of history would be well-nigh impossible. Historical sources come fragmented and partial, invariably tainted by their limited perspective. Historians must go beyond the mass of detail offered by sources to discern some pattern or intelligible form. To do so, they rely on inference, the raw material of Collingwood's imaginative web. Inference is the connective tissue that binds sources together, which allows them to come together in narrative.[3] Relying on information from sources, and using a store of personal knowledge, experiences, and creative mental processes, the historian builds a representation of the event (rE), a representation of past people and past events.

Event is used here in its broadest sense, recognizing that the term carries with it some dubious connotations. Fernand Bruadel, in particular, pits the Annalist's approach[4] of the *longue durée,* history of the great duration, against *historire événementielle,* or history that focuses on the fleeting event, the type of history, or, so the argument goes, that is ultimately distorted when not viewed in the grand scheme of things. I use the term to refer not only to what happened, but also to questions of causality, why things happened, and combine under this rubric both the history of the *longue durée* and *historire événementielle.* Beyond that, the rE embraces the thoughts, feelings, views, hopes, and fears of the human agents that acted within the contours of that event. It also subsumes what the *Annales* school refers to as *mentalité,* or the world views held by entire societies over the course of centuries.

How do readers go from the words of the text to the worlds of the text, from the decoding of written symbols to the reconstruction of mental and physical states of people who lived in the past? To explore this question, consider FA's comments in Table 4.2 which came in response to the first line of Document 4. FA was a medievalist who specialized in the conception of history held by the Kar'aites, a breakaway sect of Jews who rejected the Oral Law. He began the task with little knowledge of the events at Lexington, but by the end of the task had a sophisticated understanding of what went on.

Though the phrase "long ford up to our middles" says nothing about the climate in eastern Massachusetts, the physical conditions endured by the marching soldiers, or the discomfort they felt, FA constructed a representation that integrated all of these aspects. These elements were not "in" the text, but were part of the event that FA reconstructed from it, and it was this set of inferences, rather than the actual text, that guided FA's reading of this and later documents. Thus, when he read in

---

[3]For Collingwood (1946), the "web of imaginative construction" is not the same thing as historical reality. Indeed, Collingwood's use of the phrase "reality which it represents" in the quotation is prescient. In a later chapter in *The Idea of History* he remarks that historical inference is "never compulsive, it is at best permissive, it never leads to certainty, only to probability" (p. 262).

[4]The term "Annalist" refers to a member of the *Annales* group, taken from the name of the French journal (*Annales d'histoire sociale et économique*) dedicated to "history in the round," broad historical analyses that embrace social and economic changes spanning centuries. See, for example, Braudel (1979).

TABLE 4.2
FA's Comments on Barker, Document 5

First Reading
19th. *At 2 o'clock we began*
our march by wading
through a very long ford up
to our middles

                  it must've been cold in April too

after going

                  ooh yeh, they are going to be wet and cold

Second Reading
19th. *At 2 o'clock we began*
our march by wading
through a very long ford up
to our middles

                  you come out of Boston and you have to cross the,
                  what is it, the James, the Charles? So it means that
                  they are really cold, from 2 o'clock in the morning—
                  they may not have dried out all night. These guys
                  may have been cold and wet all night.

the following document that British troops had "advanced some miles on their march," he returned to his earlier representation of Barker's account: "Now remember [the soldiers'] legs were cold." For FA, the coldness of the men's legs is not an embellishment that is added to his representation of the event, but the key to understanding Barker's later admission that his troops became "so wild they could hear no orders." In FA's rE, the soldiers' behavior resulted from the tension produced by military confrontation, a tension that was exacerbated by their being cold and wet. In this brief example, we see how this historian's rE is not just a description of an event but is itself an explanatory framework for it. The rE offers much in the way of a causal account: The soggy clothing of tired soldiers added to their nervousness, and it was this nervousness that led them to disobey orders.

Inside Versus Outside of Events. The rE operates at two basic levels, the *inside* and the *outside* of events (cf. Collingwood, 1946). An event's outside refers to its visible (or audible) aspects, those aspects available to sense perception and that might be observed by a vigilant eyewitness. In the context of Lexington, it would refer to how the forces were arrayed, the layout of the land, the configuration of buildings on Lexington Green, and whether the British Major Pitcairn truly raised his sword commanding his troops to fire. But the outside of events tells only half a story. The other half, the inside of the event, chronicles those things that cannot be seen, heard, or touched: the motivations, intentions, hopes, beliefs, and fears of historical agents. What were the colonists thinking as they assembled on Lexington Green? Did they really believe they could repel a British force that outnumbered and outgunned them? If not, what was the point of assembling in the first place? If the outside of events gets at what happened, the inside of events provides insight on why it happened.

To explore this distinction further, consider the comments of two historians on the same sentence from Lt. John Barker's diary (Document 4): "We had a man of the tenth light infantry wounded, no one else hurt." Barker is sketchy about the circumstances behind this casualty. Did it result from the first "one or two shots" mentioned earlier, or did these shots in turn set off a larger volley between the British soldiers and the minutemen? As the representation of text base shows in Fig. 4.2 (using the notation system of Norman & Rumelhart, 1975), the text base is silent. Consider, however, the comments of MJ, a Berkeley-trained Americanist who specialized in the history of Native Americans, immediately after the sentence just quoted.[5]

> I tend to feel that if they only had one man wounded they probably weren't getting that much return fire—it's not even clear that anyone is firing at them at this point. It doesn't say where he was wounded, how he was wounded, if he was wounded by his own men.

The tracks of MJ's thought go from fact to cause—from the fact that, according to Barker, only one man was wounded, to the idea that there must have been little return fire by the minutemen. The first thing MJ does in reconstructing the event is to go beyond the text base by drawing an inference that is highly probable, but not logically necessary (cf. Spiro, 1980). But MJ's next move is more subtle. He represents the event by consciously noting what cannot be known. He carefully avoids drawing an inference made by most of the other historians: that the infantryman's wound came from the opposing side. As the semantic representation of Barker's sentence shows in Fig. 4.2, the node for the agent responsible for the wounding of the British soldier is unspecified. However, the push toward making this inference is aided by what might be called a generic battle schema. Typically, when a source enumerates losses in battle, the battle schema assigns responsibility for these losses, in the absence of other information, to the opponent. Here MJ resisted such a schema-driven reading of this text. He first wanted to know

---

[5]MJ was completing his dissertation at the time he was interviewed. Six months before, he had taken his comprehensive exams in American history. He was the only historian among the eight to make specific reference to the monographic literature of Lexington and Concord (e.g., Gross, 1976).

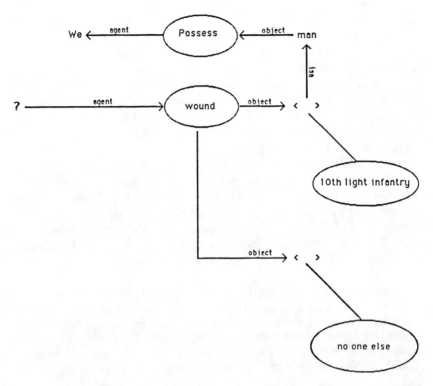

FIG. 4.2. Propositional representation following the notation of Norman and Rumelhart (1975).

where the soldier was wounded, a question presumably related to his questions about "how he was wounded." MJ suggested two possibilities that serve as alternatives to the schema-driven inference: (a) that the wound was self-inflicted (a possibility that might have been strengthened had MJ known that the soldier was wounded on the leg), and (b) that the wound came as a result of being shot by his own men in the pandemonium that broke out after the first shot was fired. But MJ curiously avoided intentionality, and so his reading stays entirely within the realm of the outside of the event.

A second example illustrates the distinction between representations of the outside and the inside of events. In response to the very same line in Barker's diary, TP, a Wisconsin-trained specialist in British history, commented: "That does suggest that the minutemen were not just, you know, seeking to really get into a heavy duty battle or they would've certainly wounded more people." The similarities between TP's and MJ's comments are apparent but there are also some important differences. First, embedded in TP's comment is the inference that the infantryman was the victim of a colonist's bullet, the same inference MJ resisted. But note that TP goes beyond a model of "what happened" to construct a model of the intentions of the minutemen who stood on Lexington Green facing seven hundred British soldiers. Reasoning from the lone casualty suffered by the British, TP infers that it was not the colonists' intention to engage in a full-fledged battle; in other words, if a serious battle had been their intention, many more casualties would-have been inflicted on the British. TP's comment signals an important leap from action to intention: In her mind, what occurred that April morning was not serendipitous, but part of a plan gone awry.

TP's interpretation that the intention of the colonists, at least initially, was not to inflict maximum injury on the British is highly plausible. Indeed, it is the same conclusion reached by Tourtellot in his study of Lexington and Concord. Citing Captain Parker's deep familiarity with guerrilla tactics from his experience as leader of Rogers's Company in the French and Indian War, Tourtellot (1959) stated:

> If Captain Parker had it in mind to challenge such a force, he knew how to do it. Before the road from Boston leveled out a straight line stretched before Lexington Common, it passed between two wooden hills. In ten minutes Captain Parker could've had his militia—out of range and out of sight of the British—raining bullets down on the heads of the enemy. Instead, he lined them up hopelessly ineffective on the Common. (p. 22)

The distinction between the representation of the outside and the inside of events is a useful one, but we should not think that the distinction has a psychological reality in the mind of the historian. The distinction is heuristic in that it allows us to describe different features of the rE. But the representation of the outside and the inside of events seems to go on spontaneously and unpredictably in the minds of historians. The comments of WL, a Stanford-trained specialist of American educational history, reflect this. Commenting on the first sentence of Barker's diary, WL paused:

> "19th we began our march by wading through a long ford" Okay, what, this again reminds me that one has to try to put themselves in the minds and the bodies of the British. They're starting out early in the morning, they must be walking quickly, I'd have to figure out how many miles between the barracks where Pitcairn and his troops left and how fast they were walking, because that would give me a sense of, that might help explain if they were really fatigued and then the adrenaline started to flow in the battle, that they may have lost control. They may have been angry, a whole range of other kinds of things. So the physical dimensions of when they left, the fact that they had to go through a river up to the

middles of their bodies means that they were wet, I suppose the entire time, so if I wanted to get a sense of the veracity of these accounts, then I would want to pick up on some of these details.

The separation of outside from inside would be artificial here—each is indispensable to WL's representation of the event. In his first pass through Barker's entry, WL was startled by the lieutenant's admission that his troops went wild. But the above comment, coming at the beginning of the second reading, shows how WL's rE becomes increasingly elaborated to account for this discrepant detail. Both aspects of this representation, the outside—the wetness of the men, their fatigue, their march through unfamiliar territory—and the inside—their tension, anger, and feelings of losing control—are central to WL's rE. Aside from the fixed points provided by the text (the verbs *marched* and *ford*, and Barker's admission that his men went wild), WL's comments exemplify how the historian puts the inside and outside together in representing the past. Indeed, WL says it best: Historians must put themselves "in the minds and bodies" of those they seek to understand.

The Document as Event. To this point I have focused on the outside and inside of events, or the actions and thoughts of historical agents. But an important aspect of representing historical events is understanding the nature of historical sources, particularly the circumstances under which these sources came into being. Considerations such as the position of witnesses vis-à-vis the events they report, the quality of information available to them, and their ability to tell the truth (provided that is their intention), as well as other situational factors, affect the quality of testimony and influence how historians represent events. In short, it is not just what a document says but how it came into being that is important when historians represent events.

The notion of the "document as event" is, at first glance, a peculiar thought. Ordinarily we conceive of events as battles, speeches, momentous decisions, acts of courage and the like, and documents as those linguistic entities that describe them. But for historians, a document's creation sometimes emerges as more important than the actual event it describes. Two examples appear in Table 4.3.

We see that almost immediately MJ rejected Barker's claim that Document 4 was a diary entry for the 19th of April, the day of the confrontation at Lexington. He based his judgment on knowledge about the aftermath of the encounter at Lexington; MJ knew that after leaving Lexington the British marched onto Concord where they faced stiff resistance, and they returned to Boston only after sustaining heavy loses. MJ reasoned that it would be unlikely for Barker, awake since the

TABLE 4.3
Examples of Representing the Document as Event

Excerpt from MJ on Document 4
19th

As soon as I see that I want to stop and see where it came from

entry for April 19th, diary of
Lieutenant John Barker, an
officer in the British Army.[a]

My guess is that this probably wasn't written until that night or probably not until the next day. He is going to be too busy marching around to stop and write in his diary, so he's had some time to think.

At 2 o'clock we began our
march

and having time to think and knowing that with what happened there was going to be possibly some kind of inquest or something like that, that it was important, he probably would be very very careful about what he is going to write.

Excerpt from WL on Document 6, Stiles
This account Major Pitcairn
himself gave Mr. Brown of
Providence who was seized
with flour

What does that mean? I don't understand what that means.

who was seized with flour
and carried to Boston a few
days after the battle; and
Gov. Session told it to me.

So, let me see if I have this now. This is a diary entry and the source for the diary entry is a Mr. Brown, who Major Pitcarin talked to, that's one, and then told—well, you don't know how many other people were told before it got to Gov. Session—who then told it to Ezra Stiles. So we have a "telephone communication," so to speak, one telling another and another, and we have at least 2 people, but you could say that there are more than 2 people. I don't know if Mr. Brown knew Gov. Sessions. So what we have is an account that has traveled through a minimum of 2, perhaps more people, before it got to Ezra Stiles.

[a]MJ skipped down to the bottom of the document at this point to read the attribution.

previous evening, to record the day's events on the 19th. And so MJ created an elaborate scenario in which Barker returns to Boston worried that his superiors might blame him for the debacle at Lexington and Concord, going so far as to convene an inquest into the day's events. Believing that he might be implicated for issuing the order to fire,

Barker, in MJ's scenario, crafts a diary entry to exonerate himself of wrongdoing. In other words, the diary entry is exactly the opposite of what it claims to be. Instead of a spontaneous outpouring of feelings, this document, according to MJ's reading, is a calculated attempt to provide Barker with an alibi should he later need one. Thus, the focus of this rE becomes not the Battle of Lexington, but how a document about the Battle of Lexington came into being.

In the second example, WL's concerns are not related to when events were recorded as much as to the quality of information available to the recorder. WL carefully reviews the document before him: a diary entry based on information that has passed through a minimum of two hands. But WL realizes that it is impossible to know just how many hands touched the information before it reached Stiles. Although Pitcairn may have given his account to Brown, it is unclear whether Sessions heard it directly from Mr. Brown, or from a third, fourth, or fifth party. WL is well aware of the distortions that creep into such "telephone communications" and ultimately questions the veracity of the source because of such distortions.

Both examples demonstrate how historians weigh documentary evidence by reconstructing in their minds the circumstances of a document's creation. In MJ's case, the represented "event" was not only what happened on Lexington Green on April 19, but the events of this day placed in their temporal context—Lexington as part of a sequence of events that resulted in a worried lieutenant, back in his Boston barracks, planning a strategy to get himself off the hook. For WL, what emerges as central is not what his source says about Lexington as much as how his source comes to know about Lexington: What happened to information as it made its way from eyewitnesses on April 19 to the pages of Ezra Stiles' diary on August 21? By constructing these cognitive models, historians have some guide for adjudicating among competing accounts. When aberrations or irregularities were detected in these models, a kind of search procedure was initiated in the mind of the historian that resulted in an informal judgment of the document's trustworthiness. And it is these judgments that figured prominently in how historians weighed competing accounts.

Event Model.   Historians do not view documents in isolation, but as belonging to something infinitely larger: a corpus of evidence. The "facts" presented by a new document are checked against what the historian has learned from previous documents and what he or she brings to the document in terms of background knowledge. As Fig. 4.1 shows, individual rEs converge into an overall *event model* in which the representations from individual documents are combined, with some details raised to the level of facts, others rejected as falsehoods, and still others placed in that historical purgatory of "perhaps" or "maybe." The event model becomes a cumulative record that is added to, refined, deleted from, and updated according to new evidence that is processed and new interpretations of that evidence that are formulated by the historian.

When MB reached the phrase in Document 5 *"The troops returned their fire and killed several of them,"* she made the following comment: "It sounds like rather excessive fire power for a minor event, but on the other hand, they were very nervous." To this point in the collection of documents, there had been nothing in the text base that had spoken of the "nervousness" of the troops, and one might have concluded that MB was drawing on her own knowledge of warfare had not the continuation of her comment offered this clue: "They were wet from marching and tired." Recall that the notion of wetness was something inferred from Lieutenant Barker's description of fording the Charles in a previous document. Thus, this representation of wet, tired, and nervous men is carried from Document 4 to Document 5, so that when MB encountered a description that seems discrepant with what she might have expected (i.e., the excessiveness of the firepower) she accessed her developing event model to help explain how it could be so.[6]

It is not an easy matter to predict what textual elements become incorporated into a historian's event model, for it is not as if one document is deemed worthy of admission and another denied. Historians exercise a kind of line-item veto, accepting some statements offered by their sources while still rejecting others. This approach characterizes modern historiography, attuned as we are both to the fallibility of memory and to the human capability to combine truth and falsehood in same breath. But things were not always so. For instance, in 17th-century historiography, one could either accept or reject a source, but it was considered illegitimate to pick and choose from among those details offered by a source (cf. Collingwood, 1946, chapter 4). The modern historian, in Collingwood's words, treats sources "not as true and false accounts of the fact of which they profess to be accounts, but as other facts which if he knows the right questions to ask may throw light on" (1946, p. 183).

We gain some insight into this stance vis-à-vis texts by examining MJ's comments on the minutemen's deposition (Document 2). In evaluating the deposition of the 34 minutemen, MJ viewed the document with grave suspicion, finding himself unable to imagine how a group of men who described themselves in a state of disorder could

---

[6]FA, on reading the beginning of the same document made a similar comment. After the phrase "Colonel Smith finding" FA commented: "now remember their legs are cold."

have all had their backs turned at precisely the same moment. From MJ's comments at the end of the document—"I'm not getting at these people, somebody else wrote this up"—one might conclude that MJ dismissed the evidentiary value of this document. But this conclusion is premature, as MJ's comments on the following document demonstrate (Table 4.4).

Despite the fact that MJ distrusted the deposition, he nonetheless integrated into his event model the minutemen's version of the chronological sequence of events. ("About 5 o'clock in the morning," was encoded as "about dawn.") Apparently MJ felt that he could accept this detail while still rejecting the minutemen's account of what happened. Thus, when MJ read about "bayonets glittering in the sun" in Howard Fast's account (Document 3), he referenced his event model, which led him to reject this account based on the fact that the sun would not be strong enough to "glitter" at 5 o'clock on an April morning in eastern Massachusetts. This example illustrates how the event model is both a cumulative record of what has been read and a touchstone against which new information is judged.

Another way to think about the event model is to view it as a *reader-based* model, while viewing each rE as primarily *text-based*. (For clarity's sake, let me reiterate that the event model goes across documents, whereas a separate rE is formed for each individual document.) The differences between the two are illustrated in WL's comments on the deposition (Document 2) presented in Table 4.5. In the early stages

TABLE 4.4
Excerpt from MJ on Document 3, April Morning [a]

Major Pitcairn screamed at us: "Lay down your arms, you lousy bastards! Disperse, you lousy peasant scum!" Clear the way do you hear me, get off the kings' green. At least, those were the words that I seem to remember. Others remembered differently, but the way he screamed in his strange London accent, with all the motion and excitement [†]with his horse rearing and kicking and the fixed bayonets glittering in the sunshine	
	now I had figured that it was right around dawn, "fixed bayonets glittering in the sunshine" I would have to take a look, at this point I glance down, excerpt from the novel, maybe that accounts for some of the glittering on the bayonets.

[a]Dagger indicates a place in the excerpt where additional comments not related to the example have been deleted for ease of reading.

TABLE 4.5
Excerpt from WL on Document 2, Mulliken

First Reading
*that about five o'clock in the morning,
hearing our drum beat,*

April 19th, I have to figure out whether
five in the morning, is there sufficient
light or not, that would be important to
me . . . are they doing this in the dark, is
it dawn at the time, is there sufficient light
to see a number of people because I don't
know exactly when the firing begins and
the degree of light, for me, would be
important in terms of determining the
weight that I would give to particular
accounts

*hearing our drum beat, we proceeded
towards Lexington Green, and soon
found that a large body of troops were
marching towards us, some of our
company were coming up to the
parade, and others had reached it, at
which time the company began to
disperse, whilst our backs were turned
on the troops,*

That's curious, well first of all, this is
curious because 32 people are testifying
that this is the account that they all agree
on. That raises some questions in my mind
about eyewitness testimony and what I
know about eyewitness testimony—it is
very hard to get this kind of an agreement
on this particular phrase

*some of our company were coming up
to the parade, and others had reached
it, at which time the company began to
disperse, whilst our backs were turned
on the troops, we were fired on by
them, and a number of our men were
instantly killed and wounded, not a
gun was fired by any person in our
company on the regulars to our
knowledge before they fired on us, and
they continued firing until we had all
made our escape.*

Well, I'm imagining a very confused
situation and I'm hard pressed to believe,
given my own experience and my own
knowledge of eyewitness testimony that
these people could have all agreed that all
their backs were turned and that not a

Continued)

108

TABLE 4.5 *(Continued)*

gun—*was fired by anyone in the Lexington militia before they fired on us, and they continued firing until we had all made our escape.*

I have doubts about that. I don't doubt that they swore to this and I don't doubt that they believe that that's what happened but that doesn't necessarily mean that's exactly what happened. And to distinguish between the perceptions of what happened and what actually happened, if that's possible, to get what actually happened.

Second Reading
whilst our backs were turned on the troops, we were fired on by them,

That strikes me as being too definitive for a situation that I would characterize as confusing—by the light, not knowing how much light was available; by a situation in which people would be fairly frightened, seeing a large body of the British, they knew the British were coming, they had that information, they saw them presumably at this time. I know that the British were marching in formation, and that they would have—I don't know whether they heard the orders because it says "we were fired on by them"—to the degree that I know about British battle formation, there would have been commands to fire, and that you cannot fire when you're walking, you have to stop and fire, given my knowledge of the muskets at that time. So it makes it appear by this deposition that the British were marching toward us, it says nothing about that they had stopped, taken aim, or anything like that, and it makes it seem that it was close to this massacre business I mentioned earlier. They were trying to tell the inhabitants these depositions are further ammunition for the cover letter that Warren sent, that this was a heinous act committed by the British on loyal subjects.

of WL's comments, we see him constructing an elaborate rE. Initially, he uses information about the time of day to speculate about the amount of light that morning, a determination that would help him understand the clarity with which the participants could have viewed their own circumstances. WL's comments in the next section take a different turn.

Questions raised about the amount of light on that morning highlight questions about the nature of eyewitness testimony, and the improbability of 34 men agreeing that they all saw the same thing.

By the last section, the conflict between the text-based rE and reader-based event model comes to a head. WL accepts the representation offered by the document of men coming and going ("some of our company were coming up to the parade, and others had reached it, at which time the company began to disperse"), and sees in his mind a "very confused situation." It is this acceptance of the "confused" state of affairs that becomes incorporated into WL's event model, and that ultimately leads to his rejection of the text-based rE. Ultimately, WL dismissed as implausible the notion that the minutemen, supposedly in a state of utter confusion, were suddenly able to act uniformly and turn their backs in unison. As he said in his second reading, this portrayal "strikes me as being too definitive for a situation that I would characterize as confusing."

To summarize, then, WL rejected the portrayal of the event presented in the text, but in order to do so he first needed to represent that event using cues from the text—cues that present a picture of confusion and uncertainty, as well as cues about the time of day and the amount of light available. WL's success in "seeing" this event, and then checking it against his own reader-based event model (informed by the other documents and the background knowledge about eyewitness testimony brought to the task) enables him to reject the minutemen's account of how things happened. However, in rejecting this account, WL was not accusing the men of lying, or even doubting that they truly believed events happened this way. Rather, he exercised the historian's right to reconstruct events in a way that goes beyond the partial and self-interested accounts of eyewitnesses.

A Counterexample. This example shows how the reader's event model leads to a rejection of the representation of the event prompted by the text. But change can go in the other direction as well, when readers refine their event models by accepting information they initially found improbable. An example of this occurs in the continuation of WL's comments from the last example. He finds further reason to distrust the minutemen's account based on his knowledge of British military procedure:

> To the degree that I know about British battle formation, there would have been commands to fire, and that you cannot fire when you're walking, you have to stop and fire. . . . This deposition . . . says nothing about they had stopped, taken aim, or anything like that.

The fact that the document leaves out such details makes it more suspicious in WL's eyes. But consider how WL revises his views when he later encounters Lieutenant Barker's description of what happened (Table 4.6). At first Barker's description raises doubts. WL calls it "interesting" and "curious" that a British officer would admit that he lost control over his troops. WL is not willing to accept this information at face value and "wants to know more." But as he reads on, the analogy he draws to the Chicago riots of 1968 signals a shift in his understanding. Can the behavior of the British troops at Lexington be compared to the riotous behavior of Major Daly's policemen at the 1968 Democratic convention?

By the second reading, this view of events—a confused scene in which troops go wild—becomes part of WL's event model. His earlier knowledge-driven representation of events (orderly troops patiently waiting for the command to fire) is abandoned as he comes to accept the British lieutenant's admission that he violated his own military customs. WL is quite explicit and self-aware about how his understanding changes:

> The inference that I had earlier from the colonial depositions that the British marched up in formation and then fired in formation under the control of their officers would not be sustained . . . and I'd drop that inference.

Representing Texts and Events: A Summary. Historical sources are fundamentally incomplete objects that tell partial stories of the past. Success in reconstructing the past using historical sources rests in no small measure on the meeting of text and historian. Texts offer clues for the construction of meaning, but without historians to decipher these clues, the past would remain a jumbled collection of contradictory statements and accounts. To be sure, texts provide a body of fixed points, but the historian's job is to spin a "web of imaginative construction," or to see a pattern between these fixed points.

As Kintsch and his colleagues have noted, readers' ability to move from a representation of the text ("one man wounded") to a representation of the event ("if only one man was wounded there probably wasn't much return fire") is a key to learning from the text as opposed to learning the text. The representation of the event has two major aspects. The first is what an eyewitness might see or experience—the chronology of events, the physical layout of the setting, the actual conditions of context, the structure of the event as it might appear to an observer. These aspects of events are subsumed by under the category *outside of events*. But events are not made up merely of actions but of

TABLE 4.6
WL on Revising Understanding (Document 4)

First Reading
upon *which our men without any*
orders, rushed in upon them, fired and
put them to flight; several of them were
killed, we could not tell how many
because they were got behind walls and
into the woods; we had a man of the
10th light Infantry wounded, nobody
else hurt.

Now, this is interesting in a couple ways. He clearly says that they fired first. Then he says "upon which our men, without any orders"—that's a curious thing— "rushed in upon them, fired and put them to flight"—is he saying that he lost control of his own unit? I'm not quite clear about that, I'd have to know more.

We then formed on the Common, but
with some difficulty, the men were so
wild they could hear no orders;

So what we have might be called a British riot, like the police riots in Chicago.

we waited a considerable time there,
and at length proceeded on our way to
Concord.

So this fellow suggests that the others fired first, that without any orders, his own troops rushed in and could not be controlled even to the point of forming, reforming the British on the Common. And he says "the men were so wild they could hear no orders," that they were caught up in the battle.

Second Reading
but on our coming near them they fired
one or two shots, upon which our men
without any orders, rushed in upon
them, fired and put them to flight;

It completely contradicts the other, the depositions. But it gives the sense here that the British lost control, the British officers lost control of their men. So the inference that I had earlier from the colonial depositions that the British marched up in formation and then fired in formation under the control of their officers would not be sustained by the British's own accounts and I'd drop that inference.

actors, and it is the thoughts, intentions, feelings, beliefs, hopes, aspirations, fears, and prejudices of these actors that form the *inside of the event*. The representation of the event also extends to the viewing of the document as event, or a representation of the circumstances of a document's generation. The representation of the document as event looms large when the historian turns to questions of probity, or evidential value, of the historical source.

Individual rEs converge into the cumulative representation of the event, the event model. The event model grows from document to document, incorporating new details and winnowing out less reliable ones. The event model serves as a touchstone for evaluating new information, sometimes integrating it automatically, other times rejecting it after careful review. The Event Model not only combines information from the corpus of evidence available to historians, but takes advantage of the resources they bring to the task—their knowledge, skills, beliefs, and personal experiences.[7]

REPRESENTATION OF THE SUBTEXT

Consider, for a moment, a hypothetical situation. Imagine that Catherine Drinker Bowen, the distinguished biographer and author of *Miracle at Philadelphia* (1966), set out to write a biography of Benjamin Franklin. (Although Franklin figures prominently in *Miracle at Philadelphia*, the following example is fictitious.) Imagine that Bowen wanted to combine two facts about Franklin into a complex sentence: Fact 1, that Benjamin Franklin was a scientist (someone who experimented with electricity, optics, and a host of other scientific fields of his day); and Fact 2, that at a certain point in his career, Franklin condoned mob

---

[7]There is a caveat to this summary, for I have studiously avoided a discussion of the ways in which the different facets of the rE are stored in memory. The evidence that this study provides is indirect and we can only speculate about the mechanisms of memory. Part of the rE is probably stored semantically in LTM, a case exemplified by MJ's encoding of "about 5 o'clock" and recalling in the next document that the minutemen "arrived about dawn." Other cases are more suggestive of a kind of visual encoding, or mental imagery. For example, one of the historians says in reviewing the minutemen's deposition: "It's a great image of these guys all mulling around in the dark, probably with torches and lanterns and all that." There is also a question about whether people can distinguish between textual information and inferences made in response to that information, for example, FA's inferences about the "wetness" of the British troops. A study by Seifert, Robertson, and Black (1985) suggests that readers are unable to differentiate between inferences they made during reading and explicit textual statements. Unfortunately, the nature of the data collected do not allow that question to be answered.

violence as a means of stirring sentiments against the British. Listed below are six candidates for this sentence:

1. Franklin was a scientist, but believed in mob violence.
2. Though Franklin was a scientist, he believe in mob violence.
3. While Franklin was a scientist, he believed in mob violence.
4. Franklin was a both scientist and a believer in mob violence.
5. Franklin believed in mob violence, but was a scientist.
6. Franklin, being a scientist, believed in mob violence.

Each of these sentences achieves the goal of combination yet each tells us something different about the relationship between science and beliefs about the usefulness of violence. From the strategic placement of the word *but* in sentence 1, we learn that a commitment to science and to mob violence are at odds. We might surmise that the author sees science as the quintessence of rational thought, of clear-headed deliberate thinking, and sees mob violence as its antitheses, the brutal hot-headed mob, deaf to reason. The construction of this sentence, with the strategic placement of the word *but* (called a *positional* in linguistics), hints at all of these things, without explicitly saying any of them.

Now skip to the last sentence in the list. While we learn the same two facts about Franklin, we see their relationship in a different light. Here Franklin's belief in mob violence is not antithetical to science, but springs from it. Here science and mob violence go hand in hand. The author may believe that science represents the world of action, of getting things done, a world entirely consistent with the efficiency of mob violence.

Attached to each of these sentences is a complex web of ideas — ideas about cause and effect; ideas about the relationship between what one does and what one thinks; ideas about how world views connect. Each of these examples, while telling us about Franklin, tells us much about Franklin's biographer. This is so because language communicates more than facts. The use of three simple and seemingly innocuous words like "while," "though," and "but" drastically alters the underlying meaning, or *subtext*, of each of these sentences. Indeed, this is the point behind Carr's oft-quoted injunction that "before you study the history, study the historian" (1961, p. 54).

Building a model of implicit textual information, of what a text does as opposed to what it says, is embraced by the *representation of the subtext* (rSB). To understand historical texts readers must discern clues about their authors, clues that authors may have wished had remained hidden: convictions they may have been unaware of or, if aware, certainly did not want to display openly. The representation of the subtext views documents as entities that reveal their authors' assumptions, beliefs, biases, convictions, commitments, hopes, fears—in sum, the totality of their world view. Of course, texts vary in the degree to which they disclose these elements; in some texts they are easily discerned while in others they are carefully obscured. But in all cases, the construction of the subtext is a representation; the rSB is a hypothesis about the author's intentions or beliefs, it is not isomorphic to them. This is so because the cues in the text that allow construction of subtext are by no means infallible. In the words of the intellectual historian Peter Gay: "If past words were addressed to the chosen few, and if we have lost the key that will unlock their message, the intentions of the writer, and with them the full bearing of his utterance, will remain opaque" (1974, p. 234).

The rSB can be divided into two spheres. The first sphere, the text as *rhetorical artifact*, is most closely aligned to the common understanding of rhetoric, and relates to how readers reconstruct the willful intentions and purposes of authors. The second sphere, the text as *human artifact*, relates to how texts frame reality and disclose information about the author's assumptions, convictions, and beliefs.

Text as a Rhetorical Artifact

Writing is a purposeful act. In representing the text as a rhetorical artifact, readers reconstruct the purposes and intentions behind the document: What do authors want to prove? How do the words or phrases they use advance their argument? What rhetorical techniques are used to convince readers of the rightness of their cause? In short, what is the polemic, or underlying argument, of the text?

Purpose can be construed at local (word or phrase) and global (paragraph or whole document) levels. Consider, first, an example in which the reader constructs the global purpose of the document. These are FA's summary comments on Warren's cover letter (Document 1):

> Okay, it's like a letter to the editor; it's a way to try and get people in England to see things their way; it's encouraging loyalty to the king but it's saying the government has messed up. It clearly shows that the Regular troops are guilty of the violence at Lexington. . . . The purpose of the document goes beyond—it's not just a recapitulation of events, but it in fact frames events in terms of both the relationship of the crown and its government, and these are two different things. . . . It has a purpose beyond description. It wants to affect people's opinions.

This excerpt shows how FA reconstructs the broad purposes behind this document. First, the document goes beyond a neutral description of the events at Lexington. Its purpose is to "affect people's opinions" by reassuring them that, despite the events at Lexington, the colonists still pledge "allegiance to the King." But beyond this reassurance, the document tries to construct reality, to set the terms on which these events are to be construed. In FA's words, the document "frames events" in terms of the relationship of the crown to its government, with the colonists pledging loyalty to the former while indicting the policies of the latter. By thus casting events, the king is absolved of guilt, which is laid at the feet of his appointees. For FA, this construal of the events at Lexington was a calculated move that guided the composition of the document and served as the larger framework for authorial decision-making within it.

Local Purpose.   Representations of local purpose go on at the word or phrase level, and can be situated on what the linguist Roman Jakobson (1960) called the "vertical axis of selection." Along this axis, authors make rhetorical decisions among words that satisfy the same grammatical constraints. For instance, the textbook excerpt (Document 7) notes: "The English fired a volley of shots that killed eight patriots." Using the vertical axis, a host of grammatically and logically correct alternatives could replace *patriots*, such as *men, farmers, hotheads, criminals, peasants, people,* or *rebels*. However, the author's use of *patriots* carries with it dramatically different connotations from the use of, say, *criminals*; in the former case, there is the sense that these men were brave and just and died in a righteous cause; in the latter, there is the sense that these men deserved to die. Consider EM's reactions to the same sentence from Document 7:

> "Patriots," not "eight colonists," and the "English," not "the troops," but "the English." So these foreigners, that's what it sounds [like] because "English" to us is a foreign people. There's a great deal of interpretation going on here. . . . Students would never know that there were a great deal of colonists that supported "the English."

For EM, a Wisconsin-trained historian of the American Southwest, "patriots" and "the English" are not simply labels for the combatants but descriptions that maximize the righteousness of the colonists' cause while emphasizing the strangeness of the British troops. (Later in his reading, EM offered what he considered to be more accurate terms— *colonists* and *troops*—because colonists at this time were often as "English" as the troops who opposed them.) This reading views word choice as neither automatic nor whimsical, but guided by motive and design. The connotations called up by certain words are not "in" the text but carried in the mind of the reader, and the process of using words with rich connotations does not automatically achieve the author's purpose. Often connotation-laden words can backfire and actually hamper the achievement of author's purpose. For some readers, the use of *patriot* in this selection may set off associations of jingoism and mindless flag waving, and cause the reader to lose faith in the author's credibility.

A second example shows the representation of purpose at a slightly higher level: the level of *information selection*. MB made the following comment on this line from the Document 5: "Several guns were fired upon the King's troops from behind a stone wall, and also from the meeting-house."

> "Meeting-house" would be . . . more likely it's a church and therefore, it's very interesting that they are noting that shots would be fired from the church because that's supposed to be sanctified . . . and you are not supposed to fire from a church. So the implication there is that there's something a little bit off, unfair, not kosher, about firing from a meeting-house.

This comment is telling in several respects. First, there is nothing in the text about a church or about the social strictures against using firearms in one: These are all part of the resources brought by the historian to the text—in this case, a Harvard-trained historian who knows about the dual role filled by Massachusetts' meeting houses. But beyond this, we see how an elaborate construction of purpose can rest on an easily overlooked detail. Whether shots were fired from a meeting-house may or may not be true, but MB views its inclusion (as opposed to including details about the color of the buildings or the clothing of the colonists) as motivated by the goal to cast the colonists in the worst possible light—as defilers of holy places and people who used places of worship as places of war.

A related way of representing local purpose is the detection of specific rhetorical moves, strategies, and tactics. This does not mean that historians comb the text applying the labels of *reductio ad absurdam, ad personam, tu quoque,* and *a fortiori* to particular textual features. (In fact, there were no places in the protocols in which historians used classical rhetorical terms to describe the texts.) Rather, the process goes on less formally, as the examples in Table 4.7 attest.

Both TP and EM reacted to the same textual feature in Howard Fast's (1961) excerpt (Document 3): the use of a direct quote from the British commander followed by the narrator's disclaimer that "others remembered differently." Both historians saw this phrase as an escape clause

TABLE 4.7
Noting of Rhetorical Textual Features

EM (United States)
Major Pitcairn screamed at us: "Lay
down your arms, you lousy bastards!
Disperse, do you hear me! Disperse,
you lousy peasant scum! . . . At least,
those were the words that I seem to
remember. Other remembered
differently. . . .

Nice way for the novelist to cover up the
fact that they were probably never spoken.

TP (Great Britain)
Others remembered differently . . .

He is at least covering . . . himself from
the accusation that he's being inaccurate
in that he's saying others remembered
differently . . . the novelist is saying, you
know, I'm not claiming that everyone who
was involved in this battle remembers it
this way

that protected the author from the charge that he has debased history by fabricating quotations. Unknown to either historian, however, was the fact that Howard Fast's use of this quotation rested on more than poetic license. Thomas Rice Willard, an eyewitness to the event, claimed that a soldier rode up to the minutemen and hollered, "Lay down your arms, damn you, why don't you lay down your arms" (cited in Bennett, 1970). In any event, Fast altered this quotation, and his disclaimer may indeed be a technique to cover himself.

Historians detected other rhetorical techniques as well. For example, MJ saw the Mulliken et al. (Document 2) repeated use of "the said" as a technique to give the document a legal flavor, making it seem more authoritative than it really was. BS, a British social historian who received his doctorate at Stanford, saw the textbook's (Document 7) use of quotation marks around "rebels" as conveying the sense that the encounter at Lexington was not an unintended incident but purposeful and planned. And, contrary to the way MB read "it will appear" in a previous example, WL interpreted this phrase as a rhetorical device to show that the author was not a partisan but actually a disinterested observer trying to piece together the best account of what happened.

Part of deciphering the author's purpose includes the representation of the intended audience for the document. In this regard, historical documents present special problems. For unlike the election flier, the cigarette ad, or the newspaper editorial, all of which are designed for the person who reads them, primary texts were written for audiences of which the reader is usually not a member. Historians must eavesdrop on conversations between dead authors and dead audiences, trying to reconstruct the goals and reactions of both.

We see an example of this in Table 4.8. FA begins by constructing the document as event, and positing that this letter, though sent to Franklin, was meant for public distribution.[8] On reaching the phrase "friends and fellow subjects," FA put himself in the place of the audience of concerned British citizens. FA was no longer the detached historian, or even the historian trying to understand the motivations of the author, but was now someone who tried to imagine what it might have been like to have been a British citizen reading this document. He concluded that "all of this looks bad." But his representation of audience does not end there. Seeing the Warren cover letter and the Mulliken deposition (Documents 1 and 2) as part of the same package (which they were), FA, later in his reading, ultimately rejected their claims: "If I was General Gage or someone in England reading this letter I would say 'this guy is a damned liar' . . . it's just too clean, just too nice." (It is interesting to note that this was the official British reaction to the Boston communiqués; see Tourtellot, 1959).

This example shows how the skillful reader of historical documents becomes more than a single reader. FA assumes at least three perspectives: that of the historian eavesdropping on a conversation, that of the author, and that of the author's intended audience. In adopting these perspectives, the reader plays the role of stage director, monitoring the processes of comprehension, but also plays all of the other roles as well. Instead of a single executive directing a top-down process, historians seem to create inside their heads an executive board, where members clamor, shout, and debate controversial points (see Wineburg, 1991a). The complexity of these cognitive mini-dramas is evident in TP's reaction to the salutation ("Friends and Fellow Subjects") of Joseph Warren's cover letter (Document 1) to Parliament: "I think I dealt with the rhetoric there, you know, we know that once you know the true story, you will sympathize with us." This congeries of pronouns simulates the give and take of social exchange, the rhetorical positioning and posturing of supplicants and their audiences. Texts emerge as "speech acts" (Searle, 1972), social interactions set down on paper that can only be understood by trying to reconstruct the social context in

---

[8]The Warren communication and the attached depositions were sent to London 9 days after the official dispatch set sail from Boston. The official British report was sent on a ship laden with cargo, while the colonists chartered a speedy schooner to carry their message. This schooner beat the Gage's dispatch by 2 weeks. Franklin circulated these letters to members of Parliament and to the press. For 2 weeks, the London press was filled with accounts giving only the colonists' side of the story.

TABLE 4.8
Representation of the Audience, Excerpt from FA on Warren
(Document 1)

To the inhabitants of Great Britain:	
	It has been written very soon, days after the event. When he says "In Provincial Congress," I'm assuming he is writing as a representative and it doesn't necessarily mean that they convened to write this letter. The "inhabitants of Great Britain" makes clear that the letter, while to inform Franklin, it is really Franklin's duty to inform public opinion in England at the time.
Friends and fellow subjects:	
	Very clear what they are aiming at there— They are approaching the audience as friends and fellow subjects, they have something in common, they have this political allegiance together to the king.
Second Reading *and first began hostilities by firing on said Lexington Company, whereby they killed eight and wounded several others;*	
	Simply an elaboration of the previous statement; they started the thing by firing, the result was eight killed several others wounded; all of this looks bad to those for whom this letter portends [intends?] to be aimed at.

which they occurred. The comprehension of text reaches beyond words and phrases to embrace intention, motive, purpose and plan—the same set of concepts we use to decipher human action.[9]

Text as a Human Instrument

We cannot read Namier's *Structure of Politics at the Accession of George III*, with its resolute anti-intellectualism, its affectionate portrayal of the political microcosm of mid-century England, without detecting in Namier,

---

[9]The discourse analyst Nancy Struever puts this more formally in her discussion of the theories of Quentin Skinner: "For Skinner . . . historical explanation is illocutionary redescription, a process of recovering the agent's intended illocutionary act by decoding the social conventions that govern the linguistic exchange" (1985, p. 251).

the minute researcher, a hidden Namier, in love with English civility so infatuated that he must be a foreigner. (Gay, 1974, p. 234)

The second way in which the subtext is represented is by constructing the text as a *human artifact*, an artifact that discloses the features of its author. These features can include the author's character, biases, assumptions about the world, convictions, commitments, hopes, and fears. When considering these aspects, the reader goes beyond the representation of author as rhetor, beyond the consideration of the intentions of the author. In fact, the representation of text as a human artifact often yields interpretations that work at cross-purposes with the author's intentions, such as the reader's detection of authorial bias that then detracts from the persuasiveness of the text. But the representation of text as human artifact is broader than the detection of bias or even the determination of point of view. It is a representation that leaps from the words authors use to the types of people authors are—their attitudes, convictions, values, ways of viewing the world and constructing reality. It is a representation that sees in Sir Lewis Namier not just a hard-nosed historian, but a lover of British civility, an admirer of the culture he wished to understand.

The examples in Table 4.9 show two aspects of the text as human artifact. In the first example, FA sizes up Warren's account as "clearly the comments of an advocate," and is an example of the type of "point of view" comment found in the protocols of every historian. The second example is a case in which the author's point of view turns against itself. By the time SY reached Document 7, he had built an event model that depicted two armed forces, albeit in unequal numbers, facing each other, with the colonists possibly trying to impede the advance of the British on their way to Concord. SY comments on the connotations of the word *atrocity*, a word choice intended to slant events in a particular way. But here is an example where the use of a loaded term backfires; the discrepancy between the associations conjured up by *atrocity* and SY's event model are so great that SY rejects this document entirely. In other words, this characterization of events is so implausible, so revealing of the author's tainted views, that SY will not consider it.

Beyond identifying the biases and interests of the author, readers construct images of the author as person. Texts vary in their disclosure of their authors. For example, the newspaper columns of William F. Buckley, with their learned vocabulary and complex sentences, convey a temperamental, witty author. Those of Andy Rooney (no middle initial), written in ordinary prose, convey the sense of a simple, down-to-earth man, certainly no highbrow. Authorial style is not an adornment, but central to understanding the author behind the text.

TABLE 4.9
Examples of Text as Human Artifact

Example 1, from Document 1
These, brethren, are marks of
ministerial vengeance against this
colony, for refusing, with her sister
colonies, a submission to slavery.

This is clearly the comments of an
advocate for the colonies and has a
perspective that one has to keep in mind
in reading both this cover letter and I
suspect the depositions [FA].

Example 2, from Document 7
It was not long before the swift-riding
Paul Revere spread the news of this
new atrocity to the neighboring
colonies.

Well "atrocity" is obviously a heavily
freighted word, a loaded word . . . it
seems to me that that's as uncalled for
word under the circumstances—it was not
an atrocity by any means. It was an
unfortunate confrontation, but it wasn't
like they came in and murdered women
and children in their beds. They fired on
armed men who were presumably going
to, or they perceived as trying to impede
their advance to Concord [SY].

"Manner is indissolubly linked to matter," wrote the historian Peter Gay
(1974, p. 225). "Style shapes, and in turn is shaped by substance."

For example, consider the kinds of comments that MB (Asian history)
made about the author of Document 5, Ezra Stiles. Stiles, whom MB had
not heard of prior to this task, was judged to be a "classist" (based on his
haughty tone and his use of *peasants*), a cleric (based on textual cues and
MB's background knowledge), well educated but probably not a
member of the aristocracy (more background knowledge), and a hypo-
crite (based on the discrepancy between Stiles' patriotism and his
reference to his compatriots as peasants). While elsewhere MB talks
about Stiles' motivation for writing, the focus of her comments here is
not the intentions of the author but the man himself.

Perhaps the most vivid example of the representation of the author
came not from the eight historians in this study, but from a graduate
student in Portuguese history interviewed during the pilot phase of this
study. In his summary comment about Ezra Stiles, this student dramatically deepened his voice and dangled his pencil from his mouth,
pretending it was a pipe:

I'm thinking [voice deepens] "a nice Yale man trying to say something, you know," [voice deepens again] "Major Pitcairn was a veeeeery good man." I'm just thinking that this is the voice of reason, Ivy League high Episcopalian Orthodoxy. . . . "Peasants"—it's just a great word . . . I mean here we are reading about the American Revolution, after all it's supposed to be a bunch of yeoman farmers vigorously defending their rights and here is the President of Yale . . . whose ancestors came from England and who made enough money to send him to Yale and get him to be president of Yale . . . this is the elite talking about the peasant.

Such readings highlight how readers construct authors. Texts are not strings of words printed on a page, but the keys to unlocking the character of human beings, people with likes and dislikes, biases and foibles, airs and convictions. Ezra Stiles is not a faceless conduit of information about Lexington but someone whose assumptions about the world are embodied in his text. Words have rhythm and shape, and it is their almost tactile quality that lets readers sculpt images of the authors that use them. In these examples, we see how the reading of history moves from a reconstruction of past events to a reconstruction of witnesses to these events.

The Subtext as Hypothesis

Sometimes a subtext jumps out at the reader. But other times, the rSB remains tentative, one of a series of possible readings of an ambiguous text. The examples in Table 4.10 are instances in which the representations of the subtext are hypotheses for how passages might be interpreted.

All three examples share a common feature: Each raises the representation of the subtext as a hypothesis. In the first example, BS wonders if the disclaimer "those are the words I seem to remember" is a rhetorical feature to protect the author (in this case, the "speaker," as author Howard Fast cannot be equated with the characters he invents) or whether it is simply a more mundane instance of a novelist trying to be "chatty" with his readers. Likewise, TP is not sure how to construe "country people," wondering whether she should represent it as part of the text (rT), a neutral appellation for the minutemen, or whether she should regard it as a calculated move to disguise the fact that the minutemen were a long-standing militia. In the last example, MJ suggests two possible ways of reading Stiles' description of Pitcairn: First, he could take it at face value, reading it as Stiles' true feelings

TABLE 4.10
Representation of Subtext as Hypothesis

BS on Fast (Document 3) *At least those were the words that I* *seemed to remember*	
	Suggesting for some reason he wanted to save his face in case he was later accused of libel, well, I don't know. Maybe it's because this is a novel . . . it's different I suppose. Maybe he's just trying to be chatty.
TP on London Gazette (Document 5) *upon arrival [of the British troops] at* *Lexington, found a body of the country* *people under arms,*	
	Here he describes them as country people but they're under arms. He doesn't identify them as the militia and I would want to know what the rhetoric was. Was there an effort still in communications to British people to minimize the extent to which the colonists were militarized? In which case you wouldn't want to describe them as a "militia," you wouldn't use the word "minutemen," you would say that they were "country people." Nevertheless, you would definitely want to say that they were armed.
MJ on Stiles (Document 6) *He does not say that he saw the* *colonists fire first. Had he said it, I* *would have believed him, being a man* *of integrity and honor*	
	The "integrity and honor" is a nice—it could be one of two things. He could actually believe him to be a man of integrity and honor. Or by making that statement it . . . makes Stiles sound that much more impartial. It's hard to say.

about Pitcairn, or alternately, he could read it as rhetorical tactic to make Stiles look more credible as a witness. In other words, first compliment your adversary to appear evenhanded, and then knock him down. Mustifer Sherif (1936), using Lewinian terminology, called this technique "preparing an unstructured field" and cited its wide use by journalists. Its use, wrote Sherif "helps to keep the established attitudes of [the journalist's] readers, which may be hostile to his attitudes, in a quiescent state and thus help to make their first reactions neutral" (p. 119).

These examples highlight some of the differences between historical understanding and problem solving in well-structured domains. According to Newell and Simon (1972), the problem solver in well-structured domains knows when a solution has been attained since a "test exists . . . that will determine whether an object proposed as a solution is in fact a solution" (p. 73). But in these examples, we see that "solutions"—if we want to call them that—are not attained but imposed. There is no way to tell, for instance, whether Stiles was genuine in his praise for Pitcairn or whether, knowing that his memoirs were likely to be published, he simply wanted to appear magnanimous. Historical questions often have more than one right answer. Ultimately the historian chooses among competing answers or simultaneously holds them in mind for later confirmation or rejection. Or sometimes the choice is simply not to choose, to hold in abeyance the determination of meaning and live with the uncertainly this entails.

Summary: Representation of the Subtext

Historical texts contain information about events, but not all information is of equal value. In forming historical interpretations, historians must weigh conflicting information, determining which information to consider and which to discard. Central to this process is the representation of the subtext of historical documents. The first component of the rSB represents the text as a rhetorical artifact, and embraces the reader's representation of authorial purpose and intent. The second component represents the text as a human artifact, the text as mirror of the author who composed it. Both forms of the subtext guide the reader in making judgments of probity, the determination of the evidentiary status of texts and the authors who wrote them.

CONCLUSIONS AND IMPLICATIONS

Despite the wide variation in background and specialization of these historians, there were striking commonalities in how they approached these historical documents.[10] Irrespective of specialization, all historians

---

[10]One indication of the similarity in historians' readings comes from their ranking of documents based on trustworthiness, a task completed at the end of the reading session. Kendall's coefficient of concordance was used to measure the amount of agreement: for all eight historians, $W = .69$, $\chi^2(7) = 38.92$, $p < .001$. The amount of agreement among

engaged in process of textual model building.[11] Documents were not viewed in isolation but as belonging to a corpus of evidence that, in its totality, rose above the particulars of any one text. As historians built models based on these texts, these models came to wield ultimate authority over new texts that were read. In other words, once a certain point had been reached in the task (and this point was not the same for each historian), new documents were judged not on the basis of how they compared to previous texts, but how they compared to the cognitive model formed as a result of the historian's encounter with previous texts. In addition, these event models, the cumulative results of this intertextual encounter, were joined by cognitive models of the author of these texts. These models, or authorial images, were then interrogated about what they intended and did not intend. As historians endowed inanimate texts with voices and proceded to engage these voices in conversation, these readings took on a striking social quality very different from the dispassionate images of "cold cognition" that continue to dominate information-processing models of reading (cf. Wineburg, 1991b).

What can we say about the generality of the cognitive representations that have been described here? Are they solely a function of these particular documents or could we expect a similar typology to emerge if the documents related to the Boston Massacre, the Tea Pot Dome Scandal, the Bay of Pigs incident, and so on? Although the data of this study do not allow us to go beyond speculation, the three types of cognitive representations, representations of the text, the event, and the subtext, seem broad enough to describe some of what goes on when historians read various historical documents, whether these documents are papyri from the Essene community in the Qumran desert or are photocopied memoranda adduced in the Iran/Contra hearings. But the question of generality can be phrased differently: Would we expect to find different representations if different historians participated in this study? For instance, might historians dedicated to the *Annales* approach

---

historians of different specializations was virtually identical, $W = .73$ for Americanists, $W = .74$ for non-Americanists. The average correlation (Spearman rho) between any two historians yielded was high, $r = .65$ (Hays, 1972, p. 803). A similar analysis with gifted high school history seniors produced a scant correlation, $r = .14$ (Wineburg, 1991a). Despite stereotypes of historians' penchant for disagreement, these findings point to a generalized way of approaching texts, one might even say a historical "cast of mind."

[11]When asked to engage in an exercise aimed at reconstructing what happened on a particular morning in history, historians without large amounts of factual knowledge could make do on what they had. However, had the goal of the task been different, had the medievalist or the Japanese specialist been asked to place the events at Lexington into the broader sociocultural milieu of the 18th century, surely their lack of specific factual knowledge would have shown through more clearly.

become impatient with the purview of these documents, seeing them as representatives of *l'histoire eventementielle*, the fleeting history of minor events? To a certain extent, BS, a British social historian, reacted this way. At one point, he became noticeably impatient with the painstaking detective work this task required and commented:

> You've got . . . a series of depositions describing the riot and you can go through like this and you can carefully map out who was where and did what and at exactly what point, but in the end it's not always very interesting and useful. That kind of reconstructing of the specific event does not always tell you very much about the bigger questions that you are interested in. . . . What I want to know as a historian is, what created the context in which this took place, what is the broader context, why are the British there?

BS was a "good subject" who went along with this task, but the questions that most concerned him, questions about the broader social context of the American Revolution, could not be answered by the evidence he was presented. In light of the perspective he brought to this task, we cannot know what cognitive representations he might have constructed had he been presented with the documents that most interested him. Certainly the constraints of the task situation historians found themselves in contributed to the commonalities present in the protocols.

The work presented in this chapter marks a psychological entry into the world of historical interpretation. Other lines of work in this research program attempt to uncover the cognitive strategies historians use to form historical interpretations (Wineburg, 1991b), the process by which historians recreate historical contexts (Wineburg & Fournier, 1992a, 1992b), and the relationship between the kinds of interpretive strategies displayed by historians and those of high school students and teachers (e.g., Wilson & Wineburg, 1988, in press; Wineburg & Wilson, 1991).

The types of issues examined in these studies carry implications that go beyond the domain of history. History offers a storehouse of ill-structured, indeterminate, and partial (in both senses of the word) texts, not unlike those that confront us every day. Such texts require an interpretative acumen that extends beyond the "locate information in the text" skills that dominate most reading comprehension tests (Resnick & Resnick, 1991). Understanding how historians engage in these interpretive processes would not only provide a knowledge base for improving school history but would inform more general theories of reading comprehension concerned with the sophisticated processes of textual interpretation and judgment.

ACKNOWLEDGEMENT

The support of the Spencer Foundation in funding this research is gratefully acknowledged.

APPENDIX: SET OF WRITTEN DOCUMENTS
USED IN THIS STUDY

Material in parentheses, designated by the dagger, is provided for bibliographic purposes. Only the reference material in italics was provided to subjects.

Document 1

In 1775, Benjamin Franklin was the colonial representative in London. After the events in Lexington and Concord, the Massachusetts Provincial Congress put together 21 sworn depositions about the events and sent them to Franklin with the following cover letter:
To the inhabitants of Great Britain: In Provincial Congress, Watertown April 26, 1775

Friends and fellow subjects: Hostilities are at length commenced in the Colony by the troops under command of General Gage; and it being of the greatest importance that an early, true, and authentic account of this inhuman proceeding should be known to you, the Congress of this Colony have transmitted the same, and from want of a session of the honorable Continental Congress, think it proper to address you on the alarming occasion.

By the clearest depositions relative to this transaction, it will appear that on the night preceding the nineteenth of April instant, . . . the Town of Lexington . . . was alarmed, and a company of the inhabitants mustered on the occasion; that the Regular troops, on their way to Concord, marched into the said town of Lexington, and the said company, on their approach, began to disperse; that notwithstanding this, the regulars rushed on with great violence, and first began hostilities by firing on said Lexington Company, whereby they killed eight and wounded several others; that the Regulars continued their fire until those of said company, who were neither killed nor wounded, had made their escape.

These, brethren, are marks of ministerial vengeance against this colony, for refusing, with her sister colonies, a submission to slavery. But they have not yet detached us from our Royal Sovereign. We profess to be his loyal and dutiful subjects, and so hardly dealt with as we have been, are still ready, with our lives and fortunes, to defend his person, family, crown, and dignity. Nevertheless, to the persecution and tyranny of his cruel ministry we will not tamely submit; appealing to Heaven for the justice of our cause, we determine to die or be free. •*Joseph Warren* [*President pro tem*] (Document reprinted in Bennett, 1970)[+]

Document 2

We NATHANIEL MULLIKEN, PHILIP RUSSELL, [followed by the names of thirty-two other men present on Lexington Green on April, 19, 1775], . . . all of lawful age, and inhabitants of Lexington, in the County of Middlesex, . . . do testify and declare, that on the nineteenth of April instant, about one or two o'clock in the morning, being informed that . . . a body of regulars were marching from Boston towards Concord, . . . we were alarmed and having met at the place of our company's parade [Lexington Green], were dismissed by our Captain, John Parker, for the present, with orders to be ready to attend at the beat of the drum, we further testify and declare, that about five o'clock in the morning, hearing our drum beat, we proceeded towards the parade, and soon found that a large body of troops were marching towards us, some of our company were coming up to the parade, and others had reached it, at which time the company began to disperse, whilst our backs were turned on the troops, we were fired on by them, and a number of our men were instantly killed and wounded, not a gun was fired by any person in our company on the regulars to our knowledge before they fired on us, and they continued firing until we had all made our escape. •*Lexington, April 25th, 1775, NATHANIEL MULLIKEN, PHILIP RUSSELL, [and the other 32 men] [Duly sworn to by 34 minutemen on April 25th before three justices of the peace]* (Document reprinted in Sawtell, 1968)[+]

Document 3

Major Pitcairn screamed at us: "Lay down your arms, you lousy bastards! Disperse, you lousy peasant scum!" . . . At least, those were the words that I seem to remember. Others remembered differently; but the way he screamed, in his strange London accent, with the motion and excitement, with his horse rearing and kicking . . . with the drums beating again and the fixed bayonets glittering in the sunshine, it's a wonder that any of his words remain with us. . . . We still stood in our two lines, our guns butt end on the ground or held loosely in our hands. Major Pitcairn spurred his horse and raced between the lines. Somewhere, away from us, a shot sounded. A redcoat soldier raised his musket, leveled it at Father, and fired. My father clutched at his breast, then crumpled to the ground like an empty sack. . . . Then the whole British front burst into a roar of sound and flame and smoke. •*Excerpt from the novel, April Morning, by Howard Fast, published in 1961*

Document 4

19th. At 2 o'clock we began our march by wading through a very long ford up to our middles; after going a few miles we took three or four people who were going off to give intelligence; about five miles on this side of a town called Lexington, which lay in our road, we heard there were some hundreds of people collected together intending to oppose us and stop our going on; at 5 o'clock we arrived there, and saw a number of people, I believe between 200 and 300, formed in a common in the middle of the town; we still continued advancing, keeping prepared against an attack though without intending to attack them; but on our coming near them they fired one or two shots, upon which our men without any orders, rushed in upon them, fired and put them to flight; several of them were killed, we could not tell how many, because they were got behind walls and into the woods; We had a man of the 10th light Infantry wounded, nobody else hurt. We then formed on the Common, but with some difficulty, the men were so wild they could hear no orders; we waited a considerable time there, and at length proceeded on our way to Concord. •*Entry for April 19th, 1775, from the diary of Lieutenant John Barker, an officer in the British army* (Document reprinted in Dana, 1877)[+]

Document 5

Lieutenant Nunn, of the Navy arrived this morning at Lord Dartmouth's and brought letters from General Gage, Lord Percy, and Lieutenant-Colonel Smith, containing the following particulars of what passed on the nineteenth of April last between a detachment of the King's Troops in the Province of Massachusetts-Bay and several parties of rebel provincials. . . . Lieutenant-Colonel Smith finding, after he had advanced some miles on his march, that the country had been alarmed by the firing of guns and ringing of bells, dispatched six companies of

light-infantry, in order to secure two bridges on different roads beyond Concord, who, upon their arrival at Lexington, found a body of the country people under arms, on a green close to the road; and upon the King's Troops marching up to them, in order to inquire the reason of their being so assembled, they went off in great confusion, and several guns were fired upon the King's troops from behind a stone wall, and also from the meeting-house and other houses, by which one man was wounded, and Major Pitcairn's horse shot in two places. In consequence of this attack by the rebels, the troops returned the fire and killed several of them. After which the detachment marched on to Concord without any thing further happening. •*Newspaper account from The London Gazette, June 10, 1775*
(Document reprinted in Bennett, 1970)[+]

Document 6

There is a certain sliding over and indeterminateness in describing the beginning of the firing. Major Pitcairn who was a good man in a bad cause, insisted upon it to the day of his death, that the colonists fired first. . . . *He does not say that he saw the colonists fire first.* Had he said it, I would have believed him, being a man of integrity and honor. *He expressly says he did not see who fired first*; and yet believed the peasants began. His account is this—that riding up to them he ordered them to disperse; which they not doing instantly, he turned about to order his troops so to draw out as to surround and disarm them. As he turned he *saw* a gun in a peasant's hand from behind a wall, *flash in the pan without going off*: and instantly or very soon two or three guns went off by which he found his horse wounded and also a man near him wounded. These guns he did not see, but believing they could not come from his own people, doubted not and so asserted that they came from our people; and that thus they began the attack. The impetuosity of the King's Troops were such that a promiscuous, uncommanded but general fire took place, which Pitcairn could not prevent; though he struck his staff or sword downwards with all earnestness as a signal to forbear or cease firing. This account Major Pitcairn himself gave Mr. Brown of Providence who was seized with flour and carried to Boston a few days after the battle; and Gov. Sessions told it to me. •*from the diary of Ezra Stiles, president of Yale College, entry for August 21, 1775*
(Document reprinted in Dexter, 1901)[+]

Document 7

In April 1775, General Gage, the military governor of Massachusetts, sent out a body of troops to take possession of military stores at

Concord, a short distance from Boston. At Lexington, a handful of "embattled farmers," who had been tipped off by Paul Revere, barred the way. The "rebels" were ordered to disperse. They stood their ground. The English fired a volley of shots that killed eight patriots. It was not long before the swift-riding Paul Revere spread the news of this new atrocity to the neighboring colonies. The patriots of all of New England, although still a handful, were now ready to fight the English.
•*From The United States: Story of a Free People, a high school textbook by Samuel Steinberg, Allyn and Bacon, publishers, 1963*

Document 8

To the best of my recollection about 4 o'clock in the morning being the 19th of April the 5 front companies was ordered to load which we did. . . . It was at Lexington when we saw one of their companies drawn up in regular order. Major Pitcairn of the Marines second in command called to them to disperse, but their not seeming willing he desired us to mind our space which we did when they gave us a fire then run off to get behind a wall. We had one man wounded of our Company in the leg, his name was Johnson, also Major Pitcairn's horse was shot in the flank; we returned their salute, and before we proceeded on our march from Lexington I believe we killed and wounded either 7 or 8 men. •*Ensign Jeremy Lister, youngest of the British officers at Lexington, in a personal narrative written in 1782*
(Document reprinted in Lister, 1931)[†]

REFERENCES

Bailyn, B. (1963). The problems of the working historian: A comment. In S. Hook (Ed.), *Philosophy and history* (pp. 93–101). New York: New York University Press.

Barthes, R. (1975). *S/Z*. London: Penguin.

Barzun, J. (1974). *Clio and the doctors*. Chicago: University of Chicago Press.

Barzun, J., & Graff, H. F. (1962). *The modern researcher*. New York: Harcourt, Brace, & World.

Bell, J. C. (1917). Editorial: The historic sense. *Journal of Educational Psychology, 8*, 317–318.

Bennett, P. S. (1970). *What happened at Lexington Green?* Menlo Park: CA: Addison-Wesley.

Bereiter, C., & Bird, M. (1985). Use of thinking aloud in identification and teaching of reading comprehension strategies. *Cognition and Instruction, 2*, 131–156.

Berkhofer, R. F. (1988). The challenge of poetics to (normal) historical practice. *Poetics Today, 9*, 435–452.

Bowen, C. D. (1966). *Miracle at Philadelphia*. New York: Bantam.

Braudel, F. (1979). *Structures of everyday life: Civilization and capitalism, 15th–18th century*. New York: Harper and Row.

Brown, A. L. (1980). Metacognitive development and reading. In R. J. Spiro, B. Bruce, & W. Brewer, *Theoretical issues in reading comprehension* (pp. 453–481). Hillsdale, NJ: Lawrence Erlbaum Associates.

Bruner, J. (1985). Narrative and paradigmatic modes of thought. In E. Eisner (Ed.), *Learning and teaching the ways of knowing* (pp. 97–115). Chicago: University of Chicago Press.

Cantor, N. F., & Schneider, R. I. (1967). *How to study history.* New York: Crowell.

Carr, E. H. (1961). *What is history?* New York: Knopf.

Chi, M. H. T., Feltovich, P. J., & Glaser, R. (1981). Categorization and representation of physics problems by experts and novices. *Cognitive Science, 5,* 121–152.

Collingwood, R. G. (1946). *The idea of history.* London: Oxford University Press.

Collins, A., Brown, J. S., & Larkin, K. M. (1980). Inference in text understanding. In R. J. Spiro, B. C. Bruce, & W. F. Brewer (Eds.), *Theoretical issues in reading comprehension* (pp. 385–404). Hillsdale, NJ: Lawrence Erlbaum Associates.

Dana, R. H., Jr. (1877). A British officer in Boston. *Atlantic Monthly, 39,* 389–401.

Davidowicz, L. C. (1975). *The war against the Jews 1933–1945.* New York: Bantam.

Dee-Lucas, D., & Larkin, J. H. (1988). Novice rules for assessing importance in scientific texts. *Journal of Memory and Language, 27,* 288–308.

Degler, C. (1963). Do historians use covering laws? In S. Hook (Ed.), *Philosophy and history* (pp. 205–211). New York: New York University Press.

Degler, C. (1976). Why do historians change their minds. *Pacific Historical Review, 55,* 167–184.

Degler, C. (1980). Remaking American history. *Journal of American History, 67,* 7–25.

Derrida, J. (1976). *Of grammatology.* Baltimore: Johns Hopkins University Press.

Dexter, F. B. (Ed.). (1901). *The literary diary of Ezra Stiles.* New York: Charles Scribner.

Durkin, D. (1978–1979). What classroom observations reveal about reading instruction. *Reading Research Quarterly, 14,* 481–553.

Ericsson, K. A., & Simon, H. A. (1984). *Protocol analysis: Verbal reports as data.* Cambridge, MA: MIT Press.

Fast, H. (1961). *April morning.* New York: Crown.

Fish, S. (1980). *Is there a text in this class? The authority of interpretive communities.* Cambridge, MA: Harvard University Press.

Flower, L. (1988). The construction of purpose in writing and reading. *College English, 50,* 528–550.

Gardner, H. (1985). *The mind's new science.* New York: Basic Books.

Gay, P. (1974). Style in history. *American Scholar, 43,* 225–236.

Goodman, N. (1978). *Ways of worldmaking.* Indianapolis: Hackett.

Gossman, L. (1978). History and literature: Reproduction or signification. In R. H. Canary & H. Kozicki (Eds.), *The writing of history: Literary form and historical understanding* (pp. 3–39). Madison: University of Wisconsin Press.

Graves, M. F., & Slater, W. H. (1986). Could textbooks be better written and would it make a difference? *American Educator, 10,* 36–42.

Gray, W. (1959). *Historian's handbook.* Boston: Houghton Mifflin.

Gross, R. A. (1976). *The minutemen and their world.* New York: Hill and Wang.

Harlan, D. (1989). Intellectual history and the return of literature. *American Historical Review, 94,* 581–609.

Hays, W. L. (1972). *Statistics for the social sciences.* New York: Holt, Rinehart, & Winston.

Hexter, J. H. (1971). *On historians.* Cambridge, MA: Harvard University Press.

Hexter, J. H. (1979). *Reappraisals in history* (2nd ed.). Chicago: University of Chicago Press.

Hilberg, R. (1967). *The destruction of European Jewry.* Chicago: University of Chicago Press.

Hirsch, E. D. (1976). *Validity in interpretation.* New Haven, CT: Yale University Press.

Hollinger, D. A. (1989). The return of the prodigal: The persistence of historical knowing. *American Historical Review, 94,* 610–621.

Jakobson, R. (1960). *Linguistics and poetics.* In T. A. Sebeok (Ed.), *Style in language* (pp. 350–377). Cambridge, MA: MIT Press.

Kintsch, W. (1986). Learning from text. *Cognition and Instruction, 3,* 87–108.

LaCapra, D. (1985). *History and criticism.* Ithaca, NY: Cornell University Press.

Larkin J., McDermott, J., Simon, D., & Simon, H. (1980). Expert and novice performance in solving physics problems. *Science, 208,* 1135–1342.

Lister, J. (1931). *Concord fight.* Cambridge, MA: Harvard University Press.

McCloskey, D. N. (1985). The problem of audience in historical economics: Rhetorical thoughts on a text by Robert Fogel. *History and Theory, 24,* 1–22.

Mink, L. O. (1987). *Historical understanding.* Ithaca, NY: Cornell University Press.

Nevins, A. (1962). *The gateway to history.* Chicago: Quadrangle.

Newell, A., & Simon, H. A. (1972). *Human problem solving.* Englewood Cliffs, NJ: Prentice-Hall.

Norman, D. A., & Rumelhart, D. E. (1975). Memory and knowledge. In D. A. Norman, D. E. Rumelhart, & the LNR Research Group (Eds.), *Explorations in cognition* (pp. 3–32). San Francisco: W. H. Freeman.

Norris, S. P., & Phillips, L. M. (1987, April). *Explanations of reading comprehension: Schema theory and critical thinking theory.* Paper presented at the meeting of the American Educational Research Association, Washington, DC.

Novick, P. (1988). *That noble dream: The "objectivity question" and the American historical profession.* Chicago: University of Chicago Press.

Oxford English Dictionary. (1986). New York: Oxford University Press.

Perrig, W., & Kintsch, W. (1985). Propositional and situational representations of text. *Journal of Memory and Language, 24,* 503–518.

Resnick, L. B., & Resnick, D. P. (1991). Assessing the thinking curriculum: New tools for educational reform. In B. R. Gifford & M. C. O'Connor (Eds.), *Changing assessments: Alternative views of aptitude, achievement and instruction* (pp. 37–75). Boston: Kluwer.

Sawtell, C. C. (1968). *The nineteenth of April, 1775: A collection of first hand accounts.* Lincoln, MA: Sawtell of Somerset.

Schoenfeld, A. H. (1985). *Mathematical problem solving.* Orlando, FL: Academic Press.

Searle, J. (1972). What is a speech act? In P. P. Giglioli (Ed.), *Language and social context* (pp. 136–154). Middlesex, England: Penguin.

Seifert, C. M., Robertson, S. P., & Black, J. B. (1985). Types of inferences generated during comprehension. *Journal of Memory and Language, 24,* 405–422.

Shafer, R. J. (1969). *A guide to historical method.* Homewood, IL: Dorsey.

Sherif, M. (1936). *The psychology of social norms.* New York: Harper.

Shiffrin, R. M., & Schneider, W. (1977). Controlled and automatic human information processing: Detection, search, and attention. *Psychological Review, 84,* 1–66.

Spiro, R. J. (1980). Constructive processes in prose comprehension and recall. In R. J. Spiro, B. C. Bruce, & W. F. Brewer (Eds.), *Theoretical issues in reading comprehension* (pp. 245–278). Hillsdale, NJ: Lawrence Erlbaum Associates.

Stanford, M. (1986). *The nature of historical knowledge.* New York: Basil Blackwell.

Stein, N. L., & Glenn, C. G. (1977). An analysis of story comprehension in elementary school children. In R. Freedle (Ed.), *Discourse processes: Multidisciplinary perspectives* (pp. 255–282). Norwood, CT: Ablex.

Steinberg, S. (1963). *The United States: Story of a free people.* Boston: Allyn and Bacon.

Stern, F. (1972). *The varieties of history: From Voltaire to the present.* New York: Meridian.

Struever, N. S. (1985). Historical discourse. In T. van Dijk (Ed.), *Handbook of Discourse Analysis* (pp. 249–271). Orlando, FL: Academic Press.

Thorndyke, P. (1977). Cognitive structures in comprehension and memory of narrative discourse. *Cognitive Psychology, 8,* 77–110.

Tompkins, J. P. (1980). *Reader-response criticism: From formalism to post-structuralism.* Baltimore: Johns Hopkins University Press.

Tourtellot, A. B. (1959). *Lexington and Concord: The beginning of the war of the American Revolution.* New York: Norton.

van Dijk, T. A., & Kintsch, W. (1983). *Strategies of discourse comprehension.* New York: Academic Press.

White, H. (1973). *Metahistory: The historical imagination in ninteenth-century Europe.* Baltimore: Johns Hopkins University Press.

Wilson, S. M., & Wineburg, S. S. (1988). Peering at history through different lenses: The role of disciplinary perspectives in teaching history. *Teachers College Record, 89,* 525–539.

Wilson, S. M., & Wineburg, S. S. (in press). Wrinkles in time and place: Using performance assessments to understand the knowledge of history teachers. *American Educational Research Journal.*

Wineburg, S. S. (1991a). Historical problem solving: A study of the cognitive processes used in the evaluation of documentary and pictorial evidence. *Journal of Educational Psychology, 83,* 73–87.

Wineburg, S. S. (1991b). On the reading of historical texts: Notes on the breach between school and academy. *American Educational Research Journal, 28,* 495–519.

Wineburg, S. S. (1992). Probing the depths of students' historical knowledge. *Perspectives of the American Historical Association, 30,* 20–24.

Wineburg, S. S. (in press). The psychology of teaching and learning history. In D. Berliner & R. Calfee (Eds.), *Handbook of educational psychology.*

Wineburg, S. S., & Fournier, J. E. (1992a). Thinking in time. *Mosaic: Newsletter of the Center on History-Making in America, 2,* 2–3.

Wineburg, S. S., & Fournier, J. E. (1992b). *Finding home in a foreign country: The nature of contextualized thinking in history.* Paper presented at the Conference on Cognitive and Instructional Processes in History and the Social Sciences, Autonoma University, Madrid, Spain.

Wineburg, S. S., & Wilson, S. M. (1991). Subject matter knowledge in the teaching of history. In J. E. Brophy (Ed.), *Advances in research on teaching* (pp. 303–345). Greenwich, CT: JAI.

Wood, G. (1982, December 16). Writing history: An exchange. *New York Review of Books,* 59.

CHAPTER 5

Students as Authors in the Study of History

Stuart Greene
University of Wisconsin—Madison

Reading and writing in school often entail demonstrating a knowledge of facts and, at times, analyzing or interpreting ideas from a single source of information. Less familiar to beginning college writers are the kinds of literate acts that entail writing from sources, that is, creating a text from other texts. Such tasks in history often encourage students to think critically about what they read, form arguments and counterarguments, and establish an intellectual project of their own. But if we are to help students learn to read and write critically about historical events, then we need to know how students' understanding of history and writing influence the character, development, and expression of their ideas in representing historical events.

The purpose of this chapter is to examine how two different writing tasks affected the ways students in a college-level course on European history constructed meaning in writing from sources. The tasks, a report and a problem-based essay, required students to synthesize information from their prior knowledge and information from six different source texts in creating their own texts. A report, or historical account, entailed discussing issues surrounding an historical event. The problem-based task invited students to speculate about how a particular set of actions could have been improved upon. These two tasks imply two very different notions of historical writing: to review information, on the one hand, and, on the other, to define a problem, speculate about alternative actions, and reformulate information from sources in supporting a point of view. Still, historians appear to value both the writing of reports and problem-based essays as academic tasks because they can help students acquire new knowledge and think critically about historical issues (cf. Stanford, 1986; Walvoord & McCarthy, 1990). But what precisely makes these two kinds of writing distinctive? How do students respond to such tasks? And to what extent do students and historians share the same assumptions about what it means to write reports and solve problems in history?

Of particular interest to this investigation are the kinds of thinking that each task fosters, including the ways students structure information in creating a text from other texts, the extent to which they are willing to include their own ideas, and the kinds of rhetorical moves they make as authors. By authorship, I mean students' attempts to contribute knowledge to a scholarly conversation that is not necessarily found in sources, but that is carefully linked to the texts they read. These sources can provide the basis for students' writing in the form of support and elaboration (Kaufer & Geisler, 1989). The construct of authorship can provide a critical referent for understanding what is involved as students attempt to establish their own intellectual projects by adapting information from sources and prior knowledge and restructuring meaning. Here restructuring may entail supplying new organizational patterns not found in the sources, appropriating information as evidence to support an argument, and making connections between prior knowledge and source content to create a novel text.

A sense of authorship can afford students opportunities to understand the extent to which the processes of selecting, arranging, and sequencing ideas are intimately related to the beliefs and values that guide one's thinking and to the problems posed within history. They can also begin to see the place of interpretation and evidence in formulating arguments and supporting claims in different contexts. Thus, learning history may entail acquiring knowledge about text conventions and even knowledge about a topic, but developing a sense of authorship also encompasses learning about the nature of facts, evidence, and interpretation. Those who become enculturated within this field must learn the ways in which different genres respond to rhetorical situations, the techniques of reference that reflect a community's acknowledgment of authority, and the epistemological assumptions that inform its discursive practices (cf. Devitt, 1991).

In the broadest sense, this study addressed the question of how students used information from sources and prior knowledge to think critically about a series of historical events that led up to and included the European Recovery Program after World War II. More specifically, this research explored four questions:

1. How are the problem-based and report tasks interpreted by the students who performed them?
2. How do historians construe these same tasks?
3. How do the tasks affect the structure of writers' texts?
4. Do these tasks differently affect students' selection of information in writing, including the rhetorical moves they make?

Answers to these questions about how writers structure meaning or generate relevant content from different sources of knowledge can potentially enlarge our understanding of what is involved in learning to report information or solve problems in history. If as teachers we begin to observe how students interpret complex reading-to-write tasks, we can better understand the factors that motivate writers to integrate, adapt, and transform information in writing about history. Though history instruction and learning is emerging as an important field of educational research, we are only beginning to understand how students learn the discursive practices of a discipline such as history, which does not have agreed-upon methods of analysis or generalized principles for presenting evidence (cf. Stone, 1979).

In what follows, I provide some key assumptions that inform the questions I raise and the methods I used in this study to explore how students construct texts within a specific classroom context.

BACKGROUND

Researchers studying discourse synthesis have suggested that, as writers "transform source texts to create new texts," they organize textual meaning, select information based on some relevance principle, and make connective inferences between the information they select from sources and the content they generate from prior knowledge and experience (Spivey, 1990, p. 257). Writers can embellish what they read with examples and counterexamples (Stein, 1990), thinking critically about what they read in light of their goals as writers, and can structure information in order to build a coherent representation of meaning. This representation or configuration of meaning facilitates understanding and enables writers to access relevant strategies so that they can use what they know effectively (Spiro, Visopel, Schmitz, Samarapungavan, & Boerger, 1987). The extent to which writers rely on sources or contribute something original depends in large part on whether a writer has sufficient background knowledge (e.g., Ackerman, 1991), or whether the relevant information is in the sources (Spivey, 1990).

Research on writing from sources can, in turn, provide a useful way to think about how different kinds of writing can affect how writers construct meaning. As writers perform different tasks, such as writing a report (Spivey, 1984; Spivey & King, 1989), a comparison (Spivey, 1991), or an analytical essay (Ackerman, 1991), they built different representations of meaning because these tasks appear to invite people to organize, select, and connect information differently. Different transformations of meaning would result because these tasks appear to require different methods of reorganization and a different basis for selecting information from sources.

What is missing from these accounts of writing from sources, however, is the important role that interpreting a task plays in constructing meaning. The ability to succeed in school depends on a writer's ability to specify what is asked for in a given assignment (cf. Flower, 1990a; Penrose, 1993). We cannot separate task and interpretation. When students read and write, they invoke knowledge about discourse, their beliefs about writing in school, and their knowledge about a given topic or problem. In turn, each of these sources of knowledge can affect the goals students set in planning what they want to write and can influence how they will organize and select information in putting together information from different sources. Seen in this way, writing actually begins in the act of understanding or "reading" an assignment. Ruth and Murphy (1984) pointed out that the initial act of reading comprehension and subsequent rereadings at any stage of composing "call into play all of the forces" that make a text meaningful: "activation of schemata or frameworks; interpretations and inferences about an instructor's expectations and assumptions; determination of the relative importance of text elements essential to understanding and carrying out the task" (p. 413). This interpretive act is itself made of other texts formed on other occasions, thus calling attention to the intertextual nature of this process. Learners make sense of new texts and new situations by making connections to familiar tasks and contexts (Rowe, 1987).

Nelson (1990) also underscored contextual factors that can shape students' evolving interpretations of a given task and the strategies they use in writing research papers. Her study of college freshmen suggested that students' approaches to writing in a number of different fields depend, in large part, on the quality and frequency of teachers' feedback on students' drafts, teachers' criteria for evaluating writing, and their stated goals for assigning writing. Similarly, Herrington's (1985) study of students writing proposals and lab reports in chemical engineering demonstrated how both task and context can shape the social purposes for writing, the persona writers adopt in composing, and their understanding of what it means to think and act in different disciplinary forums. Whereas this research provides insight into some of the ways in which "context can give shape and direction to students' performance" (Marshall, 1987, p. 31), what are some possible ways an instructional context can motivate how students transform meaning as they organize and select information in creating a text from other texts?

THE STUDY

Participants

The participants in the study were 15 juniors and seniors enrolled in an advanced course in social history, "European Lifestyle and Culture," at a major university in the eastern United States. Four of the students were history majors with a background in decision science and applied history. The remaining students, with backgrounds in chemistry, engineering, psychology, and management, had taken, on the average, two history courses in addition to "European Lifestyle and Culture." The group of students was stratified by the researcher according to year in school and whether or not the students were history majors. A stratified random sampling procedure was used to assign students to one of two task conditions, report or problem.

Context and Instructional Setting

To examine the nature of the classroom context and its possible influences on the ways students approached the tasks of writing either a report or problem-based essay, I collected all course documents (e.g., assignments, exams), observed each class hour for 12 weeks, and took extensive notes on the questions the instructor posed and the answers students provided. I did not participate in any class discussions. I also interviewed the instructor on two occasions in order to understand the learning goals of the course and the philosophical assumptions informing his approach to teaching history.

The theme of the course, "European Lifestyle and Culture," focused in part on the social and political structures of France, Germany, and Britain in the 19th and 20th centuries. Students also examined national differences in European countries and national differences in periods of pan-European crisis. The Second World War was one of those experiences and served as a backdrop for the writing tasks that students completed for this study.

The Instructor's Theoretical Assumptions in Teaching History. In large part, the instructor questioned what some historiographers have called a tradition of archivism, a tradition that reflects a strong faith in the objectivity of history and the belief that history is a cumulative science based on the amassing of facts (cf. Kellner, 1989; Megill & McCloskey, 1987). What is important in an archivist view is not readers—their beliefs and values, the times they live in, or questions they ask—but historical sources. Seen in this way, the historian's chief task is to establish as firmly as possible events and states of affairs in the past and find the best words with which to describe them (cf. Stanford, 1986).

As an alternative to a seemingly objectivist view of language and knowledge, the instructor called attention to the tenuous nature of historical explanation; history is the study of probabilities and possibilities, an expression of the rhetorical nature of history (cf. LaCapra, 1983, 1985; White, 1987). Indeed, historians base their interpretations on rigorous methodology, requiring verification of facts and their logical relations, accuracy, and caution in drawing inferences. But historians do not mirror the historical field of naturally occurring and human events in their rendering of history. After all, historical understanding is an act of judgment made on the basis of historical evidence and an historian's interpretive framework that guides his or her selective attention. To an extent, this framework looms as large as the evidence itself, as historians determine significance and draw inferences about the basis for historical change.

Preparing Students to Write from Sources. Although students were not given direct instruction in writing from sources, the sequence of assignments in the course provided students with skills in using different types of sources and with a theoretical grounding in the constructive, rhetorical nature of historical writing. For example, students compared a documentary film's treatment of the student demonstrations in Paris in 1968 with a written analysis of these same events 3 weeks before they wrote about the European Recovery Program (ERP). In comparing these two sources, the instructor pointed out that his students confronted the relationships between the "power of written analysis and the emotional impact of a film," recognizing that there is a point of view in historical argument. Students also examined the strengths and weaknesses of these two media in conveying what happened in Paris in the context of crisis.

The instructor talked directly about writing historical arguments when he returned the graded assignment on the Paris demonstrations to the students, about 2 weeks before they wrote their papers on European recovery. In this context, he discussed the criteria historians use in judging the adequacy of an argument. He emphasized (a) the importance of "marshaling" evidence, (b) formulating an argument that is directed toward the evidence, and (c) looking critically at the nature of the sources that historians use in constructing an argument, that is, what is said and what is overlooked.

Source Texts

Students used six source texts in composing either a report or problem-based essay. These texts included *The Harriman Report* (1947), authored by the President's Committee on Foreign Aid, and the U.S. Economic Cooperation Administration's *Report on Recovery Progress and United States Aid* (1950). Students also read chapters from four contemporary historians' analyses: Hogan's (1987) *The Marshall Plan: America, Britain, and the Reconstruction of Western Europe, 1947–1952*, llgen's (1985) *Autonomy and Interdependence: Western Europe and Monetary and Trade Relations, 1958–1984*, Milward's (1984) *The Reconstruction of Western Europe, 1945–1951*, and Wexler's (1983) *The Marshall Plan Revisited: The European Recovery Program in Economic Perspective*. These sources provided information about the historical circumstances that triggered a need for a recovery program in Europe. In addition, historians' analyses focused on the conflicting positions that arose in the United States and Europe about the nature and extent of aid, and the types of provisions and conditions that were to be attached to the aid program.

The Writing Tasks

The writing tasks, designed by both the instructor and researcher, were a required part of the course and reflected the instructional goals of "European Lifestyle and Culture": to expose students to a body of knowledge about different ways of understanding historical events; to see links among different arguments in a variety of source texts; and to learn how to write clear and defensible arguments based on primary and secondary sources that introduced students to different rhetorical approaches.

Report Task.

Recently, historians have begun to review the effects of the European Recovery Program (ERP), also known as the Marshall Plan, a program that was instituted a little more than forty years ago. Historians of the plan have pointed out that American decision-makers had a number of important political, economic, and strategic goals in mind when they conceived of the ERP, but faced opposition both here and in Europe, which affected planning and implementing the program. *Write a paper that presents your understanding of issues surrounding the European Recovery Program, basing your discussion on the sources that you have been given.*

Problem-Based Task.

Recently, historians have begun to review the effects of the European Recovery Program (ERP), also known as the Marshall Plan, a program that was instituted a little more than forty years ago. Historians of the plan have pointed out that American decision-makers had a number of important political, economic, and strategic goals in mind when they conceived of the ERP, but faced opposition both here at home and in Europe, which affected planning and implementing the program. *Write a paper in which you consider issues surrounding the ERP and, based on your understanding of the sources you have been given, propose conditions or options that planners might have attached to the ERP to insure that it would be more responsive to both European and American interests.*

PROCEDURES

Data for this study were collected over a 3-week period. In class, just before students received the writing assignment, all students were tested for prior knowledge in order to determine whether the two groups of students—those writing reports and those writing problem-based essays—were equivalent. If students in each task group had significantly different levels of background knowledge, then prior knowledge would be used as a covariate for analyzing qualitative changes in knowledge. Students were asked to jot down (e.g., free-write) what they knew about the European Recovery Program after World War II, the North American Treaty Organization, and free-market economy.

Next, students were given one of two writing assignments in class, either a report-writing task or a problem-based task. Students had 10 days to read the source materials and write a 3-to-5-page essay.

After all students had received one of the two assignments, they were asked to provide think-aloud protocols for 10 min in whatever setting they chose outside of class. These were intended to capture students' initial impressions of the writing task, as well as their attempts to specify for themselves what was required and how they might proceed. In particular, students were asked to read the assignment from start to finish, commenting and thinking aloud into a tape recorder as they read. When they finished reading, students were instructed to explain in detail how they thought they might go about completing the task.

Three historians, including the instructor of the course, also provided think-aloud protocols as they read the report and problem-based tasks described earlier. These protocols were intended to throw into relief students' and historians' understanding of how to write about historical events. Like the students, the historians were instructed to "Read this assignment from start to finish, stopping at various points to comment and think aloud as you read. Explain how you think you might go about completing the task."

MEASURES

Think-aloud protocols were transcribed and then analyzed to see how students and historians interpreted how they might perform the tasks they were given. Three separate analyses of students' essays were also made in order to understand how different tasks of writing influence the ways students organized and selected information in writing their essays.

Students' and Historians' Interpretations of Writing Reports and Problem-Based Essays

If students and historians appeared to rely on the texts they were given as the primary source of information, their interpretation of the task was coded as *text*, as shown here in an illustration from a student's protocol:

(1) really vague—discuss [issues surrounding the ERP] could mean anything . . . not really interested in formulating an opinion . . . try to understand what each article was saying . . . write a thesis that can cover everything and *get specifics from the texts*.

(2) write about what the plan was . . . the goals of Marshall aid . . . motives for Marshall aid as a major section and political, strategic, economic as subsections . . . opposition to the plan with *specific examples*.

Protocols were coded as *text* × *self* when students and historians
indicated they would rely on their prior knowledge (e.g., the role that
interest groups play in determining policy, their knowledge of economic
theory) as well as on the sources they were given. Cues that distinguished this category from text included comments such as "have to
draw conclusions from the articles" and talk about "what was plausible." Here are excerpts from one student's protocol coded as text × self:

(1) . . . issues surrounding planning and implementing of the ERP . . . He
wants us to *assume the role of a decision-maker* . . . what could have been
done to make the plan more responsive to American and European
interests.

(2) Consider issues (e.g., whether the program was effective or not), the
goals of the recovery program, the consequences, and the alternatives . . .
Detail different country's positions . . . *Propose conditions or options* . . .
Argue with evidence about whether the plan did what it set out to
accomplish.

Analysis of Students' Essays

Analyses of students' essays included (a) the organization (i.e., top-level
structure) that framed a given essay, (b) origin of information (i.e., the
extent to which students relied on borrowed or added information), and
(c) appeals to authority (i.e., rhetorical moves).

Organization. For the analysis of organization, each student essay
was read and analyzed in order to pinpoint the underlying logic, or
frame, informing a given essay. As in Haswell (1986), the method of
analysis consisted of identifying the top-level structure, that is, "the one
logically coherent arrangement of ideas that embraces the largest
number of words in the main body of the essay" (p. 403). Analysis of
each essay consisted of finding the organizing principle that subsumed
all of the content and relationships in the essays (e.g., causal connections). Categories used for classifying top-level structure were taken
from Meyer's (1985) taxonomy of logical relations that operate in a text.
These included collection, causation, response (i.e., problem–solution),
comparison, and description. Two structures were identified in students' essays: collection and problem–solution.

Origin of Information. To examine the origin of information in
students' final texts—borrowed or added information—I constructed a

template (cf. Spivey, 1983) of content units in the source texts and students' essays. This measure was designed to examine the extent to which students in each task group relied on the source texts and the extent to which they introduced information from prior knowledge in order to contribute to the scholarly conversation revolving around European recovery.

The semantic content of each source text and each student's essay was parsed into content units in a modification of Ackerman's (1989) and Kroll's (1977) procedure for analyzing clauses in written discourse. To qualify as an idea unit, a clause or phrase had to elicit a positive response to the following question: Can this clause stand as a complete, factually correct, and informative sentence in a student's essay? For example, a noun phrase and a verb phrase were counted as one idea unit, including (when present) a direct object, a prepositional phrase, or an adverbial phrase. The sentence *The forum included critics on the Left* would be considered as one content unit. Clauses and phrases joined by a coordinating conjunction (and, or, but, nor) were considered separate units if they could stand alone in a student's essay. *The Marshall Plan facilitated essential imports and eased production bottlenecks* would be parsed into two content units: *The Marshall Plan facilitated essential imports. The Marshall Plan eased production bottlenecks.* (The Appendix provides a brief excerpt of a student's text parsed into content units.)

Each content unit in a student's essay was then scored as either *borrowed*, if the idea matched the semantic content in one of the source texts, or *added*, if the information did not match the source content in the template.

Appeals to Authority. Analyzing students' appeals to authority provided a further means for understanding the basis on which students writing reports and solving problems *selected* information from sources. Of interest was whether there were differences in the ways these two groups of students cited authorities in the field in order to further their goals as writers. This analysis also sought to identify some of the rhetorical moves these writers made in *structuring* their ideas. These moves include situating their work amid what others have written; showing that there were unresolved problems the field needed to address; and advancing their own claims (cf. Swales, 1984). Finally, understanding the kinds of rhetorical activity involved in performing each task can help us to see the extent to which different reading-to-write tasks foster different kinds of thinking. Contributing to a scholarly conversation entails not only acquiring content knowledge but also learning to manage this knowledge within certain rhetorical and linguistic conventions (Berkenkotter, Huckin, & Ackerman, 1988).

Students' essays were first read and then their explicit appeals to authority were coded according to the function these appeals served in presenting information about European recovery (cf. Kaufer & Geisler, 1991). Three ways that students cited the sources they used are shown by examples taken from students' essays:

1. To use as a source of content: The writer used the work of an author as a source of information.

In *The Marshall Plan: America, Britain and the Reconstruction of Western Europe, 1947–1952*, Michael Hogan suggests that American decision-makers had a number of important political, economic, and strategic goals in mind when they conceived of the European Recovery Act or Marshall Plan.

2. To locate a faulty path: A faulty path may be a line of argument that a writer thinks is mistaken or simply misses the mark and that a reader ought to reconsider or even avoid such an argument. Locating a faulty path consists of comparing points of view as illustrated here, but it also entails showing an alternative path signaled by words like however.

Critics, such as Milward, argue that the hard work of the European citizens and the skill of their leaders contributed more than the Marshall Plan to the recovery of France, Italy, Belgium, West Germany, and Austria. In fact, some claim the ERP hurt Western Europe and the US more than it helped . . . Ilgen points out that austere living conditions requested during General De Gaulle's terms in office moved France back to a position of power in the foreign trade arena. *However, restored competitiveness of European products in world markets and the return of currency convertibility, as provided by the Marshall Plan, were responsible for such opportunities.*

3. To support a claim: The writer appealed to an author to support his or her own line of argument.

Although problems and disputed ideologies existed during the time the Marshall Plan was implemented, there is evidence that the plan itself was successful for Western European countries. *The late 1950s yielded the European Common Market which proved that European exports could compete successfully in world markets as well as European monetary recovery* (Ilgen, p. 28).

TABLE 5.1
Summary of Measures Used in the Study

	Measure	Coding
Students' and historians' interpretations of task	Think-aloud protocols	Text, text × self
Organization of students' essays	Top-level structure	Collection, problem–solution
Students' selection of information	Origin of information	Borrowed, added
	Appeals to authority	Source of content, faulty path, support a claim

SUMMARY

Table 5.1 provides an overview of the measures used in this study and how the data were coded. To summarize, this study examined both students' and historians' understanding of what they believed is involved in writing reports and solving problems. Analyses also focused on how students' interpretations of the two tasks guided the ways they organized their essays and used information from sources and prior knowledge in writing from sources.

Reliability of each measure was established by asking a second rater to read a random sample of at least 20% of the data. There was 100% agreement in coding the protocols and in identifying the top-level structures of students' essays. Cohen's kappa was used to test the reliability of the scoring procedure for determining origin of information, $\kappa = .80$, and students' appeals to authority, $\kappa = .86$. The high agreement between raters can be attributed to the second rater's training.

RESULTS AND DISCUSSION

The results of this study indicated that the report and problem-based tasks had different effects on the ways students interpreted these tasks, organized information, and generated content from sources or prior knowledge and experience. An analysis also revealed that both task groups were equivalent in terms of their background knowledge of European Recovery, so that prior knowledge was not used as a covariate in any of the analyses focusing on students' selection of information (e.g., borrowed or added information).

In presenting these results with more detailed explanations, I first discuss the ways these students and three historians construed the tasks of solving problems and writing reports. Of particular interest was whether the students and historians understood their task as one that required them to rely on sources or invited them to use their prior knowledge about history. A post hoc analysis of students' and historians' think-aloud protocols helped to bring into focus the goals they set, the strategies they invoked to further their goals as writers, and the extent to which they were aware of why the strategies they used were appropriate (cf. Flower, 1990b). Identifying matches and mismatches between the ways students and historians interpreted these tasks called attention to some important differences between what it means to write within the culture of school and the discipline of history. Understanding the nature of these differences can provide some ways to think about teaching students about both the subject matter of history and what it means to think like a historian (cf. Wilson & Sykes, 1989; Wineburg & Wilson, 1991).

This comparison between historians' and students' approaches to writing reports and solving problems is followed by a three-part analysis of how students' interpretations got played out in the texts they wrote: (a) how students organized information, (b) the extent to which they relied on the sources they were given or relied on prior knowledge in writing essays, and (c) the rhetorical moves they made in either writing a report or problem-based essay.

Historians' Understanding of Writing Reports and Problem-Based Essays

Differences between how students and historians interpreted the task of writing a report or solving a problem can, in part, be explained by historians' rhetorical knowledge. Rather than writing for a specific audience, the instructor of the course suggested that "historians often write for an indeterminate number of readers in different fields" within the discipline in their attempts to make past events intelligible to the present. As the following analyses also show, historians were more likely to answer questions that they posed for themselves in light of their understanding of the discipline than respond directly to the prompt of a given assignment. In any event, an emphasis on differences does not necessarily imply a judgment that one approach is better than the other; instead, each interpretation reflects a set of options for performing a given task that may or may not have been a part of students' repertoire for writing about history.

I do make one qualification in presenting the analyses that follow.

Since the historians in this study did not actually write a report or a problem-based essay, it is possible that historians' interpretations of the two tasks may have been different had they been expected to write an essay based on sources. Still, their interpretations of these tasks not only called attention to the kinds of rhetorical moves that experts make in constructing meaning, but foregrounded as well the difficulties that students faced as they worked through these same tasks.

Historians' Interpretations of the Report Task. The three historians envisioned their task as requiring them to rely on the sources in writing about issues surrounding European recovery; they also saw the possibility of using information from the texts they were given as a source of evidence for an argument and for contributing a novel perspective. Developing an argument entailed making connections among different issues and establishing why focusing on a given set of issues might be important. One historian, Professor A, revealed a plan for writing that embodied just such an approach:

> . . . the first paragraph might indeed begin, "American decision-makers had several important political goals in mind. In this paper I will only explore two of them. They are linked and they are linked by the fact that . . ." and that's your first paragraph.

His goal was to show the significance of at least two specific issues among those that historians had previously discussed in the sources, pointing out the basis on which these issues were related. Such a plan also implied a set of strategies that consisted of selectively evaluating the issues presented in the readings in order to define the writer's own sense of what should be discussed.

For Professor B, providing one's understanding of the issues entailed playing issues off one another, in addition to determining importance and justifying one's decisions. Her interpretation of the task emphasized, even more than Professor A's interpretation, that the task required both a discussion of key issues and an argument that established why the two or three issues they chose were important. Professor B saw the sources as a means for discussing contemporary arguments about the plan in order to identify the main points of agreement and disagreement. In large part, Professor B wanted to see "the extent to which maybe I feel like a couple of issues haven't been given sufficient emphasis." In her think-aloud protocol, she reflected on the need to "marshal evidence to justify the notion that these were the principal issues." By doing so, she could find a way to enter the conversation without "parroting what other historians have already established."

Although Professor B believed that she would rely on sources in writing a report or historical account, her interpretation suggested that in doing so she could still contribute her own ideas in ways that met the expectations of historians, which includes adding something new. It would not be useful, she commented in thinking aloud, to "identify main lines of interpretation for their own sake."

Discourse and topic knowledge provided an interpretive framework that enabled the instructor, Professor C, to classify, categorize, and make judgments about a given body of information. In his think-aloud protocol, he demonstrated the important role that topic knowledge played in the way he interpreted the task. In turn, this interpretation set in motion a well-developed plan for writing a report on the ERP:

> In my mind, I would be preparing a grid. And the grid would have columns and rows. And the columns would be national participants and it would have different interest groups within different nations. And the rows would be periods of time. . . . I would be interested in trying to disentangle the interest groups within different nation states . . . isolate these interest groups, the nations, and the time periods . . . select what is important and organize information, for example, societies, nations, classes, changes over time.

According to Professor C, this kind of reasoning "inevitably leads to questions of significance," so that linked to a comparison of different issues was an argument that established the importance of discussing a certain group of issues, a strategy that the other two historians believed was important. He instantiated a schema for historical writing that fulfilled the assumption that any discussion of issues must be set in the context of what others have said and that these issues should be explained in relation to one another. Moreover, as Professor C thought aloud, he also reflected upon the extent to which he could contribute his own perspective, even if his work was linked to the sources:

> We're not asked to include our own ideas . . . we're asked to compare, however, and therefore asked to conceptualize because you have to compare in terms of something. And the way in which they formulate what is to be compared will reflect some of their own ideas. That's to say their own language for discussing these things.

In the end, Professor C demonstrated his awareness of the rhetorical strategies that enabled him to establish a point of view that, as is shown later, some students felt that they could not take in writing a report.

Historians' Interpretations of the Problem-Based Task. All three historians saw the task as requiring them to base their evaluation of the recovery program and alternative proposals on the readings they were given. Even though Professor A suggested in his think-aloud protocol that the "main focus is to propose conditions or options," he also underscored the need to master "a body of factual information." His view was consistent with the instructor's sense that in order to ask "what if?" and speculate upon what might have happened, "one must know exactly what happened. You will never know the probabilities you're altering unless you know what actually happened." Similarly, Professor B said that "you've got to handle some of the problems of interpretation and motivation that are suggested in the first part of the assignment." For her, this would mean sorting "through the combination of explicit and implicit motivations" discussed in the readings "to figure out what really caused a particular development." Based on this understanding, "you've got to develop some sense of the other ways that could have been pursued, of other options in relation to the *field* [my emphasis]. . . . So it's an evaluation exercise."

Professor B's reference to the field is significant because she calls attention to the larger context that she invoked in constructing an interpretation of how to go about solving a problem in writing history. This context extended well beyond the one that surrounded students' attempts to solve problems in school. In addition to knowing about decision-making structures in the governments involved, as Professor A pointed out, Professor B observed that solving a problem also entailed having an awareness of the constraints in developing foreign and domestic policies:

> . . . when you deal with a foreign policy issue which this is fundamentally you want to remember more than diplomatic historians usually do. That there are lots of domestic constraints. It's not just policy makers bravely marching out and then maybe interacting with the foreigners to whom their policy applies. They also have domestic constraints.

Thus, identifying a problem not only required that historians go beyond the information in the sources, but also required them to marshal evidence within the larger context of what it means to think like an historian in speculating about possible options and alternatives to the European Recovery Program.

As in writing a report, the role that prior knowledge played in construing the problem-based task was brought into focus by the instructor's interpretation. This knowledge guided his construction of the task and how he would proceed:

> I would expect them to raise hypothetical situations and then try to judge what the likely effect of those would have been. . . . Suppose for example

that the cold war mania had not been allowed to dominate American foreign policy and the lawless wing of the democratic party in '48 had emerged much stronger in the elections. What would it have meant to the face of the post-war Europe to have actively sought to include Eastern Europe in the program from the beginning?

> . . . You can sketch scenarios. I don't know how else to do it . . . You're asking them to go back to the environment of '47, '48. Take options that were available then and see what pursuing them might have been like. Now one of the options of course was to take the Taft position. And to refuse to support the ERP on the grounds that it would undercut the American economy and its development and to think what it would have meant to America to have conceived of its economy without European clients. Probably would have had much lower rate of inflation. We would have had much more insular foreign policy. We would not have been involved in the cold war position.

To engage in this kind of hypothetical reasoning required having knowledge about what happened at the end of World War II—politically, strategically, and economically. He was also sensitive to the need to balance individual contribution with accountability, showing an awareness of what others have argued. The ability to strike this balance, taking charge of one's own thinking, on the one hand, and invoking authorities in the field, on the other hand, reflects a level of critical literacy that students are often asked to engage in as they perform complex academic tasks of writing, but that they may not be adequately prepared to do in their work.

Students' Understanding of Writing Reports and Problem-Based Essays

With some understanding of the ways historians construed these two tasks, I want now to turn to a comparison between students' interpretations. As expected, the two groups of students differed significantly in the ways that they interpreted these two tasks, differences that are, on the surface, consistent with the historians' interpretations. More of those writing reports saw their tasks as one that required them to rely on the sources to write their essays, as shown in Table 5.2. Most of those writing problem-based essays were apt to see that they should integrate prior knowledge with information in the source texts.

Students' Interpretations of the Report Task. Protocol transcripts indicated that six of the seven students recognized that writing a report

TABLE 5.2
Observed Frequencies of Two Task Interpretations of Students
Writing Reports or Problem-Based Essays

	Report (n = 7)	Problem (n = 8)	Total
Text	6	2	8
Text × self	1	6	7

required them to rely primarily on the source texts and therefore constrained the extent to which they could include their own ideas or opinions. One student saw the report task as requiring him to "understand what each article was saying" and formulate a "thesis that [could] cover everything." Fulfilling these criteria meant getting "specifics from the texts." In contrast to the historians, he decided that he was really not interested in formulating an opinion, that there was not a strong view that he could take. Instead, his main goal was to demonstrate that he read the sources and cited each of the authors. He also wanted to make sure that he did not leave anybody out: "I didn't really try to say this is my view and try to defend it. I didn't try to push anything. I didn't see a strong view I could take."

His response reflected a typical concern described by five of the seven students writing reports, one that revealed the extent to which these students felt accountable to the sources they read. Their understanding of what was required may not be surprising because students often see writing as a test of what they know, not as an invitation to use writing as a means for exploring their own ideas, challenging received opinions, or making their own interpretations, as was the case for the historians in this study (cf. Applebee, 1981, 1984; Barnes, 1976; Walvoord & McCarthy, 1990). Still, reliance on the sources and a certain reluctance to take a stance on the issues did not prevent this student from appropriating the report-writing task: "Maybe the opposition was in the assignment, but I focused on why the ERP was starting—I felt that was more important."

Three other students also gave evidence that it was possible to include their "own opinions" or their "own understanding," but one student chose not to, typifying in her comments the attitude these others had adopted about writing in school: "It's much more difficult when you say that this is your opinion. I'd want to be right. I think you leave yourself open for more, especially when [the instructor] is reading your paper. You've got to know what you're talking about." The more advantageous move, for her, was to rely on sources, not to risk stating an opinion within the evaluative climate of the classroom. Although the instructor valued independence in thought and action, this student weighed the costs and benefits of presenting her opinion. When she wrote her essay, she deferred to the authority of the sources, citing a single author throughout her essay, thus subordinating ideas from prior knowledge and experience. The six other students writing reports did not defer in this way, but such a comment calls attention to the way in which the notion of audience influences how students construe a given task. In her view, her writing was sanctioned by the teacher, the sole audience of her paper.

A striking contrast to this student was a student who constructed an image of the teacher as someone who valued the ideas of students and appreciated students' willingness to go beyond the task. This is consistent with her prior experiences in school where she was a member of the debate club and where she had often been rewarded for her ability to raise questions and challenge accepted ideas. With such an image in mind, she decided that she "couldn't go straight from the assignment." In a think-aloud protocol, she asserted that she had to give her own opinion. It was more important than simply repeating what was in the texts. "I didn't think it would be as helpful to my reader to simply recite. . . . It was more important to express what I felt was important."

While her essay was provocative, suggesting that the ERP was not a sound investment for the United States, she cited only two sources in making her argument, relying, instead, on her own ideas about the limitations of this foreign policy initiative. Thus, at issue is whether personal expression is sufficient in the context of writing a report for a history class where students were expected to demonstrate their understanding of a shared body of knowledge in developing an intellectual project of their own. This latter point is made quite clear in the ways that historians, including the instructor of the course, interpreted what it means to write a report in history.

Students' Interpretations of the Problem-Based Task. The problem-based task appeared to provide students with a more explicit prompt to incorporate ideas from prior knowledge in their essays than did the report-writing task. Interestingly, there was little variation in how students and historians envisioned this task. Students and historians, alike, recognized that they were accountable to the sources in proposing conditions and options to the recovery program. Moreover, most of the students saw that solving a problem entailed weaving source information with prior knowledge in supporting their view of what could have been done to improve upon the recovery program.

Six of the eight students interpreted the problem-based task as inviting them to speculate, assuming the role of decision maker. And, like the historians, they saw the assignment as an evaluation task. One student believed she would have to "argu[e] with evidence about whether the plan did what it set out to accomplish." In turn, she specified what she needed to do in order to fulfill her goals. Her strategies included "draw[ing] conclusions from the articles. [After all] proposing conditions entails speculating but it has to be based on the articles." Similarly, as did her instructor, another student emphasized the importance of striking a balance between introducing her own observations about what might have been proposed to make the ERP more responsive to the United States' and Europe's needs and making use of the sources:

> The most important thing that he's looking for is more insight . . . putting together everything that was given to us . . . taking bits and pieces out of each specific source and putting it together into one uniform paper. He wants us to really consider options . . . what could have been done. . . . Why did some things work, what were the reasons why other things didn't work.

Her comments also indicated her awareness of audience. The choices she made were in keeping with her goals as a writer, but they were also shaped by her sense of her reader's expectations, in this case her teacher's. Knowledge about what she was going to write and an understanding of why such an approach might be appropriate underscored this student's ability to monitor the choices and possibilities that may or may not be open to her in this situation.

To sum up, most of the students writing reports envisioned their task as one that required them to rely on the sources; however, there was little sense that they understood the need to link these issues in ways that the historians did or to establish an argument justifying their decisions to focus on a given set of issues. Most of those writing problem-based essays interpreted the task as one that invited them to incorporate their own ideas with information from the sources. In keeping with the historians' interpretations, they also saw the need to develop an argument in proposing possible options or alternatives to the original plan. Perhaps the most striking differences, among others, included students' and historians' sense of audience. Students saw their audience as the teacher, someone who would evaluate their work. Although the historians did not make explicit references to a reader or audience, they seemed to construct a representation of the task that was consistent with the discipline's expectations of what it means to write reports and solve problems.

Analysis of Students' Essays

Three separate analyses focused on students' essays: (a) the organization (i.e., top-level structure) that framed a given essay, (b) origin of
information (i.e., the extent to which students relied on borrowed or
added information), and (c) appeals to authority.

Organization. Based on differences between the reasoning students
engaged in as they interpreted what it meant to write a report and a
problem-based essay, one could speculate that the resulting structures
of their essays would be quite different as well. An analysis of the
top-level structure (Meyer, 1985) of students' essays, shown in Table 5.3,
revealed that in fact students in each task group structured information
in different ways. Students writing reports organized their essays in a
collection structure, a loose pattern of organization that included a set of
descriptions about issues surrounding European recovery. These issues
were grouped on the basis of topic or association. For the most part,
those writing problem-based essays organized their ideas about the
recovery program in a "response" or problem–solution structure, a
pattern of organization in which students grouped their ideas on the
basis of some sort of causal relationship. Students' proposals for
improving upon the decisions made about European recovery were a
direct consequence of having established the existence of a problem.
Moreover, there was some overlap between the description of the
problem (i.e., the topic content) that students framed and the solutions
they offered.

Figure 5.1 provides a visual description of the organizing principle
that framed students' reports, again a loose collection of ideas grouped
by association or topic. This principle is illustrated in one student's essay
in which she first provided background information about European
recovery in order to set up her discussion of issues surrounding the
program. This approach was taken by five of the seven students in this
group.

TABLE 5.3
**Observed Frequencies of Two Text Structures for Two Task
Conditions**

Structure	Report	Problem	Total
Collection	7	2	9
Problem–solution	0	6	6

FIG. 5.1. Collection structure.

After World War II Europe was faced with the problem of reconstruction. This was a difficult task which involved both economic and political restructuring and development. The United States helped in this effort through its European Recovery Program (ERP) which was also known as the Marshall Plan. The plan spanned almost four years from 1943 to 1951, in which time the United States spent almost $12.4 billion mostly in the form of grant aid to the countries involved in the ERP (Wexler, pg. 249).The main objectives of the United States in supplying this aid were not only economic but political and strategic as well. . . . Various issues were raised with respect to the Marshall Plan as a result of this. Some of the major issues were: balance of power in Western Europe, integration of Western Europe both economically and politically, and the extent and type of aid to be given.

After noting "that various issues were raised," she went on to develop these three issues, linking them together numerically, rather than establishing possible connections among these issues or justifying why these issues are important:

The balance of power Western Europe was to have after the reconstruction was a major issue involved in the Marshall Plan. . . . A second important issue surrounding the ERP was the issue of European political and economic integration. . . . The last issue surrounding the European Recovery Program to be discussed is the extent and type of aid to be given.

Interestingly, the pattern of her writing—an introduction, three points, and a conclusion—took the form of a five-paragraph essay, reflecting a legacy of schooling that appeared to influence her understanding of what it meant to write a report in history. This approach is in contrast to the instructor's view that writing a report inevitably leads to questions of significance and an argument establishing the importance of discussing a given set of issues.

Figure 5.2 provides a visual description of a problem–solution struc-

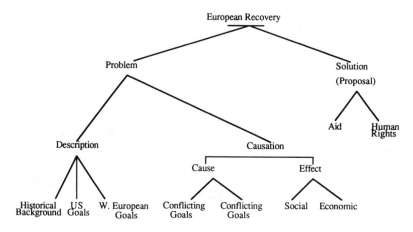

FIG. 5.2. Problem–solution structure.

ture. A major portion of students' problem statements was devoted to
providing historical background on U.S. and western European goals
for economic and political development after World War II. This kind of
background information helped show that some sort of recovery program was necessary in order to rebuild Europe as a result of the
economic, social, and political devastation caused by the war. An
important part of students' problem statements also entailed explaining
why the actions policymakers took were not adequate, particularly
because U.S. and Europe's goals for recovery often came into conflict.
These conflicting goals often led to actions that adversely affected the
social and economic structures of a given country. Once students
established that these actions could have been more sensitive to the
needs of all countries involved in the recovery program, they offered
possible solutions.

In a typical example of a problem-based essay, one student led up to
a statement of the problem by providing a sense of the political climate
in Europe at the end of World War II:

> World War II wreaked havoc on all nations concerned, and the United
> States was no exception. Though the United States emerged from the war
> in a much better position than any other major power, the devastation of
> Europe and the seemingly rapid expansion of Communism were a direct
> threat to its economic stability. The task of rebuilding Europe was
> therefore a major concern for American policy makers. The European
> Recovery Act which was created to address the situation in Europe,
> strongly reflected the United States' own domestic goals. Because the
> strategic, economic and political goals of the United States were the
> foundation of the recovery program, European needs were sometimes

overlooked. While economic reconstruction was successful in many respects it may have been more so had the United States been more sensitive to the particulars of European society.

In developing his ideas, this student suggested that the Marshall Plan "was too oriented toward industrial productivity and neglected the needs of individuals and social classes." Here he identified two conflicting goals: the need to stabilize the European economy, and the need to improve the standard of living for individuals living in western European countries. For him, industrialization took precedence over concerns for individuals, creating gains of one sort, but deprivation as well, thus producing adverse effects in both economic and social arenas. The program, he argued in posing alternative options and conditions (his solution), could have included "domestic measures, such as insuring adequate food supplies and restoring the stability of the family unit." This student demonstrated that he knew the issues, interweaving his "own" ideas about how the ERP could have been more responsive and providing a possible solution, one that was directly related to the problem.

By examining the specific relationships of the content structure of students' essays, the analysis just performed actually goes beyond the top-level structure that framed their texts, but such an analysis helps to show that students from each group tended to construct different representations of meaning that can be explained by the different transformations they performed. In particular, they used different principles to restructure information from the sources. The problem-based task appeared to invite students to restructure information by supplying a "new" organizing pattern not found in the sources. Students writing reports combined and recombined information in creating their own texts, but they did not restructure meaning from text as extensively.

Origin of Information. A key assumption in this study was that different principles of organizing a text in writing a report or solving a problem would influence the basis on which students selected information from prior knowledge and the sources they were given. Because students writing problem-based essays were invited to propose solutions to an unresolved problem, one might have expected them to include a larger proportion of information from prior knowledge than those students asked to discuss issues based on their reading of the sources.

Findings showed that the proportion of information from sources included in students' essays was not significantly different. The mean proportion of source units to the total number of content units included in students' problem-based essays was.62 (SD = .16), and the mean for those writing reports was.71 (SD = .19).

One possible explanation for why there were not significant differences is that students in both task groups appeared to rely on sources in composing their essays to demonstrate that they had done the reading and that they knew what the key issues and problems were. Another explanation is that writing a report entailed discussing controversial issues in a course that encouraged students to think critically and independently. As a consequence, some students may have begun to apply the problem-solving strategies introduced and discussed in the course they were taking to writing their reports. Analyses showed that two students writing reports included a relatively large proportion of information from prior knowledge. In each case, 35% of the information they included was from prior knowledge, which is closer to the mean for those writing problem-based essays (38%) than for those writing reports (29%). One of these two students, mentioned earlier, explained that she "couldn't go straight from the assignment," that she had to give her own opinion. The other student used her knowledge of economic theory to discuss issues surrounding the ERP and point out some flaws in this program.

Appeals to Authority. Given the theoretical assumptions of this study, one might have predicted that students writing reports and problem-based essays would appeal to sources in significantly different ways. Those writing reports were expected to rely on source content more than those writing problem-based essays and to make more overall appeals to authorities primarily as sources of information. Those writing problem-based essays were expected to invoke authorities less as a source of information and more as a source of evidence to support their claims about how a given set of actions might have been improved upon.

Again, however, these expectations belie what was actually happening. An analysis of students' appeals to authority indicated that both task groups tended to follow a similar pattern in their use of citations as sources of information rather than as resources for supporting an argument or locating a faulty path. Table 5.4 shows the overall means and standard deviations for each type of appeal.

Both groups of students appealed to authorities in the field as important intellectual touchstones, demonstrating to a reader—their instructor—an awareness of key issues or problems. Relying on sources can suggest a lack of confidence in one's own ideas, but it does not preclude making a contribution to a scholarly conversation. Doing so entails using published authorities in different ways: to lay out what has

TABLE 5.4
Means and Standard Deviations for Appeals to Authority

Appeals to Authority	Report	Problem	All
Total appeals	10.29	12.13	11.21
	(9.27)	(7.18)	(7.96)
Content	7.71	6.88	7.26
	(8.67)	(3.64)	(6.25)
Faulty path	0.57	1.50	1.03
	(1.13)	(2.14)	(1.74)
Support an argument	2.00	3.75	2.93
	(1.30)	(3.50)	(2.76)

been said about a topic, issue, or problem; to support one's argument in light of what others have expressed; and perhaps to use one's ideas to criticize another perspective in order to establish one's own point of view. Some students in both task groups saw the opportunity to critique a position, appealing to authorities as a source of evidence. In doing so, some students writing reports and problem-based essays adapted and transformed source information in order to make a contribution, playing one discourse off another in order to introduce their own perspective or propose their own alternative to a plan designed to aid European recovery. That is, they strategically placed information in the texts they wrote and used points of information presented in the source texts to support a claim in order to fulfill their goals as authors.

The ways in which students appealed to authority might have reflected a fundamental tension that existed in the classroom context described earlier and can provide us with a picture of their attempts to learn how to enter what for some was a new discourse. This tension points to students' need to invoke the authorities of a discipline in order to demonstrate their awareness of issues, on the one hand, and the degree to which students could take charge of their own ideas, on the other hand. Although the instructor encouraged students to think critically about the nature of historians' representations of historical events, considering both what was said and what was left unsaid, most students tended to appeal to authorities in the field as sources of information. Those who appealed to authority to advance their own ideas or to locate a faulty path in a historian's argument to set up their own position had apparently learned part of what it means to write and think like a historian, at least from the point of view of one who sees the writing of history as an interpretive, constructive act. Indeed, this is the philosophical position taken in the course, "European Lifestyle and Culture." That others had not employed these kinds of rhetorical moves, particularly those students writing problem-based essays, calls attention to the potential difficulties of entering a new discourse and of knowing how to set up a scholarly project. Such a project entails adapting and transforming source information to meet one's own discourse goals. In the end, what strategies are involved in constructing a historical interpretation? The answer can vary, depending on whether they see historical representation as an act of judgment that can be challenged, or perceive history as a chronicle of facts, adopting an archivist view of history.

SUMMARY OF RESULTS

This study examined four questions related to the issue of how different tasks of composing from sources influence the ways in which students construct meaning in writing about history:

1. How are the problem-based and report tasks interpreted by the students who performed them?
2. How do historians interpret these tasks?
3. How do the tasks affect the structure of writers' texts?
4. Do these tasks differently affect students' selection of information in writing, including the rhetorical moves they make?

Because the sample size was relatively small and the instructional context appeared to influence some students' responses, it is difficult to generalize beyond this particular context and these two tasks. Still, the decision to study a small group of students provided a way to look closely at students' intellectual activities from a number of different perspectives. It was also important to study students' writing within a fairly naturalistic setting where students' work was very much a part of the instructional goals of the course they took. Although we may need to maintain some control of the setting to insure that our results are valid, we can also try to increase our understanding of how the "special nature of school settings" influences students' writing (Nelson, 1990, p. 363). A key point is that students' interpretations revealed the extent to which writing is a constructive act. Students relied on previous schooling and cues from the immediate classroom setting in deciding how to use different sources of information in creating their own texts.

The results cited in this section did help to specify some differences that manifest themselves in two relatively structured assignments of writing from sources. Students writing reports uniformly understood their task as one that required them to rely largely or exclusively on the sources to write their essays. Most of those writing problem-based essays felt that they should integrate prior knowledge with source information. Of particular interest was the extent to which these students' conceptions of writing either a report or a problem-based essay rested on their sense of what their teacher expected. In contrast, historians envisioned the tasks of writing reports and solving problems in light of their understanding of what readers in the field expected.

The comparison between students' and historians' approaches to writing a historical account also suggested the difficulties some students had in writing a report and setting up a scholarly project. Educators often think of writing a report as a generically simpler task than writing an analysis or problem-based essay (e.g., Applebee, 1984), but students in this study had trouble writing a report because they lacked the kind of disciplinary knowledge that would have enabled them to set their ideas in context and justify the issues they chose to write about. In contrast, students writing problem-based essays appeared to have a wider range of options than those writing reports, enabling the problem solvers to draw upon different kinds of information and to use this knowledge in relatively conventional ways.

Differences in the ways students organized their essays provided concrete descriptions of how students' interpretations of task play themselves out in constructing meaning in both reading and writing. Their essays revealed the kinds of structural transformations that different tasks of writing appear to invite and the potential differences in thinking that different kinds of writing can foster.

IMPLICATIONS FOR TEACHING AND RESEARCH

Although discussions about writing have primarily existed outside the domain of history teaching and instruction (Giroux, 1988), the present study connects with prior research focusing on classroom instruction because it has also emphasized the role that context can play in student learning. Prior research has thus far explored the relationship between different types of historical explanations and students' ability to reason in history (Leinhardt, 1990a, 1990b; Halldén, 1986), the relationship between teachers' subject-matter knowledge and instruction (Wineburg & Wilson, 1991; cf. Wilson & Wineburg, 1988), and the kind of instruction that can foster students' abilities to think and act like historians (Wilson & Sykes, 1989; Wineburg & Wilson, 1991). Perhaps the research presented in this chapter can provide the groundwork for studies designed to examine further the ways in which students learn to write historical accounts and solve problems, engaging in the kind of reasoning that historians value. For example, researchers might investigate the relationship between prior knowledge and the transformations readers and writers perform as they select information, add information in strategic ways, and restructure information. What is the role of a writer's evolving topic and conceptual knowledge in constructing meaning in complex reading-to-write tasks? An equally important concern is how a writer's strategic knowledge (i.e., goals, strategies, and awareness) motivates these kinds of transformations.

Finally, this study points to a need to probe more deeply into contextual factors that can influence performance, such as teacher–student interactions that occur within the classroom (cf. Leinhardt, 1990a, 1990b) and in teachers' evaluation of students' written work. What kinds of questions does the instructor ask? What kinds of reasoning do these questions promote? How does the experience of the classroom relate to the kinds of writing students are asked to produce? What concerns does the instructor address in commenting upon students' papers? How does the nature of a given task affect the kinds of comments an instructor makes? By answering these questions in a study that examines how students perform different tasks, we can be in a better position to discuss those factors that influence students' willingness or ability to create novel texts in writing about history.

This study does have some pedagogical implications as well that underscore the need to provide students with an enlarged repertoire of strategies, so that students can negotiate complex tasks of reading and writing in history. If students are to make a contribution as authors, we can help them to weigh options in setting goals, to use strategies appropriately and flexibly, and to monitor the appropriateness of their choices and decisions in a given situation. These strategies include knowing how to establish a scholarly project by placing one's own ideas amid what others have said, citing sources as both intellectual and social touchstones, and justifying one's decisions in determining what is important. Of course, students need to have opportunities to develop the thinking skills historians value as well. It is one thing to get students to "absorb" information about a given set of issues (cf. Wilson & Sykes, 1989). It is quite another to engage students as active participants in their learning as authors who need to think critically about what they read, integrate information from different sources with their own knowledge, and structure their work in ways that adhere to certain habits of mind in history. Toward this end we can give students occasions to write informally as a means for helping them to explore their ideas and for acquiring new knowledge. Writing-to-learn can also include more structured writing tasks that focus on the outcomes of new knowledge and facilitate students' entry into a scholarly conversation. In the end, although different kinds of writing can encourage different intellectual activities, we cannot ignore the many sources of knowledge that influence how students construct writing tasks in school.

ACKNOWLEDGMENTS

This study was conducted with the support of a grant from OERI and the Center for the Study of Writing. Portions of this chapter appear in Greene (1993) and are included here with permission.

The author would like to thank his colleagues, Deborah Brandt and Martin Nystrand, for their careful readings and suggestions throughout the process of writing this chapter.

APPENDIX: SOURCE TEXT INFORMATION PARSED INTO CONTENT UNITS

Original Text

In the Spring of 1948, American officials began framing the Foreign Assistance Act and working with their European partners to implement the commitments outlined in the preliminary report of the CEEC. Although the forum now widened to encompass congressional and private leaders, including critics on the Left and Right, most of those involved were able to maintain the earlier consensus on fundamental points.

Content Units

1. American officials began framing the Foreign Assistance Act
2. In the Spring of 1948, [American officials began framing the Foreign Assistance Act]
3. [American officials began] working with their European partners
4. [American officials began framing the Foreign Assistance Act and working with their European partners] to implement the commitments outlined in the preliminary report of the CEEC

5. Although the forum now widened to encompass congressional leaders, most of those involved were able to maintain the earlier consensus on fundamental points
6. [Although the forum now widened to encompass] private [leaders, most of those involved were able to maintain the earlier consensus on fundamental points]
7. [The forum now widened to] include critics on the Left
8. [The forum now widened to include critics on the] Right

REFERENCES

Ackerman, J. M. (1989). *Reading and writing in the academy.* Unpublished doctoral dissertation, Carnegie Mellon University, Pittsburgh.

Ackerman, J. M. (1991). Reading, writing, and knowing: The role of disciplinary knowledge in comprehension and composing. *Research in the Teaching of English, 25,* 133–178.

Applebee, A. (1981). *Writing in the secondary school* (Research Monograph No. 21). Urbana, IL: National Council of Teachers of English.

Applebee, A. (1984). *Contexts for learning to write.* Norwood, NJ: Ablex.

Barnes, D. (1976). *From communication to curriculum.* Hammondsworth, UK: Penguin.

Berkenkotter, C., Huckin, T., & Ackerman, J. (1988). Conventions, conversations, and the writer: Case study of a student in a rhetoric Ph.D. program. *Research in the Teaching of English, 22,* 9–44.

Devitt, A. (1991). Intertextuality in tax accounting: Generic, referential, and functional. In C. Bazerman, & J. Paradis (Eds.), *Textual dynamics of the professions: Historical and contemporary studies of writing in professional communities* (pp. 336–359). Madison: University of Wisconsin Press.

Flower, L. (1990a). The role of task representation in reading-to-write. In L. Flower, V. Stein, J. Ackerman, P. Kantz, K. McCormick, & W. Peck. *Reading to write: Exploring a cognitive and social process* (pp. 35–75). New York: Oxford University Press.

Flower, L. (1990b). Negotiating academic discourse. In L. Flower, V. Stein, J. Ackerman, P. Kantz, K. McCormick, & W. Peck. *Reading to write: Exploring a cognitive and social process* (pp. 221–252). New York: Oxford University Press.

Giroux, H. (1988). *Schooling and the struggle for public life.* Minneapolis: University of Minnesota Press.

Greene, S. (1993). The role of task in the development of academic thinking through reading and writing in a college history course. *Research in the Teaching of English, 27,* 46–75.

Halldén, O. (1986). Learning history. *Oxford Review of Education, 12,* 53–66.

Haswell, R. (1986). The organization of impromptu essays. *College Composition and Communication, 37,* 402–415.

Herrington, A. (1985). Writing in academic settings: A study of the contexts for writing in two college chemical engineering courses. *Research in the Teaching of English, 19,* 331–359.

Hogan, M. (1987). *The Marshall plan: America, Britain and the reconstruction of western Europe, 1947–52* (pp. 88–98, 427–438). Cambridge: Cambridge University Press.

Ilgen, T. (1985). *Autonomy and interdependence: Western European monetary and trade relations, 1958–84* (pp. 22–35). Totowa, NJ: Rowman & Allenhead.

Kaufer, D., & Geisler, C. (1989). Novelty in academic writing. *Written Communication, 6,* 286–311.

Kaufer, D., & Geisler, C. (1991). A scheme for representing written argument. *Journal of Advanced Composition, 11,* 107–122.

Kellner, H. (1989). *Language and historical representation: Getting the story crooked.* Madison: University of Wisconsin Press.

Kroll, B. (1977). Combining ideas in written and spoken English: A look at subordination and coordination. In E. O. Keenan & T. L. Bennett (Eds.), *Discourse across time and space* (pp. 69–108). Los Angeles: University of Southern California, S.C.O.P.I.L. #5.

LaCapra, D. (1983). *Rethinking intellectual history: Texts, contexts, language.* Ithaca, NY: Cornell University Press.

LaCapra, D. (1985). *History and criticism.* Ithaca, NY: Cornell University Press.

Leinhardt, G. (1990a). *Weaving instructional explanations in history* (Tech. Rep. No. CLIP-90-02). Pittsburgh: Learning Research and Development Center.

Leinhardt, G. (1990b). *Towards understanding instructional explanations.* (Tech. Rep. No. CLIP-90-03). Pittsburgh: Learning Research and Development Center.

Marshall, J. (1987). The effects of writing on students' understanding of literary texts. *Research in the Teaching of English, 21,* 30–63.

Megill, A., & McCloskey, D. (1987). The rhetoric of history. In J. Nelson, A. Megill, & D. McCloskey (Eds.), *The rhetoric of the human sciences* (pp. 221–238). Madison: University of Wisconsin Press.

Meyer, B. J. F. (1985). Prose analysis: Purposes, procedures and problems. In B. Britton & J. Black (Eds.), *Understanding expository text* (pp. 11–64). Hillsdale, NJ: Lawrence Erlbaum Associates.

Milward, A. (1984). *The reconstruction of western Europe, 1945–51* (pp. 465–471). Berkeley: University of California Press.

Nelson, J. (1990). This was an easy assignment: Examining how students interpret academic writing tasks. *Research in the Teaching of English, 24,* 362–396.

Penrose, A. (1993). Writing and learning: Exploring the consequences of task interpretation. In A. Penrose & B. Sitko (Eds.), *Hearing ourselves think: Process research in the writing classroom* (pp. 52–69). New York: Oxford University Press.

President's Committee on Foreign Aid. (1947). *Harriman report: A report on European and American aid.* Washington, DC: Government Printing Office.

Rowe, D. W. (1987). Literacy learning as an intertextual process. In J. E. Readance & R. S. Baldwin (Eds.), *Research in literacy: Merging perspectives* (pp. 101–112). Thirty-sixth Yearbook of the National Reading Conference.

Ruth, L., & Murphy, S. (1984). Designing topics for writing assessment: Problems with meaning. *College Composition and Communication, 35,* 410–422.

Spiro, R., Visopel, W. L., Schmitz, J. G., Samarapungavan, A., & Boerger, A. E. (1987). Knowledge acquisition for application: Cognitive flexibility and transfer in complex content domains. In B. C. Britton (Ed.), *Executive control processes* (pp. 177–199). Hillsdale, NJ: Erlbaum Lawrence Associates.

Spivey, N. N. (1983). *Discourse synthesis: Constructing texts in reading and writing.* Unpublished doctoral dissertation, University of Texas, Austin.

Spivey, N. N. (1984). *Discourse synthesis: Constructing texts in reading and writing.* (Outstanding Dissertation Monograph Series). Newark, DE: International Reading Association.

Spivey, N. N. (1990). Transforming texts: Constructive processes in reading and writing. *Written Communication, 7,* 256–287.

Spivey, N. N. (1991). The shaping of meaning: Options in writing the comparison. *Research in the Teaching of English, 25,* 390–418.

Spivey, N. N., & King, J. (1989). Readers as writers composing from sources. *Reading Research Quarterly, 24,* 1–14.

Stanford, M. (1986). *The nature of historical knowledge.* Oxford: Basil Blackwell.

Stein, V. (1990). Elaboration: Using what you know. In L. Flower, V. Stein, J. Ackerman, M. Kantz, K. McCormick, & W. Peck. *Reading to write: Exploring a cognitive and social process* (144–155). New York: Oxford University Press.

Stone, L. (1979). The revival of narrative: Reflections on a new old history. *Past and Present, 85,* 3–24.

Swales, J. (1984). Research into the structure of introductions to journal articles and its application to the teaching of academic writing. In J. Swales & J. Kirkman (Eds.), *Common ground: Interests in ESP and communication studies* (pp. 77–86). New York: Pergamon Press.

U.S. Economic Cooperation Administration. (1950). *A report on recovery progress and United States aid.* Washington, DC: Government Printing Office.

Walvoord, B. E., & McCarthy, L. P. (1990). *Thinking and writing in college.* Urbana, IL: National Council of Teachers of English.

Wexler, I. (1983). *The Marshall plan revisited: The European recovery program in economic perspective* (pp. 249–255). Westport, CT: Greenwood Press.

White, H. (1987). *The content of the form: Narrative discourse and historical representation.* Baltimore: Johns Hopkins University Press.

Wilson, S. M., & Sykes, G. (1989). Toward better teacher preparation and certification. In P. Gagnon and the Bradley Commission of History in Schools (Eds.), *Historical literacy: The case for history in American education* (pp. 268–86). New York: Macmillan.

Wilson, S. M., & Wineburg, S. S. (1988). Peering at history through different lenses: The role of disciplinary perspectives in teaching history. *Teachers College Record, 89,* 525–539.

Wineburg, S. S., & Wilson, S. M. (1991). Subject matter knowledge in the teaching of history. In J. Brophy (Ed.), *Advances in research on teaching: Vol. 2. Teachers' subject matter knowledge and classroom instruction* (pp. 305–347). Greenwich, CT: JAI.

CHAPTER 6

Educational Ideologies and the Teaching of History

Ronald W. Evans
San Diego State University

The central aim of this investigation is to explore teacher conceptions of the meaning of history, the relationship between teacher conceptions of history and teaching style, background factors that may influence development of teacher conceptions, and the effects of teacher conceptions of history on student beliefs. What conceptions do teachers hold of the meaning of history? What conceptions do they have of the purposes of historical study, of patterns in history, of its generalizability? How do teacher conceptions of history impact the transmitted curriculum (that which is observable in classrooms)? Do certain approaches to teaching history promote the reflective testing of belief more than other approaches? What effects do various approaches to teaching history have on student beliefs about history and society?

WHAT IS HISTORY?

The continuing debate over the revival of history (Whelan, 1992), over the proper focus for social studies in the schools, is shadowed by definitional questions. What is history? What is social studies? In each case these are ideological questions, shot through with assumptions about the nature of schooling, the nature of the discipline of history, and

171

the value of various kinds of knowledge, and complicated by competing visions of a preferred future.

Historians and philosophers of history have long disagreed on the true nature of historical study. Many conceptions of history are possible. One can divide approaches to history among historians and philosophers of history into several major schools, ranging from the limited, idealist view of history, which emphasizes context and the uniqueness of each topic studied, to the cosmic, sweeping interpretations of metahistorians. Approaches to the philosophy of history vary on many counts, but most fundamental are different conceptions of the historian's purpose and of the generalizability of historical events (Evans, 1989).

Idealist historians argue that the events of the past are unique and that it is the historian's role to comprehend the unique particularity of past events, to re-create past actualities, to empathize with actors, to explain through intervening detail—in short, to tell a story.

Scientific historians take a different approach. Generally, they tend to view history as a form of scientific inquiry and tend to borrow methods from the natural sciences. Underlying this approach to history is the belief that human events are subject to external observation and that laws of behavior may be guiding human action. Generally, scientific historians view history as highly generalizable and seek to make the study of history as "objective" as possible.

On the other hand, relativist historians argue that objectivity is impossible, that every aspect of historiography is infected with preconceptions, that an objective rendering of history is impossible, and that we should recognize the relativistic nature of knowledge and pursue historical studies relevant to significant problems of the present and future. Finally, the more speculative approach to history taken by metahistorians is much broader and all-encompassing. Metahistorians attempt explanation of the human saga, or at least large chunks of it.

Each of these schools of thought takes a different perspective on the historian's purposes, on the nature of history, and on the generalizability of historical episodes. Each approach carries ideological baggage. Do teachers of history in the schools reflect these competing definitions? Do they think and act like this? Do their approaches to teaching reflect differing notions of what history is?

Certainly, competing definitions of history are at play among those involved in the debate over the revival of history. Among social studies purists, the history-as-core movement has been greeted with a considerable amount of hostility. This may be due to the fact that the movement does little to promote the goal of reflective teaching and the reflective testing of belief (defined as the critical examination of beliefs about society), an aim that many social studies theorists have long held as the raison d'être of social studies instruction. Although I share the concerns of my colleagues about the revival of history (Evans, 1992), at this juncture in curriculum history it may be most advantageous for us to ask, what approaches to teaching history are most likely to promote sustained critical reflection in students?

The general emphasis on history as the core of social studies, when viewed in historical perspective, may not seem as disastrous as many scholars are inclined to think. Despite periodic outbreaks of concern over the teaching of history in our schools, teachers tend to go about their tasks in routinized ways that have changed very little over the years. The teachers discussed in this chapter teach, for the most part, in the same ways that teachers have always taught (Cuban, 1984). Yet each teacher offers something slightly different, a nuance, an angle of vision, a philosophy, an ideology, or a technique different from the ways other teachers have taught. Do certain approaches to teaching history promote the reflective testing of belief more than other approaches? What effects do various approaches to teaching history have on student beliefs?

RESEARCH RELATED TO TEACHER CONCEPTIONS

An emerging body of research has explored teacher thinking, teacher knowledge, and teacher perspectives and their impact on school curricula. Research on teacher knowledge has focused on three kinds of teacher knowledge: subject matter knowledge, pedagogical knowledge, and curricular knowledge. As Shulman noted, research on teacher congnitions has fallen short in the "elucidation of teachers' cognitive understanding of subject matter content and the relationships between such understanding and the instruction teachers provide for students" (1986, p. 25). As Feiman-Nemser and Floden suggested, teacher knowledge is "actively related to the world of practice," and "functions as an organic whole, orienting her to her situation and allowing her to act" (1986, p. 513).

In one of the most important and relevant studies of teacher knowledge to date, Elbaz, building on Schwab, distinguished three levels of practical knowledge: rules of practice, practical principles, and images. Images capture the teacher's knowledge and purposes at the most general level, orienting the teacher's overall conduct rather than directing specific actions. "The teacher's feelings, values, needs and beliefs combine as she forms images of how teaching should be, and marshals experience, theoretical knowledge, and school folklore to give substance to these images" (1983, p. 134). Images mediate between thought and action; they guide teachers intuitively, inspiring rather than determining their actions.

Research on teacher perspectives has explored similar terrain, examining the purpose and context of particular teaching acts. Goodman and Adler (1985), in a study of elementary teacher perspectives on social studies, found six major conceptualizations of social studies expressed through their informants' beliefs and classroom actions. These included social studies as nonsubject, as human relations, as citizenship indoctrination, as school knowledge, as the integrative core of the elementary curriculum, and as education for social action.

Studies by Wilson and Wineburg (1987; Wineburg & Wilson, 1988) focusing on history teachers' knowledge of subject matter and wisdom of practice found that disciplinary perspective and depth of background have a profound impact on what history teachers teach, and how they execute their craft. Further, they suggested that knowledge of subject matter is central to teaching but not the sole determinant of good teaching.

Teacher perspectives are important because they guide the curricular decisions of teachers within the larger context of schooling. In a review of research on teacher perspectives, Stephen J. Thornton suggested that within a societal and institutional context, teachers serve as instructional gatekeepers: Their beliefs largely determine both the subject matter and experiences of students (Thornton, 1989). How teachers conceptualize history, how their conceptualizations are transformed into classroom activity, and how those activities affect students should therefore be a central concern for social studies researchers.

Two characteristics distinguish this particular study from much of the existing research. First, much of the data, and many of the insights reported, are based on interviews with students, a data source too often neglected. Students spend more time observing teachers than anyone else and deserve more attention from researchers because they can provide a rich source of information on class activities and invaluable insight into the effects on students. Second, the emerging focus on ideology, exploring the links between a teacher's ideological orientation and what occurs in his or her classroom, is, to my knowledge, an element that has also been neglected in much of the research on teaching and that, it seems to me, sorely needs further exploration.

Approaches to teaching develop within a value-laden context and are inherently ideological. (Ideology is defined as manner or content of thinking on matters social and political.) Whether conscious or not, teacher perspectives and practice represent curriculum theories played out in classrooms. By their nature, curriculum theory and practice are negotiated, compromised, contingent, and flawed; they are socially constructed. Whereas discourse in the field is fragmented, contradictory, and incomplete, often responding to professional and political forces beyond our control, debates on schooling represent discussion over visions of a preferred future—that is, conversation on what kind of society and schools we want (Cherryholmes, 1988, p. 142). Therefore, discourse among curriculum theorists and practice in particular classrooms are inherently ideological and correspond to competing conceptions of purpose, competing commitments, and competing visions of the good society.

Conflicting conceptions of purpose and differing ideological orientations seem to be played out most poignantly in history and social studies classrooms. My previous exploratory research on conceptions of history suggests that teacher conceptions of history vary; student conceptions are poorly formed; teacher conceptions help to shape the transmitted curriculum or that which is observable in classrooms; and student conceptions may be influenced by their teacher's conceptions (Evans, 1988).

In a continuation of the same line of research, this chapter describes teacher conceptions of history and explores the possible impact of particular teachers' conceptions of history in five classrooms. Questions guiding the research and data analysis include: What conceptions do teachers hold of the meaning of history? What conceptions do they have of the purposes of historical study, of patterns in history, of its generalizability and relevance?[1] How do teacher conceptions of history impact the transmitted curriculum (that which is observable in classrooms)? Do certain approaches to teaching history promote the reflective testing of belief more than other approaches? What effects do various approaches to teaching history have on student beliefs about history and society? Are the teaching of history and political ideology linked? If so, how?

---

[1]For purposes of this study, the meaning of history was defined to include four kinds of informant conceptions. First, I examined informant conceptions of the purposes of historical study and valuations of its usefulness. Second, I explored conceptions of patterns in history, informant beliefs on progress and decline. Third, I examined the degree of generalization with which informants were comfortable. And fourth, I investigated informant conceptions of the relevance of history, the relation of historical data to the present.

METHOD

The study was conducted in two distinct phases. The first explored teacher conceptions of history, focusing on teachers as the source of data. The second phase of the study explored five representative classrooms, drawing on observation and interviews with students.

The first phase of the study combined survey and interview data. Based on a previous exploration of teacher and student conceptions of history (Evans, 1988) and a review of the philosophy of history (Evans, 1989), a survey questionnaire was developed and mailed to all secondary school history teachers in six counties of central and eastern Maine ($N = 160$), located near the investigator. Seventy-one questionnaires were returned. The primary purpose of the questionnaire was to locate potential interview subjects. The breadth of the sample was intentionally limited to areas relatively close to the researcher's base. The questionnaire focused on teachers' concepts of history and personal background. An independent judge assessed content validity and the questionnaire was revised. Background items dealt with years of teaching experience, undergraduate major, level of educational attainment, semester hours in history, political affiliation and point of view, gender, and religious affiliation. Substantive items dealt with the teacher's conception of history and teaching style. The questionnaire also asked for volunteers to participate in subsequent interviews.

Data from the survey were read for patterns of teacher response, and preliminary teacher typologies based on conceptions of history were then developed. Teacher concepts of history were then cross-tabulated with background information to determine patterns of teacher background that may relate to teacher conceptions of history.

Thirty interview subjects were then selected from the survey respondents who volunteered to participate in brief interviews. Although the sample was largely self-selected, subjects were selected from volunteers based on survey responses and geographic proximity. Semistructured interviews with each informant lasted approximately 50 min and probed teacher conceptions of the meaning of history (including the purposes of historical study, patterns in history, generalizability, and relevance), a description of the informant's teaching style, and teacher perspectives on the origins of their conceptions. The interview questions included: Tell me a few of your thoughts on the purposes for studying history. Are there patterns in history? To what extent can we reliably make comparisons across time and space? Tell me a little about your teaching. What shaped your ideas about history? After each general question, similar questions phrased in a different manner were often asked; for example:

What is history for? In addition, category probes were often used. On teaching method these included textbook, lecture, discussion, and other methods.

Data analysis consisted of a frequency analysis and a preliminary development of teacher typologies. Survey responses were scored 0–6 for each respondent on each typology. Teacher typologies were then cross-tabulated with teacher background data. Teacher typologies were subsequently revised and developed in greater detail, drawing on interview data as a source for description of teacher conceptions of history. Interview and survey data were then combined to develop a comprehensive portrait of each teacher's conception of the meaning of history.

The second phase of the project focused on five teachers, each representing one of the typologies developed in phase one. Selection of the five representative teachers was based on fit with the typology; in each case, the teacher most representative of each typology was selected from the original sample of thirty teacher interviews. This selection was based on the aggregate of interview data and scores on the 0–6 scale used to rank each teacher's survey responses. Also, six student informants were selected from each site at random, two students from the upper third, two from the middle third, and two from the lower third of the class roll, based on the previous semester's grades. This selection of student informants was made in an attempt to get a somewhat representative sample.

Data collection in the second phase of the study included follow-up interviews with each teacher, in-depth observation of at least eight classes at each site, and interviews with student informants. Classroom observations focused on holistic collection of relevant data on the transmitted curriculum including recorded transcripts of class discussions and documentary evidence. Student interviews, each lasting approximately 20–30 minutes, were conducted after classroom observations and follow-up interviews with teachers were completed. Each student interviewed spent at least 6–7 months in their teacher's class. Student interviews probed student knowledge of their teacher's teaching style, student attitudes, student conceptions of the purposes for studying history, student knowledge of their teacher's political beliefs, and student beliefs. For example, interview questions on student knowledge of the curriculum included, "Tell me a little about your history class. Describe what you do." Follow-up and probing questions were based on initial informant response, and, in some cases, on category probes. For the preceding example, category probes included, "Tell me about your assignments," and "Tell me about some of your class activities."

Data were analyzed by content analysis of interview transcripts, field notes, and transcripts of class sessions. Data were coded according to preplanned categories of informants and organized by their relevance to the original research questions. Patterns and themes which emerged were then developed in an effort to create a portrait of each of the five classrooms studied.[2]

FINDINGS

Based on data from the teachers studied, conceptions of history, its purposes and meaning, seem to vary. Although teacher conceptions of history are not completely distinct, most teachers studied tend to fall into one of five broad categories or typologies: storyteller, scientific historian, relativist/reformer, cosmic philosopher, or eclectic. These typologies, based on teacher conceptions of history, combine an approach to pedagogy and an epistemology. The dominant factor seems to be a conception of purpose. Each category emphasizes a distinctly different conception of the purposes for studying history. Although conceptions of purpose range from gaining knowledge to changing the future, these are not exclusive categories. Most teachers studied possess elements of more than one typology, although most also displayed a dominant tendency, similar to favoring one hand over the other.

Data from the second phase of the study, focused on detailed study of five teachers each representing a different typology, generally supported the notion that the teaching of history is influenced by teacher conceptions of history. However, the impact is more pronounced and more readily observable in some classrooms than in others. In two cases, the storyteller and the scientific historian, teacher descriptions of what they do in classes were very similar to what I observed and to what their students reported. In each of the other cases, the connections among

---

[2]Despite the researcher's best efforts, the study has several limitations that limit generalizability. First and foremost, the intent of the study is to describe teachers' conceptions of history with the aim of developing typologies that reflect various approaches. The study is not designed to generate a random sample that will reflect the status of teacher conceptions in a generalizable way. Given the plethora of teaching deemed typical, and the voluminous research documenting its constancy, the author believes we can learn more from the diverse and the extraordinary. Second, the researcher relied on volunteers only, thus further restricting the generalizability of the sample. Reliance on volunteers was deemed necessary in order to find willing interview subjects who would openly discuss their thoughts on history and its meaning, but may make this a rather select group of research subjects. Perhaps the teachers who volunteered were those who felt comfortable answering questions about their teaching.

what teachers said they did in their classrooms, what I observed and what students told me, seemed more distant. As I spent time in their classrooms I discovered that two of the five teachers spent a good deal of their time and energy managing student behavior problems. Thus, my initial impression was one of disappointment.[3]

Storyteller

Eight of the 71 teachers, or 11.3% of the sample, fit the storyteller model. Storytellers emphasize fascinating details about people and events and suggest that knowledge of other times, people, and places is the most important rationale for studying history. Each of these teachers runs a teacher-centered classroom in which teacher talk is dominant, and storytelling is a common mode. Generally, they suggest that we should emphasize the study of people and events to help our students grasp knowledge of basic facts and a sense of time.

In looking for a comparable theoretical model, the storyteller typology resembles the idealist philosophy of history. The idealist does not explicitly address questions of meaning, instead arguing that the events of the past are unique and that it is the historian's role to comprehend the unique particularity of past events, to explain through rich detail, in short, to tell a good story. Thus, the central purpose for studying history is to gain cultural knowledge, or to pay tribute to our predecessors. Because events are unique, no patterns exist. Generalizability is nil. We study history because it explains who we are; it gives us clues to our identity. Thus, the idealist history teacher can fulfill the ubiquitous purpose of explaining "what man is" (Collingwood, 1946). Currently in vogue among historians, this approach to history does little to illuminate the process of historical explanation, its relationship to ideology, or the significance of past trends or events. It is history writ small.

The storyteller typology is apparent in the following quotes (on purposes for studying history) from teachers interviewed:

Studying history is one way we establish our identities; can't establish one's identity without having contact with the past. (John)

---

[3]Of course, there were some complicating factors. The classes taught by these teachers were tracked. The scientific historian had an Advanced Placement group, one of the storyteller's classes was an elective, the cosmic philosopher had above-average classes, and both the relativist/reformer and the eclectic taught "vocational" students. These clienteles may have had a profound impact on each teacher's efficacy.

It's not so much that I try to tell the student anything, it's that I try to make it interesting for them . . . I try to teach by storytelling. Like in ancient historic times I suppose the first teachers were the storytellers and when parents wanted to get rid of their kids for awhile, maybe there was some guy that liked to sit around telling stories and had little kids listen to him and it worked. And it works for me. I can turn almost anything into a story. (John)

With age and being exposed to more and more material, you can turn what has happened into story form. In other words you make it interesting, you don't try to justify it, you make it interesting. (John)

Knowledge is the mark of being an educated person. (Paula)

History is an escape. It's fun. It's like a giant soap opera. I talk about events and the kids love it because it's a story, and that's what history is. (Susan)

I think that, you know, really down deep, digging right into the soul here, that if a person does not know their background, that they are not a whole person; they're missing something and so I think it's very important that a person know their background, where they have been and maybe even paying tribute to those who have preceded us. Their lives were worth something. . . . Maybe it's a thing of honoring past ancestors and their accomplishments. (Charles)

Figure 6.1 provides further detail on each of these four teachers' conceptions of history. As shown in Fig 6.1, on the purposes for studying history all four suggest that knowledge of history is part of becoming educated, a key element necessary to understand ourselves. This conception of purpose is consistent with the theoretical model described above. On pattern, these teachers seem to be split. Two see historical events as unique, and two see some overarching patterns to history. They also seem to differ on the generalizability of history. Thus, these teachers seem not to fit the theoretical model in their beliefs on pattern and generalizability, or, rather, to fit it only partially. However, in their teaching style, all four fit the storyteller mode. Each mentions telling stories, often, it seems, as a means of making history come alive for students, and all four seem to rely on heavily teacher-centered methods of imparting knowledge of history.

Background data on these teachers suggests that the origins of the storyteller typology may be traceable to early experiences with historical novels and movies, parental influence, a fascination with stories, or an interest in ancestors. When asked to describe their political leanings, all four of these teachers described themselves as moderate conservatives.

	Susan	John	Charles	Paula
Purpose	History is an escape. It's fun. It's like a gigantic soap opera. I talk about events and the kids love it because it's a story, and that's what history is. What it's for is to better understand ourselves. History touches everything in our lives... past events color how we think today, they color how we act, how things will be in the future.	History is one way that I believe we establish our identities; can't establish one's identity without having a contact with the past. It's not that I try to tell the student anything, I try to make it interesting. I teach by storytelling. It makes it easier for them to remember material. You don't try to justify it, you make it interesting.	If a person does not know their background, they are not a whole person... it's very important that a person know where they have been and maybe even paying tribute to those who have preceeded us... honoring past ancestors and their accomplishments. It also helps you mature as a person.	I was always interested in the facts and in learning about people, especially ancient people. Knowledge is the mark of being educated. We study history to know more. The book might mention people and what they did, but I tell them stories about their personal lives and it makes it more interesting for them.
Pattern	I think that everything happens over and over in different time frames. It's rather like the little circles you made in penmanship class... It isn't always the same, but pretty much it's a cycle of build up, level off and decay.	I think that there would be some kind of pattern, of course. There always seem to be conflicts. I teach a world history course and stress Hegel's definition of history, that history is the unfolding of man's struggle for freedom.	If there was a pattern it would be very small, very minute because history has changed... everyone is different, society has different ideas. I would almost go to the point of saying there is no pattern. Each time period is unique.	I think that each era is unique, but it all evolves together, so I think that you can look at each one differently. It's all wrapped together, one period led to the next. But, you have to look at each event for what it is... unique.
Generaliz-ability	You can't be real general... you've got that little kid in the back row with glasses who can get you so you have to be careful. I'm not sure how much you can learn from history in terms of not making mistakes. Everybody has to make their own.	You can generalize... for example, Americans have mistreated the environment. You have to start with a general concept. You have to teach from a generality to be effective. Predictions are possible only on sureties.	Only in a very general sense. You always have richer and poorer, strong and weak, those who rule and those who are ruled. Those are all generalities. You always have problems which confront man and man trying to overcome...	Generalizations can give you a feeling for an era. You can generalize about any subject, but it's more important to get a feeling for an era. I think it is possible to take certain events from the past and look to the future.
Teaching Style	I basically talk to the kids. I lecture a lot and I tell a lot of stories because I think history is fun. Tell a story and turn it into a movie, turn it into technicolor... and it makes people more real, and makes the book more real, makes it come alive.	The way that I teach is maybe the oldest way of teaching. I teach by storytelling. If you visit my class you'd see a teacher centered classroom. I am the center and everything comes from me. That doesn't mean I'm the sole arbiter of ideas.	Sometimes you've got to spoon feed them while other times you don't have to. I like to lecture. You've got to be almost like an entertainer. Start talking about reform movements and the class is snoring away. Talk blood and guts and its great.	I have question and answer periods. I lecture some. Most of them need a push and do not read the material. I combine vocabulary, questions from the text, lecture, and worksheets. Frankly, I'm more concerned about time with my family.
Teacher Background	I always liked to read historical novels, which is a good way to learn history... it was just my way of escaping. I was a voracious movie-goer. Another way of escaping. I was not around a lot of other kids.	I was always fascinated with history. Always. I mean preschool. My mother would read me King Arthur stories so I had a concept of knights in armor and it was long ago. I'm a genealogy bug and I've got loads of ancestors.	In school history was a favorite course of mine. I liked to see what my ancestors had done. My father liked history, he has history books, and served in the Navy in World War Two.	My father used to talk about history. He used to sit down and talk about people in history and he would pick up my books and he would see a different side of it than I would and we would sit down and discuss it.

FIG. 6.1.   Storytellers.

181

A cross-tabulation of survey data on the larger sample also suggests that storytellers tend to be political conservatives. Five of eight storytellers identified themselves as right of center, as either conservative or moderately conservative. All four in the subsample also have a relatively high concentration of semester hours of study in history, ranging from 39 to 90 and averaging 70 semester hours of study in the discipline of history. Other interesting findings are that three of the four identify a religious affiliation, and that survey data show a slight tendency for beginning teachers to focus on a content orientation (66% of those teachers with 5 years of experience or less were either storytellers or scientific historians).

Although it may be impossible to make any definitive statements on the factors that may have shaped these teachers into storytellers, it seems that a tendency toward political conservatism and a strong background in the discipline of history are relevant factors. The teaching of history is shot through with ideological assumptions. Thus, a storyteller's approach to the teaching of history may develop from the interaction of an ideological base, a conception of history and its uses, and practical classroom experience. Each of these teachers has found that storytelling is an approach that works.

Susan Tells Stories.   Susan, the storyteller selected for detailed study in phase two of the project, fit this typology quite well.[4] Every lesson we observed followed a similar format. She stood at the lectern, opened the textbook to the appropriate section, and lectured, peppering her lecture with stories—not boring stories, but lively descriptions of characters in history, stories spiced with sex and violence, peppered with colorful adjectives and slang. For example, a U.S. history lesson on relations with Mexico began with the following story about Napoleon III, Maximilian, and Carlotta, his wife:

> In France, there was a dicator who named himself president and then Emperor by the name of Napoleon III. A politician, this guy could charm a little old lady out of her shopping bag. He was a charmer with the ladies. . . . Probably today he would be a very popular politician no matter where. . . . After Napoleon was defeated at Waterloo in 1815, French pride and national spirit kind of hit the skids and so when he came along and said, I will make you great again, they said terrific, let's go for it. . . . He was real smooth and he got into power.

Then, after describing the appointment of Maximilian as emperor of Mexico, she said:

---

[4]All teacher names used in this chapter are pseudonyms, with the exception of Steve Smith (Rusty), who told me he wants to become famous. He deserves to.

So now we have a situation where Napoleon decided he didn't want to spend any more money over there. He said, Max, you better come home. Max said no and he stayed. And what did the Mexicans do? Shot him full of holes. They took him prisoner and executed him in front of a firing squad. I'll tell you a little story. The description in your book says that Carlotta, his wife, went crazy and lived until 1927. She lived in an asylum. She never knew her husband was dead. He had sent her away when things got real tricky. He sent her to Europe to raise some money and get some help. . . . She went to see the Pope because they were Catholic, and at that point she was thinking everybody was trying to poison her. She wouldn't eat anything. She was losing weight like crazy. She was running around telling everybody about how poor Max was going to get killed in his own house. She went in to see the Pope and was crying all over his shoulder and he was trying to calm her down. Come nightfall when everyone is supposed to be out of the Vatican, she wouldn't leave. She was in the Pope's private conference room and she wouldn't leave. You couldn't stay overnight in the Pope's private residence so what they did is they fed her some hot chocolate and the Pope drank it first to prove to her that it wasn't poison and then they gave her a cup of chocolate and slipped a mickey in it and hauled her out, bodily, out of the Vatican. She lost it and didn't know what was going on. Never knew her husband was executed. It was all stress and being in Mexico and being constantly afraid that they were going to get attacked by Mexicans and so forth and the fact that there was a mental instability in the family. Her father ran around in high heels and lipstick, so it kind of ran in the genes, so to speak.

Stories during other lessons talked of "carousing" officials who had mistresses and illegitimate children, businessmen who "played on the side," and sailors who were "slimeballs, real skuzzbuckets," who "went berzerk" when out of the sight of land.

Susan's students seem to enjoy her class and confirm this description of her teaching. As one student said:

She'd be wonderful as a tabloid editor. As I said earlier, she has a story for everyone and everything. She'll never keep any stories from us. She'll share them with us all and most people seem to remember them. It's a fun way to learn because everyone is laughing and chuckling about what this guy did and what that guy did. Little do we know we are learning U.S. History in the process.

Susan's storytelling is enjoyable to students, but may be having little impact on student beliefs other than giving them an image of history as story with the concomitant focus on knowing for the sake of knowing. Students report that their beliefs haven't changed, but that they know more about history. Ultimately, Susan's teaching may be functioning to acculturate students by giving them an appreciation for their ancestors. Graphic and entertaining stories transmit an interest in the past on a human level and a belief that history is fun. Unfortunately, because of the basic conflicts it leaves out, and because of its didactic style, this kind of history teaching may tend to foster noncritical acceptance of the powers that be.

Scientific Historian

Thirteen of the 71 teachers surveyed or 18.3% of the sample fit the scientific historian model. These academic types suggest that historical explanation and interpretation make history most interesting and argue that understanding historical processes and gaining background knowledge for understanding current issues are the key reasons for studying history. The scientific historian suggests that in teaching history we should emphasize a mix of uniqueness and similarities among people and events, and that it is most important for students to gain insight into historical generalization and process skills of historical inquiry.

These teachers' practical philosophies resemble the scientific historian's philosophy of history. This group views history as a form of scientific inquiry and tends to borrow methods from the natural sciences. Generally, scientific historians call for rigorous reliance on evidence and critical attention to primary sources so that historian and student may objectively attempt to discover truth. They see history as generalizable but disagree among themselves over the existence of universal laws. For the most part, scientific historians see no pattern in history, but have faith in the existence of probabilities and the idea of progress.

The scientific typology is apparent in the following quotes from teacher interviews:

> Kids have to know where we've been before so they can see why we do things the way we do, why things are the way they are today and to understand what changes could be made. I think that just as a matter of culture, of passing on culture . . . you have to have at least a nodding acquaintance with these general gross tendencies and trends and the names and the people from history. (Steve)

> I don't try to put words in their mouths at the end of it all. I don't finish with a flourish and tied neatly for them; I'd rather leave them questioning . . . more questions, more questions, fewer answers, fewer answers. It's hard for teenagers to accept though, because they want answers and

every once in a while, we'll try to come to a conclusion, but I want them to test their hypothesis again and again and again and again. We write in that style; we hypothesize, we don't know in microns. Some teachers wouldn't find that comfortable, I'm sure. (Eric)

Right from the beginning in any level course I teach, I make it real clear that . . . that there are the facts, and that your interpretation of them is yours and . . . that theirs is as valid as mine at any level and I encourage them to, you know, challenge and confront the book and to confront me and to put things in their own order, and often at the beginning of the year I'll ask some question which is interpretive and then read two totally different answers and try to get them to understand that both answers are valid as long as they're supported, as long as they're based upon evidence. (Rusty)

In my years of teaching I've only had a couple of kids who were real aware of my political persuasion. . . . I usually make it to the end of the year and they don't know whether I'm a Democrat or a Republican. . . . We work hard on understanding that everybody has a position and they are entitled to that, but, I think it's part of my job to keep my opinions right at home. (Rusty)

We study history to understand the present, how we got here and the choices that have been made. We need different historical perspectives on questions like why our state tends to be economically depressed. (Sally)

Figure 6.2 provides more detail on these teachers' conceptions of history. On purpose, all four discuss skills common to the historian's trade. Three mention analytic or research skills, and all four mention perspectives or competing views or interpretations. A central element of these teachers approach to history is their attempt at scientific neutrality or objectivity.

Although all four see some patterns in human history, several seem reluctant to discuss patterns as more than trends. Rusty exemplifies the general tone of providing different theories and letting the students decide. Although each of these teachers suggests that generalizations may be of some use, all four expressed caution about the limits of analogy and their reliability. This lack of comfort with generalizations is in keeping with the theoretical model developed. In fact, the scientific philosophers of history developed as a critique of speculative systems that were regarded as indefensible.

The teaching style of each of these teachers exemplifies use of competing interpretations, the teacher as guide rather than arbiter of truth, and emphasis on thinking about important questions from

	Rusty	Doug	Eric	Sally
Purpose	Right from the beginning I make it real clear that there are the facts, and that your interpretation of them is as valid as mine... and often I'll ask some question which is interpretive and then read two totally different answers... both answers are valid as long as they're supported by evidence. History puts things into larger context.	History helps you to understand events as they develop in the world, to know the historical background and to gain a long-term perspective. I think by delving deeply into into a time period or an issue you develop some analytical skills and some research skills that will serve you in anything you want to study.	I don't try to put words in their mouths at the end of it all... I'd rather leave them questioning... It's hard for teenagers to accept though because they want answers... I want them to test their hypothesis again and again. History broadens the mind. It gives us a common vocabulary so we can communicate.	We study history to understand the present, how we got here and the choices that have been made. We need different historical perspectives on questions like why our state tends to be economically depressed. Historical understanding is necessary for us to make good decisions today.
Pattern	I don't teach "this fulfills a pattern." I try to give them a questioning framework and let them decide. I tell the kids about different theories. I think the human condition is pretty consistent. All those potentialities are there for progress or...	I think of history more as trends than patterns. I can see issues developing out of events of the past and those patterns are ongoing. I think there are patterns to a degree. There may be something to the rise and fall of great empires...	I am a devotee of the Schlesinger thesis, the cycle thesis. We have cycles and patterns that are worth studying. They give a semblance of hope to those that would like to see a return to a more caring, more thoughtful style of government.	There have been patterns of growth, then decline. Empires rise and fall... Each era has a flavor... they aren't totally different and the people involved aren't totally unique.
Generaliz-ability	Each time period has unique qualities. I try to point out similarities, parallels, although those analogies and parallels have real limits. History is not very predictable, though we should have some consciousness of the range of our capabilities.	I think there are time periods that are similar, but I don't think you can make direct comparisons. It is possible to generalize like hell if you want to. I think your danger is always generalizing and saying something is a model... a real danger...	Hard to do that. Hard to do that. A.J.P. Tayor once said, after the dawn of the nuclear age, that if history is any guide we should all be begging for our death pills. We do generalize at times but it tends to turn off the students... we risk doing lousy scholarship.	You really can't generalize. Comparisons can be made but sometimes they are of little value. Comparisons can serve as a guide only in terms of providing warning signs. Using models to explain history can be problematic...
Teaching Style	I don't lecture. I try to get maximum involvement from the students. We do simulations and I have the kids have debates. We did a simulation the other day that I designed on the strike at the mill. My overall format is chronological.	Its primarily a pretty wide open discussion kind of history class. I don't do a lot of lecturing. I ask questions... I use conflicting quotes as a lead in to get the kids thinking and then expand on that. We get into different interpretations.	I use a variety of methods. Some kids like to discuss, some kids don't. I mean really discuss, not just say yes or no. I don't lecture. I'd rather pose questions from the material, have them answer and do my best to make everyone aware...	I make controversial statements about the past like, "Hitler didn't do anything wrong," to see how they react. I don't like textbooks... We use student research, mock trials, projects... I give them a framework and they choose.
Teacher Background	I worked with professors in graduate school who were very good. They made me confront the facts, be more disciplined and more organized and wouldn't let me get by with the easy answers... but they all allowed me to make my own judgement.	I've always enjoyed history, from the time I was a little kid. In high school it was dismal and boring but in college I had a course that got into all the different controversial aspects of history and different issues and things.	Professors, in lectures, made more of an impact than the material that they required us to read. The style I have today is probably based on that idea, that I'd rather talk history than labor over reading it unduly.	In college I began to question things. I had one professor who made history fascinating by providing different perspectives. My interest in history goes back to grade school. I remember reading biographies.

FIG. 6.2.   Scientific historians.

history. Each attempts a rather transparent objectivity by posing open-ended questions for students.

Interview data from the four teachers suggest the importance of professors of history in having shaped the thinking of each teacher. Three of the four directly mention their professors' emphasis on competing interpretations, on using evidence, on providing different perspectives. Generally, this emphasis belies a process orientation centered on the skills and issues discussed by historians. The scientific historian's orientation seems to have been shaped more by formal study and less by family.

Their political orientation stands in sharp contrast to that of the storytellers. Three described themselves as liberals and the fourth as a moderate liberal. Survey data on the larger sample of scientific historians suggests that this group tends to be left-of-center or centrist politically. Eight of the 13 teachers in this category described themselves as either radical left (1), liberal, or moderately liberal, while only 3 were right-of-center. Perhaps an orientation to teaching that emphasizes students reaching their own reasoned conclusions rather than an appreciation for ancestors is more in keeping with a liberal political ideology.

Another interesting fact about this group is that three of the four in the small sample stated no religious affiliation. Perhaps this reflects a lack of strong commitments, or a scientist's attempt to remain detached from moral questions. Whichever may be the case, this fact seems to somehow fit the general world view of the scientific typology. Finally, all four teachers have a very strong background in the discipline of history. Although they range from 30 to over 100 semester hours, their average, 78 hours, is highest among any of the groups studied.

Although it may be impossible to make any generalizable statements about the background factors that have shaped each of these teachers' conception of history as a form of scientific inquiry, it seems that they were strongly influenced by their disciplinary background and seek to emulate the historians they have known. It also seems reasonable to suggest that their religious and political orientation generally provide an ideological backdrop in which fostering certain beliefs in their students is seen as less important than providing evidence and letting students reach their own conclusions. In any event, these teachers have found that the spirit of inquiry, the spirit of questioning, when played out in their classrooms, serves to stimulate student interest, activity, and thought.

Rusty Makes History a Science.   Rusty, the scientific historian selected for detailed study, exemplifies most of these characteristics. Rusty doesn't lecture. He teaches by asking questions, asking students to grapple with the stuff of history.

An example from his advanced placement (AP) "American Experience" class perhaps best exemplifies his approach in practice. One representative lesson, the immigrant roundtable, had students seated in a circle and reporting to the class in the form of first-person testimony, role-playing the immigrant lives they had studied, with teacher and other students questioning and discussing the life of each immigrant. Following student testimony and questions, the teacher said, "We want to look for some patterns, and what your experiences meant to you as individuals and to the country as a whole. What patterns do you see?

Later, he asked students to "write a thesis statement that captures the pattern, or a dominant pattern for what we have seen." The discussion went as follows:

T1:   Topic sentence, Armando.
S10: Immigrants came to America for gold streets, but found it wasn't that way.
S9:   It was not as they expected. They were able to build up the quality of their lives over time and make it better for their children.
T1:   Matt.
S3:   Many came by free will and were successful and happy.
S4:   Many were from poor backgrounds and hoped to shovel up the gold they thought was flooding the streets. The majority were stuck in factories or survived on middle class jobs.
T1:   I notice something interesting happening, you all heard the same stories, but you all have a different interpretation. That is the whole point of the course, to draw different conclusions about what history has to say. What is fact? What is a pattern? What is culture about? Can we switch now to the consequences for the country?

And the discussion continued. Every lesson we observed involved students actively, and exemplified central elements of Rusty's conception of history. For example, another lesson from the "American Experience" class involved students in a teacher-led discussion of Upton Sinclair's novel *The Jungle*. Students were asked to share "interesting, important aspects of the novel." In another lesson, a regular feature of each unit the teacher called "contemporary echoes," students were asked to bring in something from the media related to the topic under study, the teacher and other students would ask questions, and the students were asked to develop analogies.

Students report that the course is having an impact on their beliefs and report becoming more "critical," more "analytical," and more "aware." One student said, "I didn't criticize like I do now. . . . The world doesn't seem like it is everything I thought it was." Another said, "I never thought about people that were lower in society being trapped there." Judging from such comments, Rusty's "American Experience" class is having a profound impact on students' notions about history and beliefs about society. Perhaps the key reason is the questioning, process-centered orientation to history and pedagogy employed in the class. It seems a powerful mix. Although Rusty is not telling students what to believe, the course seems a liberating experience, especially when contrasted with the other teachers described in this study. As one student said, "He doesn't sit there and tell us why. I know he could but he doesn't. If we don't want to learn it, then we are not going to. I'm sure if he said it I would feel like I was scolded and go against it."

Relativist/Reformer

This is by far the largest category: 32 of the 71 teachers surveyed fit the relativist/reformer typology (45.1% of the sample). This group emphasizes relation of the past to present problems and suggests that history is background for understanding current issues. Generally, these teachers endorse developing lessons from history to guide current decisions, and argue that tentative laws are possible and must be developed and examined in light of evidence. While stressing the similarity of people and events, the relativists suggest that it is most important for students of history to grasp the relevance of history to the present.

These classroom teachers are similar in stance to the relativist philosophers of history who will serve as a theoretical model for this typology. Relativists argue that every aspect of historiography is infected with preconceptions—thus, scientific objectivity is impossible. These historians argue, as Charles Beard once did (1933), that history represents "contemporary thought about our past" and that no historian can describe the past as it actually was. Historians of this group, from the progressives to the new left, are predominantly social reformers holding an explicit vision of a better world that guides much of their work. Many of the relativists among the teachers studied hold a similar vision of social justice, of a reformed society.

The following quotes illustrate the relativist/reformers' conception of the purposes for studying history:

My approach is to teach kids what history can teach us about our own situations. It is likely that they'll have to make important decisions throughout their life, or they'll react to certain feelings, resentments . . .

so I really use historical process to teach basically why America is in the mess it's in. I try to show them where this all comes from; how this all got started and why we are sort of still stuck with it. (Warren)

I think if you can draw attention to the fact that this country has made enormous mistakes, people have handled themselves poorly in almost every respect, partly because they're human beings and partly because of ignorance and partly because they're greedy . . . but if you can draw attention to that, then I think you get them on track and looking at it and thinking about it and questioning what's happenning now. (Warren)

I see history as very much a dialectical process. I mean I have to admit there's a very, in my world view, a very Marxist sort of premise there and I do see processes through class and economic struggle but I think we can broaden that. I think there are a lot of struggles out there. . . . I think history teaches us about . . . the great triplets, militarism, racism, and economic exploitation. (Warren)

I think, mainly, it's relating the past to the present. . . . I try to draw parallels; things that happenned before, then try to apply them to what's going on now. . . . History is to be learned from. . . . If it isn't to learn from, then why do it. I think the best historians try to do that, try to draw lessons from the past. That's all I teach. That's how I try to teach anyway. (Tom)

The reasons that I see for teaching social studies [are] to help young people understand the present and it seems to me the past is actually the key to understanding what is going on today and why it's going on today and that we as people actually, people in a democracy have the ability to determine our own personal future as well as to help determine the future of the country and its effects upon the world as a whole. It seems to me that as a social studies teacher, we have a clear obligation to generate involvement in our democratic system. (Jeff)

Figure 6.3 provides a more detailed overview of four relativist/ reformers ideas about history. Each of these teachers emphasize the relation of history to the present. Perhaps the key element in each is the emphasis on making this a "better world," on trying to learn from our mistakes, and on student involvement in the community. Each teacher seems to be imposing a view that our world has many problems and that we share an obligation to seek improvment. This view is similar to an underlying assumption of the social studies movement, that is, the central aim of civic education, social amelioration (Evans, 1987).

Each of these relativist reformers sees patterns in history. Further

	Warren	Tom	Jeff	Dan
Purpose	My approach is to teach kids what history can teach us about our own situations. ...so I really use historical process to teach basically why America is in the mess it's in. History is for learning about process, it's for learning about how people get to a certain point culturally... and what you can do about it once you're there.	I think mainly its relating the past to the present and to try to learn from the mistakes that have been made. I try to draw parallels; things that happened before then try to apply them to what's happening now. Most of what we teach has happened before... If it isn't to learn from, then why do it?	The reasons that I see for teaching social studies is (sic) to help young people understand the present and it seems to me the past is actually the key to understanding what is going on today... We have a clear obligation to generate involvement on the part of our students. We have the opportunity to determine our own future.	The key thing I try to emphasize to the kids is the fact that we're human beings making decisions and affecting lives. The old adage that history repeats itself really does apply if you take a good look at it. If we can learn from the mistakes of past people and build upon them then we're going to make a better world.
Pattern	I see history as very much a dialectical process... I have to admit there's... a very Marxist premise there... the whole struggle concept: economic, class, male-female, East-West, you name it. I think all of those can be seen to run across the board.	I think there are patterns. I believe in countervailing power, like when one group develops power, then some other group opposes it, and they clash for awhile, and then the new group makes a new power. I think its a cycle but I don't think its predictable.	I think there are patterns in history... the only time any of those patterns have any relevance at all is if we actually make use of those patterns. I think we have the opportunity to determine things, and there are factors that might influence the patterns.	Everything seems to be very cyclical in nature. I don't care what civilization you look at, it seems like we go up and we go down, but that something happens and the civilization declines. I don't know if we can do something about it.
Generaliz-ability	To understand something from history and then generate solutions you have to be able to generalize or why bother. You've got to get to a deeper understanding of what makes people tick, why they're still doing the things they were doing 400 years ago.	I think we can make some comparisons. Human nature is the same whether time periods are different or not. You have to be able to generalize about history or else it's just a list of facts. I think the best historians try to draw lessons from the past.	It's very possible to make generalizations. I like my students to be able to document the generalizations they make, to have historical evidence to back them up. That isn't to say we're going to exclude or ignore the uniqueness of a particular period.	Time periods are unique but they have a common ground that you can compare. I think they are all related. Human beings are basically the same regardless where you're talking about. I like to generalize, but you have to back it with specifics.
Teaching Style	I try to keep it varied. I talk and I ask people for responses and try to get them to think about issues. I do a lot of lecture. I try to use a lot of outside readings. We study things that have a bearing on the basic issues that I am concerned with.	I use lecture/discussion. I try to provoke thought and provoke questions, and I question students, and sometimes I say kind of outrageous things to make them think. I might advocate an attack on the Soviet Union just to see what students would say.	I tend to use a very practical approach. We don't just talk about it and read about it... we have vistors and field trips and can begin to explore issues directly. I have them read a variety of sources, then I ask questions... to relate to issues of the present.	A lot of discussion and question and answer. It's very open. I do lecture but not too much. We do a lot of reading and research papers. I use the jurisprudential model a lot. It's a good way to examine both sides and get kids involved.
Teacher Background	The single most important thing that ever happened to me as far as studying history... as a first year graduate student I had a professor who was a material anthropologist. The university called him a Marxist. He changed my thinking.	Discussions. I grew up in a family that read, and I can remember historical type discussions, and all these books were around. My father was very conservative... I kind of rebelled against that. I had traditional teachers but they were provocative.	I had a fascination for historical artifacts... read the landmark books as a child. My parents were survivors of the holocaust and I was influenced by my father's pacifism and liberalism. My H.S. teacher wanted us to think about issues in historical context.	My parents had friends that came over and they always argued about politics. It was friendly arguments, but it's funny, I can always remember that. I had a history professor in college who was very provocative... and I'd like to emulate.

FIG. 6.3. Reformers.

more, the patterns they see are generally more definitive than the patterns acceptable to any of the other typologies considered thus far. Two of the relativist reformers view history as a dialectical process, and all four seem to suggest that we can influence the patterns of history through human action. Each teacher also views generalizability as a key component to the study of history and sees comparisons and analogies as the stuff of historical understanding, as a source of lessons valid as long as they are supported with evidence.

In teaching style, these teachers are similar to the scientific historians in that they pose problems for students while using a variety of methods. However, the key distinction is the source of such problems. For the scientific historian, problems come from competing interpretations of history, from the structure of the academic discipline. For the relativist/reformer, problems are drawn from present day issues and history made relevant to present concerns. Both are inquiry oriented.

What accounts for these teachers' relativist/reformer orientation? Three mention family influence, citing discussions or arguments on history and politics as they were growing up at home. All four also mention provocative teachers in high school or college. Interestingly, all four of these teachers describe themselves as liberal democrats. Analysis of survey data from the larger sample suggests that the majority (20 of 31 or 65%) of relativist/reformers are left-of-center, describing themselves as either liberal or moderately liberal. Also, all four of the teachers examined in detail have Judeo-Christian religious affiliations. Relativist/reformers in the larger sample also tended to be Christian (81%). Finally, all four have a strong content background in history ranging from 30 to 60 semester hours, though the average of 49 hours is significantly lower than that for the other typologies described thus far.

One other interesting finding: More experienced teachers tend to be relativist/reformers at a rate slightly higher than those with less experience. Of those teachers with over 5 years of experience, 49% were relativist/reformers, whereas 66% of teachers with 5 years of experience or less fit either the storyteller or scientific historian typology. This suggests that the relativist/reformer mode may also be related to years of experience.

Although this evidence is far from conclusive, each teacher's ideology, which combines liberalism and religious belief, seems to have had a major impact on the teacher's view of history, on the desire to set the world straight. Also, disciplinary background does not seem to be as strong a factor for this group. Regardless of the influences that may have shaped these teachers' conceptions of history, each has found success as a teacher through the relativist/reformer approach. Each has found that this approach can stimulate students to study history and to relate the past to issues of the present in an effort to learn what we can do about changing the future.

Jeff Tries to Change the World. Jeff, the relativist selected for detailed study in this chapter, offers a fairly typical example of the relativist approach to history. Although his teaching was hampered by discipline problems, Jeff's images of history do seem to have a major influence on his teaching. Every lesson we observed included some reference to the relationship between past and present, and in many lessons the central focus was on students' lives in the present. Unfortunately, the historical connection was sometimes lost in the shuffle. However, most of the time, connections were attempted. In discussing Jeff's teaching, it is of primary importance that we keep his audience in mind. His teaching style combines an image of history and perceptions of his clients.

A few brief examples illustrate Jeff's teaching style. A lesson on the general topic of government regulation of business and bank crises exemplified his approach. Although the lesson contained a good deal of historical content, it centered around the then current savings and loan crisis and bailout. The class period began with students entering the room and taking folders containing their notes from a box. Jeff had a list of economic terms on the board, and most of the students began writing down notes, chattering while writing. Terms on the board included "interest, collateral, corporation, common stock, monopoly, trust, outstanding stock, marketing, profit, net profit, dividend." As students wrote, Jeff announced:

T: I'm going to go over it, tie in to you.
S: We're still writing.
T: [After a few minutes] O.K., I need to begin now. The first point in relation to all this is money. [Student chatter continues unabated. Jeff, in a booming voice, simply talks over the chatter.] What this is going to lead to is savings and loan banks are in serious trouble. Why hasn't the federal reserve system worked as well as we hoped? These terms [on board] relate to forming a business. Many of you will work in business or even start your own. How is it that people get rich, Shawn. How is it possible for you?
S: Steal from a bank.
T: Are there other ways of stealing money. There are illegal ways of stealing, but there are also more refined ways of making money. Something like that happenned in terms of the bank crisis. How else can you people earn money by not stealing?
S1: Get a job.
S2: Sell drugs.

The discussion continued, centering on ways students could make money, borrow money, find loopholes in the system, and ended with Jeff stating, "to tie things up, these are the legal ways our system works and how our system makes money legally. The economy is run by people with ideas to make money legally." So most of the discussion was only tangentially related to the intended lesson focus, although relating to students' lives was presumably the teacher's motive.

Jeff often switched back and forth, from present, to past, to present, as a means of getting students interested in the past, or making issues from the past more understandable, and as a means of relating historical content to the present. Other good examples include his use of the film *Footloose*, about students who rebelled against their small town's restrictions on dancing in 1980s America, as a means for students to reach some understanding of the issues that led to the Protestant Reformation. He asked, "What were the similarities of the issues represented in *Footloose* to those of the reformation?" Also, he used the Chaplin film *Modern Times* as a means to introduce labor/management relations. In each lesson we observed, students' lives were the starting point. History was important mostly for what light it could shed on present-day dilemmas and problems. Unfortunately, the relationship between past and present was sometimes murky, not powerfully drawn. Jeff's teaching suffered from a lack of clarity as well as student disruption. Yet his conception of purpose was always present.

According to student interview responses, their beliefs about history and about society were not influenced much, if at all, by Jeff's class. When asked whether their beliefs had changed in any way as a result of the class, most students simply said, "No," or "Not really."

Jeff's reform message, calling for social participation through his teaching, is not powerfully presented. This lack of power is reflected in the management problems that beset his classes. His teaching is apparently having little impact on student beliefs. One wonders what impact a more gifted teacher might have on students, given a similar typology. A reformer I reported on in a previous investigation seemingly had a much more dramatic impact on his students' ideas about history (Evans, 1988).

Cosmic Philosopher

Although not a large group (2 of the 71 teachers surveyed or 2.8% of the sample), the cosmic typology has several distinguishing characteristics. First, the cosmic teacher sees generalizations or "laws" connecting events as the most interesting aspect of history. Second, the cosmic philosopher sees definite patterns in history; although each may see a different pattern, most suggest a cyclical view of history. Like the metahistorian, these teachers see grand theory as an essential part of history and believe that history has a profound meaning with implications for the future.

Speculative philosophers of history, metahistorians, tend to fall into one of three broad groups, the metaphysical, the empirical, or the cosmic. Metaphysical philosophers of history seek explanation that transcends observable experience, formulating universal laws to explain the powerful forces shaping the course of events. Empirical metahistorians attempt a similar synthesis of human experience, but make a stronger attempt to base speculation on historical evidence. Cosmic philosphers tend to attribute explanation to other-worldly forces, usually described as providence or God. These strains of metahistory are united by their attempt to synthesize all of human experience, to locate human experience in a grand pattern. The same may be said for the "cosmic" teachers I interviewed.

> History is the study of the human condition. The human form hasn't changed much, it's more or less the same. We still have rich and poor, we still have mysticism, war hasn't changed, societies still go through various stages quite similar to those that went before. It's all connected, humans have thought about the same things for centuries. (David)

> There are patterns in history. The example I use is that civilization emanates from a single human being, forms a group, which then goes through various stages, the tribe, the community, the city-state, the nation, and eventually the empire. Empires reach a certain point when they become cumbersome, then they disintegrate . . . and the cycle starts over again. It is a cyclical pattern, entwined with nature like the life and death cycle of a human, or a tree, or the seasons. (David)

> We don't learn from our mistakes, that is the lesson. . . . History is moving toward Armageddon because we don't learn from the past. I wouldn't want to be a teenager today. I would like . . . I try to teach optimistically, that we can learn, that we should learn, that there's hope, but if you want to be realistic we had a margin of error in the past, before we had gotten to these nuclear bombs. But we don't have much margin of error now. (Leo)

Although each of these teachers' conception of history contains elements of other typologies, each strongly emphasizes a grand pattern. As Fig. 6.4 illustrates, both of these teachers discussed humans as an animal form, taking what might be described as a biological view of

	David	Leo
Purpose	I am primarily concerned with my student's ability to think, to solve problems. I wonder how they are going to cope with the 21st century, how they are going to adjust to living, make decisions. History is the entire study of the human endeavor... an understanding of that foundation allows them to study and master the other subjects. The historical process is continual and it's all linked together. There is essentially an animal form. It has gone through various stages and experiences but they are all quite similar. Humans have thought about these similar things and they have addressed the same questions. The historical process will continue... It's all connected.	Using the past, hopefully you can communicate to kids where our species, you know, homo sapiens, has gone wrong and continues to go wrong and you know we do not learn from our historical experiences. You look at the cycles of history, you try to communicate the idea that there's a certain predictability...
Pattern	Civilization emanates from a single human being... then for whatever reason they form a group and that group goes through various stages... that extend from a domestic tribal existence into a community, a city state, and states into nations. Then if that nation comes together and everything is in its place, it extends its boundaries into an empire. Empires reach a certain point where they no longer function, then they disintegrate. The pattern is reoccurring... not any different than the life or death cycle of a tree.	The pattern is the weakness of man, his inability to resist temptation. I try to teach optimistically, but if you want to be realistic, with these nuclear bombs we don't have much margin of error. We don't learn... we're moving toward Armageddon.
Generalizability	Comparisons are constantly made, and they have to be made, but they have to be astute in the concepts of time. 1988 and 1488. What were the empires doing in 1488 that is so different than what the American empire is doing in 1988. We have to understand that in 1488 those colonial empires were very similar to the American empire. History changes because people think, but the overall human condition isn't changing. Humans can think and change the course of history... It's open ended.	I believe in generalization. We repeat the mistakes of the past, and you can show analogies that are valid. With our lack of attention to government we get what we deserve in politicians. As ye sow, so shall ye reap... We don't learn from our mistakes.
Teaching Style	My courses have a standard text. I supplement that with anything and everything that I can get my hands on, depending on what I think the students need. I lecture, engage in discussion with the students, engage in debate. Very often I play the devil's advocate. I challenge their values, their morality, whatever they think is right or wrong. I use a critical thinking process. I demand that they write essays, that they read x number of books, write critical book reviews and that they present these to the class.	I am an autocratic dictator. We get into some role-playing, I use the Nuremburg trials. We use study guides. I spend a lot of time on people and places and causation... the reasons why. I also spend a lot of effort on geography.
Teacher Background	I was going for my MBA and started taking some other courses, quite a bit of philosophy and some psych courses... then history. Two professors really turned me on to it, then I said bingo and just changed. I think I was just searching and whatever it was I found it and fell in love with it. My father used to always say he loved history in school, and it became a positive thing for me. Toynbee, I guess, has been a major influence on me. He made it interesting. And the Durant series.	Overall life experience, in Asia and Africa and the Middle East. I mean those are the formative years and they were years when I was in my late twenties and early thirties. Toynbee, H. G. Wells and his outline of the world both had an influence.

FIG. 6.4. Cosmic philosophers.

human history as a living organism. Both see a clear pattern in history, one of cycles, the other of decline. Both also view history as generalizable, and believe that generalizations can be quite reliable. Both teachers use process-centered approaches among a variety of teaching techniques. Both describe themselves as moderate liberals, and both have a strong religious connection: Leo is Protestant; David earned his masters degree from a Jesuit institution.

The small size of this group in the sample and the lack of any strong pattern make the origins of these teachers' ideas more difficult to trace. Survey data reveal little interesting insight into the cosmic philosopher, perhaps because there were only two cases. However, both did have high levels of educational attainment: one had a master's degree, the other a master's plus 45 semester hours. They averaged 49 semester hours of history. Also, both mentioned studying philosophy of history, and listed Toynbee as an influence.

Perhaps a later study can find more examples of this typology. At this point, my guess is that in each case a reading of cosmic historians and a religious background have had a profound impact on each teacher's thinking about history. Religious belief played a central role in the case of Jacob Neuman, a cosmic philosopher described in my earlier study (Evans, 1988).

David Goes Cosmic. David, the cosmic teacher examined in this study, embodies elements of cosmic thinking in his conceptions about history. David's teaching is rather eclectic, although elements of his cosmic approach to history come through. Of nine lessons observed, two involved student oral reports, several involved brief student writing exercises, and most included teacher lecture or teacher-led discussion of the topic under study. During one of our observations, David began class with a brief writing exercise as follows:

> T: Today we have a little exercise to do on a reading assignment we discussed yesterday. I want you to write on two different questions. This side [motions at left side of room] . . . What caused the great depression? Did it start abroad or in America? Other side: What caused the stock market to collapse in 1929? Is it likely to collapse in the same way again? O.K. You have 15 minutes.
>
> T: [after passage of time] Why did the market collapse? Will it do the same thing again?
>
> S: The market crashed because there were too many imports. The same thing could happen today.
>
> T: Is that similar to yours?
>
> S: It's the same.
>
> T: Where do you differ?

S2: America got into trouble with too much building on money they didn't have . . . people were gambling with money on Wall Street.

T: You hit on some of the key issues. The stock market, gambling, credit, inflation. The key reason was people were buying stocks on credit, with nothing to back it up. Ceci hit the key point, you have to put your money into business or investment. When you have money, buy . . . it keeps the economy healthy. Teresa.

S: The depression was caused by overproduction . . . America was producing too much, and couldn't sell it. Europe added to the problem. . . . President Hoover's ideology was that government should stay out of the economy.

T: People were starving, standing in bread lines, and yet we had surpluses. Money didn't get down to the lower classes. Hoover said, "We'll give money to the big boys, and it will trickle down," but the money didn't trickle down. But don't blame the depression on one individual, Hoover. His actions were coming from an ideology, individualism. Where have you heard that before? Bush, á la Reagan. That philosophy is perhaps outdated.

Thus, a lesson employing a writing exercise and beginning with the kinds of questions that historians ask became a soapbox for David to express his views, something he did with regularity. David's style of teaching reflects his cosmic orientation in minor ways, but his approach is largely eclectic, and seems to devote a good deal of attention to relating past to present. What are students taking from the class? It is difficult to say. They seem to be gaining some knowledge of the past, and a belief that history can help us in the present, although connections do not seem powerfully drawn. It is similar to his student's attitudes; they like the class, but generally are not excited about it. That lack of excitement reflects David's fatigue, and the overload he experiences as a teacher, coach, and part-time bartender. Cosmic philosophy may be present in his teaching (his students say that he sees everything "connected" to everything else), but it is not a powerful presence, nor does it seem to dictate much of his pedagogy.

Eclectic

A fairly large group, 16 of the 71 teachers surveyed or 22.5% of the sample, had no central tendency, no score of four or higher in any category on the questionnaire analysis. Though some members of this group are probably closer to a typology than the questionnaire results allow, most combine elements of two or more of the conceptions of history described earlier. The interview notes summarized in Fig. 6.5 illustrate this eclecticism.

	Betty	Sumner	Paul	Donald
Purpose	To create a greater appreciation of some of the forefathers. Also, to make them understand that history does repeat itself... and that we can find parallels. I think that there are some fun things in history, you can get away from the conventional and find something that can interest a kid, just for pleasure.	I think its important that students have a knowledge of how this country came to be. So many things hinge on the government, people need a good background in American history. Maybe we can learn by our mistakes. I use history as a good way to tell stories and emphasize how things can relate to us today.	An appreciation of the past. In any culture or society you have to feel as if there is a base. Going back a little can make you aware, you can become more involved, more educated. Knowing the past can give you a greater understanding of what is going on now. Maybe that can help the community. It extends into real life.	I'm a traditionalist. I think the roots of the present are in the past. I look upon history as a survival course. If we do not learn... nothing else will survive. Knowledge is power. Sometimes it's for the sake of knowing. We need a certain body of knowledge to function. The mind, like the body, needs exercise.
Pattern	I think that there are patterns, but they are probably clouded or over-shadowed by other things. I think that history has unique characteristics, but the overall premise is we can find some common denominators in many things that happenned.	There probably is an overall pattern. We talk about an age of peace and then there is an economic depression, then a war and this has more or less gone down through America and Europe. It's just something that keeps repeating itself. I don't think we progress.	There definitely is a pattern... a period of birth, then more advanced morals and ideals, then a nation gets more decadent. Everything seems to go in cycles. The cycles are completing faster and faster. Nothing lasts forever.	Does history repeat itself? The answer is obviously no. That would be taking a very complex situation and put a very simple answer to it. There is only a very broad, very general kind of pattern. Civilizations do rise and fall.
Generaliz-ability	I think it is possible to make generalizations about anything. The validity depends on who is saying it and where it is coming from. We can look at mistakes... kind of like sitting at an athletic event and second guessing. We have to live with decisons.	You really shouldn't draw any generalizations but you can't help but do it. It's pretty hard to look at past revolutions and not compare them to things happening today. In some cases we are bound to draw some parallels between time periods.	I don't believe we can learn from history. If you know the past and can appreciate the present... fine, that's good, but I don't think that anyone ever really learns from the past. There are too many factors involved, too many variables... all unique.	I'm constantly comparing and contrasting the past with the present. I believe that the student should understand the uniqueness of an event within the context of a country's history. I have a tendency to be careful with generalizations.
Teaching Style	A bit non-conventional in some ways. I do a lot of group work, a lot of simulations, projects and reports that are generated right here. I try to use a lot of primary documents... a lot of supplementary things. Whatever we do it has to relate to them.	When I teach it's a combination of lectures, student participation, and audio-visual... we do mock trials, and we talk about current events and how they relate. I tell stories about personalities and pretend to be them... I do anything to get the kids interested.	I try to involve the students as much as possible. I don't like to just lecture. I also involve my students in getting the material, and I like to hear their point-of-view. Sometimes I have them work in small groups. I bring in controversy.	Variety is the spice of life. Sometimes I lecture, sometimes I use group discussion, sometimes I use simulation games. My students do written research reports, they do oral reports. Variety is the spice of life. I cannot be bored in class.
Teacher Background	My grandfather was the local town historian. I listened to his stories about the lumber camps. I read biographies. I had a one teacher in high school who made it come alive. At home history was always respected as an important part of life.	My father told me stories of the Korean war. I had a 7th grade teacher who would try any ways to get the child to learn. It was just fascinating to listen to this person. He made history come alive. I think I pattern my teaching after him.	One history teacher in college was very good. I took all his courses... I remember stories told by my grandparents. My parents used to take me everywhere. It made the want to learn more... My father was engaged in politics. I tagged along.	My parents and a couple of teachers were a big influence on me. My mother and father came from the old country and used to tell stories of what Italy was like. My 9th grade world history teacher was great. So was one professor.

FIG. 6.5. Eclectics.

When asked about the purposes for studying history, each of these teachers gave multiple answers. All four mentioned knowledge or appreciation of the past. Each teacher also mentioned at least one other purpose, such as interest, telling stories, relating the past to the present, helping the community, or mental exercise. The key similarity is that each of these teachers seemingly had no dominant tendency. Although they differed on their thoughts about patterns and generalizability, a second important area of similarity was in teaching style. Each of these teachers emphasized variety and student interest. In fact, the common element seems to be a very practical orientation toward getting students interested.

If these teachers' conceptions about history and their teaching style are eclectic, it seems fitting that teacher background is somewhat eclectic as well. It may be little more than a curiosity, but all four mentioned stories told by family members, and three of the four mentioned history teachers they had in school. All had a religious affiliation, fewer semester hours in history courses, and described themselves as either political moderates or middle-of-the-road. Perhaps this moderation reflects an absence of strong ideological commitment, consistent with eclecticism. More than any other typology, this group's conceptions of history may have been tempered by the necessities of classroom teaching, by the need to somehow interest students in history.

Sumner Embraces Chaos.   For most eclectics, getting the kids interested seems to be the overarching concern. Yet if Sumner, the eclectic I report on, is any indication, the lack of a deeper and more consistent philosophy may lead to a lapse into the most basic and least sophisticated type of teaching, a style based on teacher talk and student recitation. Each of the nine lessons we observed followed a similar format. Sumner talked, students listened. Sumner asked factual questions, students tried to answer. Usually, he tried to relate the past to something in the student's lives, such as a radio station or the rivalry between two towns. Occasionally Sumner spiced up his presentations with an overhead transparency, a drawing on the board, or an artifact, which usually served to heighten student interest only temporarily.

A lesson on the Vikings, Norse gods, and mythology began with a story Sumner read to the students of the Norse gods and later included an artifact, an English version of a battle axe, which was passed around the room and seemed to generate a good deal of interest, although mostly in the axe itself. The lesson was primarily a lecture peppered with questions designed to maintain student interest.

Student interview data on Sumner's teaching style confirms this description of his teaching. Students said that "He talks and we take notes." The most telling comment came in one student's response regarding his teacher's political beliefs when he said, "This is a world history class so you don't really get into politics that much. . . . There aren't a whole lot of politics involved."

That response suggests that Sumner's rendition of history is failing to reach that student, and I suspect many others, at a very basic level. His approach is apolitical. Students really aren't asked to think, only to recall. Thus, such a comment is understandable. Data on student belief suggest that Sumner is having very little impact on student thinking.

On the whole, Sumner's approach to teaching history seems far removed from the reflective testing of belief. His students do not seem more likely to vote or to be thoughtful citizens as a result of this class. In fact, it could be having just the opposite effect, a routinization producing apathy. Although one could imagine an eclectic teacher having more profound impact on students' lives, it is possible that the lack of strong commitment exemplified by eclecticism could stand in the way of lively or provocative teaching, and could contribute to a kind of blandness brought by lack of purpose.

DISCUSSION

Although the data collected for this exploratory study are insufficient for developing firm conclusions, several findings are interesting and deserve further comment.

1. Teacher conceptions of history, its purposes and meaning, seem to vary. Teachers studied tend to fall into one of five typologies: storyteller, scientific historian, relativist/reformer, cosmic philosopher, or eclectic. Each typology may be identified with longstanding traditions in philosophy of history, in social studies education, and often with larger philosophies of education. The storyteller typology is similar to the idealist philosopher of history finding voice in the writings of Ravitch (1987; Ravitch & Finn, 1987) among others. Their emphasis on transmitting knowledge, on using teacher-centered methods, clearly places the storytellers in the citizenship transmission tradition in social studies (Barr, Barth, & Shermis, 1977).

Educationally, their emphasis on content knowledge is closest to the view held by the essentialist, a stance Brameld described as conservative "because he would solve the problems of our time by developing behavior skilled mainly in conserving rather than in changing the essential content and structure of the pre-existent world" (1955, p. 77).

The scientific historian typology is similar to the positivist philosopher. Their emphasis on open-ended inquiry into historical questions and their attempted scientific objectivity place this typology in the tradition of social science inquiry (Barr et al., 1977). This is a group that FitzGerald dubbed "mandarins," presumably because of their overuse of complex concepts from scholarly disciplines, concepts that seemed exotic to many teachers, students, and parents (FitzGerald, 1979). Educationally, this group might be seen as moderately progressive, but, because of its emphasis on scholarly knowledge, contains strong elements of essentialism as well.

The relativist/reformer is similar in outlook to the relativist philosopher, viewing history as contemporary thought about our past and seeking to help students draw lessons for the future. Its orientation to the present, its emphasis on relating the past to current issues, and its vision of studying the past to build a better future clearly place this group in the reflective inquiry tradition (Barr et al., 1977). Educationally, these teachers are progressives and reconstructionists, philosophies that Brameld described as the educational counterparts of liberalism and radicalism. They are forward looking and future-centered, respectively. In Brameld's words, "The progressivist is the genuine liberal because he would meet our crisis by developing minds and habits skilled as instruments in behalf of progressive, gradual, evolutionary change. . . . The reconstructionist is the radical because he would solve our problems not by conserving, or modifying, or retreating, but by future looking" (1955, p. 77).

The cosmic philosopher has most in common with the speculative philosopher of history. This typology sees all experience as connected, part of a larger pattern, a pattern that has profound meaning. For these teachers, the human form remains unchanged, the key elements of existence are perennial. Thus, this typology may link most closely with perennialism, a philosophy that Brameld describes as backward looking, desiring a return to an earlier time. Again, Brameld states, "The perennialist is the regressivist because he would deal with contemporary issues by reacting against them in favor of solutions extraordinarily similar to those of a culture long past—or even escaping into an intellectual realm of timeless perfection" (1955, p. 77).

Although this analysis discusses five major categories, these are not completely distinct nor are they all-inclusive. Most teachers exhibit some elements of more than one typology, but display a dominant tendency. One wonders how aware teachers are of their teaching style and its fit with educational philosophy and ideology.

2. Teacher conceptions of history seem to have a profound impact on the transmitted curriculum in two of the five classrooms we studied in depth, the storyteller's and the scientific historian's, with less impact in the other three. This suggests that the impact of teacher conceptions may vary. At this point I do not have a lot of evidence to use in speculating on the reasons for such variation, although I suspect that teacher efficacy may be strongly related. Both the storyteller and the scientific historian seemed clear about what they were doing, and effective at reaching those ends. This consonance, between their conceptions of history and the curriculum transmitted in their classrooms, reflects both the clarity of their images of history teaching and their skills as teachers. Each of the other teachers portrayed, the reformer, cosmic philosopher, and eclectic, had lower levels of consonance due to several factors, including the difficulty of effective discussion-centered teaching, less effective teaching skills, lower student motivation, constant difficulty with classroom management concerns, or teacher burnout.

3. Students in several classes reported that their teachers had influenced their understanding of history and had contributed to their knowledge of the past. Based on their comments, most students seem to learn that history can help us solve problems and help us avoid mistakes. However, students are seldom given much help in applying these ideas. Often, connections or links between past and present aren't given much explicit attention, or sufficient time to allow full exploration of analogies through socratic discussion. Just as often, similarities between historical events of different eras are raised without much discourse on differences in historical context, and, even more troublesome, without explicit, in-depth discussion of the ethical dilemmas or decisions posed by the events under study. Thus, relevance to students lives often becomes a superficial justification for learning the stuff of history. Without more powerful links and more powerful discussion strategies, it seems a rather empty justification.

Most students report no change in their beliefs about society. This is not surprising given the content orientation of most of their teachers and their teachers' weak attempts to connect past to present. If these teachers are at all representative, the teaching of history and social studies generally may be having little impact on student belief or thinking, except on knowledge of the content studied. Other research on teaching supports this notion (Goodlad, 1984; Shaver, Davis, & Helburn, 1979).

Nevertheless, a few teachers may be having a more profound impact on their students. For example, Rusty's (a.k.a. Steve Smith of Belfast, ME) students reported that their history class had made them more analytical, and had forced them to ask reflective questions about their lives, their government, and their society. Although it would be wonderful if more teachers could emulate such teaching, the reality of schooling suggests that the prospects are not all that hopeful. Even Steve has not found a way to make his larger classes with students of mixed academic skills fit his ideal vision of teaching. Small classes and sustained innovation are costly.

4. Teacher conceptions of history seem profoundly related to teacher background, teacher belief, and teacher knowledge. Among the factors mentioned by informants are previous teachers, college professors, family, books, and life experiences, although home and school factors seemed most important. In particular, political and religious background seem to play an especially important role, although the importance of each of these factors may vary considerably. For storytellers, it seems that a tendency toward political conservatism and a strong background in the discipline of history are relevant factors. For scientific historians, disciplinary background and particular professors of history seem most relevant, although political liberalism and lack of religious affiliation may also be important. For relativist/reformers, family background, liberal political belief, and religious affiliation seem important, and disciplinary background apparently played a less crucial role. For cosmic philosophers, religious belief may have played the most crucial role, and for eclectics, previous school teachers and the press of the classroom seem most important, whereas absence of strong political convictions may have prevented development of a more definitive approach.

Thus, political belief seems related to teacher conceptions of history, though the relationship is not absolute or direct. Storytellers tend to be conservatives, relativist/reformers and scientific historians tend to be liberals, and eclectics show centrist tendencies. My earlier conclusion that the teaching of history can be a potent forum for imparting values (Evans, 1988) seems to be supported, at least in the majority of cases, by the data from this study. However, the political nature of historical thinking usually lurks beneath the surface, beneath the level of daily consciousness. As in historical interpretation, political beliefs tend to creep in through the back door.

5. In most of the classrooms subjected to detailed study, judging from student comments, the teaching of history and political ideology do not seem related, at least not in an explicit way. But, if we look beneath the surface, they may be. The storyteller, a conservative, is passing on our traditions and an understanding of the past as cultural knowledge that undergirds our way of life. As Hayden White has suggested, history is the conservative discipline par excellence, and narrative its dominant, most traditional mode (White, 1978). The scientific historian, a liberal, is

liberating students, causing them to ask questions about their world, many for the first time in their lives. He is transmitting the scientist's skepticism about knowledge, and with it a questioning attitude. His approach seems to mirror a structuralist, neopositivist framework, yet the outcome, in terms of student reflection, seems to partially fulfill the poststructuralist argument for critical pragmatism (Cherryholmes, 1988).

The reformer, a liberal, although a miscast and apologetic teacher failing to succeed with most of his students, is trying to improve the world through his teaching. In that intent, he has much in common with relativists and poststructuralists, the pragmatist approach that Rorty might call "history as politics" – an attempt, only lightly veiled, to build the kind of society in which every human potentiality is given free reign (Rorty, 1989, p. 22). The cosmic philosopher, also a liberal, imparts his truths, that all things are connected and that individualism is outdated. This is an approach that Putnam has called the "God's-eye view" (Rorty, 1989, p. 15) and represents an attempt to have a God-like grasp of the realm of possibility and to have a pigeonhole ready for every event in history. Finally, the eclectic, a moderate, seems most interested in making it through the day: an approach that emphasizes functional efficiency, or a "vulgar pragmatism" that is "socially repro-ductive, instrumentally and functionally reproducing accepted mean-ings and conventional organizations, institutions, and ways of doing things for good or ill" (Cherryholmes, 1988, p. 151).

6. The typologies developed in this chapter pose some very practical questions, which cut to the core of theoretical approaches to the teaching of history. Which should we emulate? Which should we discount? How should we assess them? Of course, each teacher of history must come up with his or her own answers. At the very least, we see that the conception of history as story propagated by neoconserva-tive critics of the social studies is but one of many possibilities.

Despite the few exceptional teachers who are having a serious impact, what passes for citizenship education in most classrooms may be counterproductive, helping to create and sustain apathy and lack of caring about our society and the world. It may be better to simply cut social studies and history from the curriculum rather than continue to produce such a lack of reflection. Current practice, which is generally not reflective, only makes sense if we assume that schools exist to transmit cultural norms of selfishness and conformity, if we assume that the underlying purpose of schooling is to teach students "how not to question and how not to doubt" (Kozol, 1975, p. 7).

Of the five teachers studied in detail, only Rusty (Steve Smith) seems to produce sustained critical reflection in students, and much of what he is doing rests on an unexamined orientation, as he wrote in a letter commenting on my description of his views:

> Thanks for the disturbing but accurate paper. . . . Your accuracy is precisely what's disturbing about your work, because for the most part I have not thought about the issues you dealt with. You're right, there is a philosophy underlying my teaching, but it's the worst kind of philosophy, unexamined and unarticulated, even to myself. And, if I understand the thrust of your work, you imply that without that examination it becomes impossible to evaluate and eventually to improve what history teachers are doing, since no one, even the teachers, seems to know what they are trying to do. In my case, I have little knowledge of the 19th century historians or the New Social Studies movement, and none about the analytic positivist philosophy of history. Yet what I do know suggests that you are correct—making me an unwitting dupe of people and philosophies I don't even know. Ruefully, I must agree with you.

If Rusty's philosophy is "unexamined and unarticulated," what of the other teachers I studied? For the most part, these teachers are part of the seamless web of schooling helping to create a denatured social life, void of controversy, void of causes, void of deep caring—socializing, but not countersocializing (Engle & Ochoa, 1988). For most of their students, the teaching of history may function as a softened, diffused means of oppression. The boredom and routinization in most history classrooms produces a sense of well-being, a drowsy feeling that life is acceptable as it is, and that history has little to do with our lives and the decisions we face.

ACKNOWLEDGMENTS

Special thanks to James Hadden, who helped with data collection in the second phase of the study, and to the University of Maine, which provided necessary financial support.

REFERENCES

Barr, R. D., Barth, J. L., & Shermis, S. S. (1977). *Defining the social studies.* Arlington, VA: National Council for the Social Studies.

Beard, C. A. (1933). Written history as an act of faith. *The American Historical Review, 39,* 219–229.

Brameld, T. (1955). *Philosophies of education in cultural perspective.* New York: Dryden.

Cherryholmes, C. (1988). *Power and criticism: Poststructural investigations in education.* New York: Teachers College.

Collingwood, R. G. (1946). *The idea of history.* London: Oxford University Press.

Cuban, L. (1984). *How teachers taught.* New York: Longman.

Elbaz, F. (1983). *Teacher thinking: A study of practical knowledge.* New York: Nichols.

Engle, S., & Ochoa, A. (1988). *Education for democratic citizenship: Decision making in the social studies.* New York: Teachers College.

Evans, R. W. (1987). *Defining the worthy society: A history of the societal-problems approach in the social studies, 1895–1985.* Unpublished Ed.D. dissertation, Stanford University, Stanford, CA.

Evans, R. W. (1988). Lessons from history: Teacher and student conceptions of the meaning of history. *Theory and Research in Social Education. 16,* 203–225.

Evans, R. W. (1989, March). *Meaning in history: Philosophy and teaching.* Paper presented at the annual meeting of the American Educational Research Association, San Francisco.

Evans, R. W. (1992). Misunderstanding social studies: A response to Whelan. *Theory and Research in Social Education, 20,* 313–318.

Feiman-Nemser, S., & Floden, R. E. (1986). The cultures of teaching. In M. C. Wittrock (Ed.), *Handbook of research on teaching.* (pp. 505–526) New York: Macmillan.

FitzGerald, F. (1979). *America revised.* New York: Vintage Books.

Goodlad, J. (1984). *A place called school.* New York: McGraw-Hill.

Goodman, J., & Adler, S. (1985). Becoming an elementary social studies teacher: A study of perspectives. *Theory and Research in Social Education, 13,* 1–20.

Kozol, J. (1975). *The night is dark and I am far from home.* Boston: Houghton Mifflin.

Ravitch, D. (1987, April). *The revival of history: Problems and progress.* Paper presented at the annual meeting of the American Educational Research Association, Washington, DC.

Ravitch, D., & Finn, C. (1987). *What do our 17-year-olds know.* New York: Harper & Row.

Rorty, R. (1989). Philosophy as science, as metaphor, and as politics. In A. Cohen & M. Dascal (Eds.). *The institution of philosophy: A discipline in crisis* (pp. 13–33). La Salle, IL: Open Court.

Shaver, J. P., Davis, O. L., & Helburn, S. W. (1979). The status of social studies education: Impressions from three NSF studies. *Social Education, 43,* 150–153.

Shulman, L. S. (1986). Paradigms and research programs in the study of teaching: A contemporary perspective. In M. C. Wittrock (Ed.). *Handbook of research on teaching* (pp. 3–36). New York: Macmillan.

Thornton, S. J. (1989, November). *Teachers' views of social studies curriculum.* Paper presented at the annual meeting of the College and University Faculty Assembly of the National Council for the Social Studies, St. Louis, MO.

Whelan, M. (1992). History and the social studies: A response to the critics. *Theory and Research in Social Education, 20,* 2–16.

White, H. (1978). *Topics of discourse: Essays in cultural criticism.* Baltimore: Johns Hopkins University Press.

Wilson, S. M., & Wineburg, S. S. (1987, April). *Peering at history from different lenses: The role of disciplinary perspectives in the teaching of American history.* Paper presented at the annual meeting of the American Educational Research Association, Washington, DC.

Wineburg, S. S., & Wilson, S. M. (1988). Models of wisdom in the teaching of history. *Phi Delta Kappan, 70,* 50–58.

CHAPTER 7
History: A Time to Be Mindful

Gaea Leinhardt
Learning Research and Development Center,
University of Pittsburgh

On September 8, 1991, Simon Schama wrote in the *New York Times Magazine*:

> History was not a remote and funereal place. It was a world that spoke loudly and urgently to our own concerns. How can their sense of the dramatic immediacy be revived? In the first place, history needs to be liberated from its captivity in the school curriculum, where it is held hostage by that great amorphous, utilitarian discipline called social studies. History needs to declare itself unapologetically for what it is: the study of the past in all its splendid messiness. It should revel in the pastness of the past, the strange music of its diction. . . . History isn't a how-to manual full of analogies to explain whatever this week's crisis happens to be—Saddam as Hitler, Kuwait as Munich—and certainly not some carefully prepared tonic for ethnic self-esteem. (p. 31)

His article is a plea for seeing history as a discipline of beauty and elegance, a plea for history to retain and indeed revive its connections to the humanities. Although the *New York Times* does not so inform its readers, this article comes down on a particular side of a complex and tense discussion within history on the role of narrative as both art and analysis as contrasted with the role of analysis as a way of scientizing history. For students in high school and middle school, the major features of this debate are not critically salient, but the resolution and

209

even the process of debate itself has and will continue to seriously affect them and their teachers.

To continue with Schama, in his best-selling, popular history of the French Revolution, *Citizens* (1989), he presented the readers with three narrative/pictorial beginnings to his story:

> Asked what he thought of the French Revolution, the Chinese Premier Zhou En-lai is reported to have answered, "It's too soon to tell." Two hundred years may still be too soon (or, possibly too late) to tell. (Preface, p. xiii)

> Between 1814 and 1846 a plaster elephant stood on the site of the Bastille. For much of this time it presented a sorry spectacle. Pilgrims in search of revolutionary inspiration were brought up short at the site of it, massive and lugubrious, at the southeast end of the square. By 1830, when revolution revisited Paris, the elephant was in an advanced state of decomposition. (Prologue, p. 3)

> In the brilliant spring of 1778, Talleyrand went to pay his respects to Voltaire. Even in the society where the worldliness of the clergy was notorious, this was a little unseemly. (Chapter One, p. 21)

Each of the three beginnings is accompanied by a facing picture or map. All three beginnings portray a scene; they are well written, enticing, and informative. The beginnings involve a playfulness with respect to time frames, they invoke a bit of mysteriousness, and they use a cameralike adjustment to distance from the subject. In the first scene one can imagine the news broadcaster close in to the interviewee talking about pressing topics of the day, replete with sound bites; in the second scene one might imagine the opening shot of some epoch movie with a symbolic elephant slowly rotting away in a town square; and in the final scene one sees a stylized period drama with bewigged actors entering and exiting a drawing room. We know from his multiple beginnings of *Citizens* that Schama will work with perspectives and interpretations and that we as readers, in order to enjoy the game, must enter into that playfulness. As readers we may guess that he will use actual, if somewhat minor, events as symbols for more profound points.

There is an inherent invitation by Schama to join in an interesting and enjoyable pastime. It is, however, a pastime that demands a good deal from the reader, much more than just an 11th grade reading level, or a course in filling in the blanks of names and dates. He has asked readers to follow many constructs at once and to reflect on them: They are to know the event narrative of the story before he retells it (the elephant image doesn't really work otherwise); they are to know the themes of tension between societal segments (the comments on Talleyrand and Voltaire are empty otherwise); they are also to understand the social structures of France at the time of the tale (needed for both the elephant and Talleyrand); and they are to have a sense of themselves as a part of history and of the dialogue of the present with the past (the Zhou En-lai comment).

Schama also lays out the space of query. What does the French Revolution mean to us today? How did the interpretation of the French Revolution decay and get reborn? What is the story we might tell now of that revolution, and where should we start such a tale? The answers to these questions are the stuff of historical explanations. Building the cases embedded in such explanation is part of the stuff of historical reasoning.

Now consider the prose that starts the beginning—the only one—to a high school textbook's section on the French Revolution. "The ideals of Enlightenment thinkers, which had influenced the Americans' war for independence, also played a part in the outbreak of the French Revolution in 1789. French society was based on feudal ideals, economic inequality, special class privileges, and the absolute rule of kings" (Perry, Davis, Harris, von Laue, & Warren, 1985, p. 441). This single beginning opens with the baldly expository; narrative as well as mystery are absent. There is no hint of several tales or of multiple perspectives, no query to drive the answers home; it is an answer to an unasked question. These textual presentations by Schama and by Perry et al. suggest very different notions about what constitutes history. Further, they suggest rather different perspectives on the implied task of a learner and by inference on the implied task of those of us concerned with the improvement and expansion of the teaching of history in our schools.

OVERVIEW

This chapter describes an ongoing program of research into the teaching and learning of history, a program of research conducted in light of the current practice of history. The underlying concerns for this program are not simply to determine what constitutes effective instruction in history, but also to specify what the valuable contributions of instruction in history are and how they can impact the thoughtful analytic development of students. What might history look like if we use that valuable slice of curricular time wisely? What ought such instruction to reach for? The program of research is a part, as are the other chapters in this volume, of an emerging effort to understand and to improve history education. This program of research has made use of three quite different kinds of information: information from practicing historians, information from high school and middle school students and teachers in history classes, and information from classroom practices. Further, all of these efforts have dealt with the fact that history is a discipline based on reading, writing, and discussing texts. Thus, the program of research reported in this chapter focuses on dialogues about texts.

Methodology

A general overview of the methodology is presented here. The details of the methodology for the program of research appear in original research reports of the work (Leinhardt, 1990, 1993a, 1993b; Leinhardt, Stainton, & Virji, in press; Leinhardt, Stainton, Virji, & Odoroff, in press; McCarthy & Leinhardt, 1993; Stainton & Leinhardt, 1992). The class-room data consist of 189 transcriptions of audio and video tapes from three teachers' classes, as well as extensive interviews with teachers and their students. Sterling, a teacher with 34 years of experience, taught in a large, crowded, urban school. She had a tremendous love of history as a subject and anchored all of her teaching in the specifics and debates of history. We have data from two years of her Advanced Placement (AP) U.S. history classes and 18 lessons of AP European history. Peterbene is a teacher with 21 years of experience who taught in a middle-sized suburban school in Western Pennsylvania, with a modern school building that was very comfortable. He identified with the students' growth and maturation and anchored his teaching in their personal experiences and conflicts. We have data that samples 2 years of his teaching in two AP U.S. history classes. Pine is a middle-school teacher with 18 years of experience in rural Maine. He had a passion for the fundamental features of civics in U.S. history, for the rights and obligations of citizens. He anchored his teaching in concerns of civil rights and duties. We have 3 weeks of data from two different sections of his social studies classes.

In addition to tapes and transcripts of classroom teaching, we have collected a large set of data from practicing historians. During the academic year 1990–1991, I had the opportunity to discuss history with and observe history discussions among a group of prominent historians at the Center for Advanced Study in the Behavioral Sciences in Palo Alto. Part of the data collection effort took the form of an open-ended interview that dealt with such issues as: What is history? Why are you a historian? Why should we teach history? What does it mean to establish a case? How is something explained (or refuted) in history?

(Leinhardt, Stainton, & Virji, in press; Leinhardt, Stainton, Virji, & Odoroff, in press). A second set of interviews involved systematic, focused analyses of specific documents by three of the historians (Leinhardt, 1993a). The interviews were taped and transcribed, then analyzed.

These then are our databases for investigating the learning and teaching of history. We start the discussion by anchoring it on a working definition of what history is and what reasoning in history might look like.

DEFINING THE CONTENT

What is history? For Schama, it is the study of the past and its "messiness"; for others, it is a collection of heroic epics, one of the social sciences to be explored, or a specific set of "facts" and/or "stories" that help to define our sense of self: personal, communal, national, and global. Teachers regularly teach something that is called history. Students in history classes are faced with negotiating with their teachers its mutually understood tacit definition. Students and teachers establish the relative emphasis of causal relationships among events, the story of people, the system of social structures and institutions, quantitative analyses of patterns of movement or production, and the themes of human struggle and development. Given the multiplicity of meanings, students must come to understand that in each new learning situation one's definition of history will depend on the perspectives of history teachers, their classmates, and the perspectives of the historians whose work they read. History has multiple meanings and definitions; learning history includes understanding the sources of these meanings and articulating them.

In our research, we have discussed these differing definitions in terms of the dialogues among the multiple voices that we sense affect both teachers' and historians' lives (Leinhardt, Stainton, & Virji, in press).[1] The teachers' definitions spring from their pragmatic response to understanding the discipline of history, the textbooks and curriculum guides, the parental and school communities, policy critics, and the students' own assumptions. Although teachers are often held responsible for all that happens in their classes, they are not always free to decide what they will teach and how they will define the subject they are teaching. Teachers' definitions of history are thus a negotiated process, not simply their own personal construction.

---

[1]This section is drawn from Leinhardt, Stainton, and Virji (in press).

Historians, like Schama, also negotiate the meaning of history. They carry out their negotiations with professional colleagues, with students, and also with the society at large. However, they have greater flexibility and power in deciding what their discipline is and complete authority over how they engage in it. We used the explicit discussion of history from the set of interviews with seven historians as the basis for our understanding of the historians' view.

Teachers

To gain a sense of the range of teachers' definitions, we used the explicit statements about history that emerged during class discussions carried out in the first week of school. We considered these as views of what history is from each teacher's perspective. We further supported the inferred definition by direct interviews.

Of the two teachers we examined in this study, Sterling took a stance that was most strongly historical. Sterling loved history as an academic intellectual pursuit; she was an enthusiastic consumer both of popular history (writers such as Tuchman and Schama) and of historiography and philosophy of history. Peterbene clearly enjoyed the inherent opportunity of argumentation that studying history afforded, and he used history to focus on the personae, and on the social and moral development of the adolescents he was teaching. We chose to observe these two teachers in part because of their expertise (as defined by the reputations they had among their former students and by their students' consistently high and similar performances on the AP history exam), and in part because of their very different approaches to teaching history.

Figure 7.1 is a web of concepts and connections designed to display the views of history that emerged in Sterling's class over the first five lessons. The web of ideas associated with history emerged as part of the class discussion based on evolving understandings and formal readings. In Fig. 7.1 history is shown as linked to five constructs: themes, methods, events, interpretation, and construction by historians. The methods of history were discussed as including analysis, synthesis, periodicity, and interpretation. Events, interpretations, and construction were interconnected in class discussions, and formed a loop of ideas. Change was the link and, as such, formed a key idea for defining history. History was seen as both documenting change and itself changing. The change of history is shown because interpretations change over time and because different historians with their own intellectual, social class, and cultural identities each could be expected to

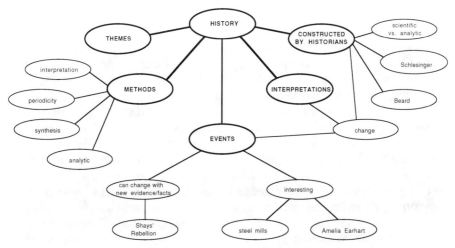

FIG. 7.1. Sterling: What is history?

take a different view. Change in history happened when new evidence or facts came to light. As is noted on the web, specific references exemplified the discussions over the first week of classes. Sterling's definition was grounded in the specifics of history itself as well as in the practice of historical inquiry.

Peterbene's class gave a different set of emphases in their discussions about history, as the net in Fig. 7.2 shows. Peterbene wanted to challenge the notion that students might have held that history was facts and dates alone. Therefore, the discussions led by Peterbene merged

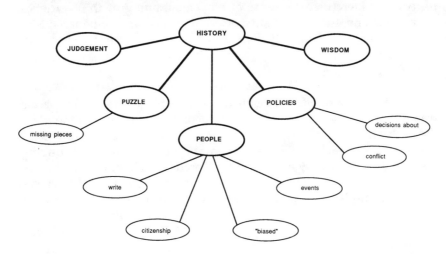

FIG. 7.2. Peterbene: What is history?

issues of purpose and content. For example, acquiring knowledge of history was deemed important because it helped to develop wisdom and ensure social justice. As shown on the net, history was described as consisting of puzzles, people, and policies. Of Peterbene's central nodes, people is the one most elaborated upon: People write history; people are citizens; people are biased in writing and interpreting history; and people live events. His ideas were less interconnected and the discussions less specific than Sterling's in terms of examples from historical writing or analysis. On the other hand, the discussions of historical events were embellished by Peterbene's own personal experiences and those of the students. Woven through the dialogues in the first few days was the strong suggestion that knowledge of history both helped to inform decisions and was about critical decisions made by individuals. Issues of interpretation and change were hinted at through the idea that historians themselves were biased by their own identities. The discussion was grounded on the pragmatics of history as useful and guiding information.

When we examined our interviews with historians we discovered with some surprise that all of the major concepts that became teacher nodes in Figs. 7.1 and 7.2 (except for Sterling's "themes") were mentioned by our historians. We thought that teachers might have communicated ideas about history in their classes that historians simply would not mention. It was only in specific examples, such as Shays' rebellion, that teachers discussed ideas not mentioned by historians. On the other hand, historians mentioned with some frequency ideas that were not mentioned by either teachers or their students. For example, historians frequently referred to ideas of causality, the relationship between history and literature, the sense of movement and growth of societies over time, and the distinction between history and antiquarianism; these topics were not directly discussed during the classes we observed.

Historians

Perhaps the most significant distinction between teachers and historians was not in specific ideas but in the structural relationship of the ideas themselves. In order to reveal this, we selected one historian's discussion for a closer analysis. Figure 7.3 shows the central ideas surrounding the definition of history expressed by Florencia Mallon, a Latin Americanist and distinguished professor of history. Mallon said, "History is a principled and humanistic dialogue between us and our ancestors . . . [it] is the reconstruction of past events, through a dialogue between surviving evidence about the past and existing analytical, theoretical, and political concerns in the present" (Leinhardt, Stainton, & Virji, in press, p. 14).

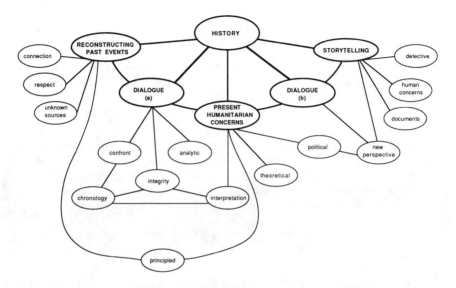

FIG. 7.3. Mallon: What is history?

The net representing Mallon's ideas shows that she emphasized the tensions inherent in a set of dialogues or discourses. Two dialogues anchored her definitions: one between reconstruction of the past and concerns of the present, the other between concerns of the present and principled story telling. These dialogues and their respective concepts (past, present, storytelling) in turn link to other systems. Reconstruction of the past required a chronology as well as principled understanding of the circumstances of the past. Principles and perspectives formed a second strand of connections, tying the central dialogues together. The ideas that Mallon used to help define history (reconstruction, dialogues, present concerns, storytelling) were themselves all interconnected. Many of the second-level ideas, such as interpretation, also served to connect the first layer of concepts. Thus, the core ideas were both directly connected and also interconnected through the attributed concepts. Mallon and the other historians built their ideas from several traditions of history: humanities, analytic social science, applied social science (political science, economics, sociology), and descriptive reconstructive sciences such as archaeology and anthropology. These traditions mapped onto the central nodes of Mallon's definitions as well. For example, storytelling mapped onto humanities, whereas reconstructing mapped onto anthropology.

Schama identified some key ideas expressed by the teachers and historians in this study. Like Peterbene, he described history as a discipline that "spoke loudly . . . to our concerns" (Schama, 1991, p.

31). Like Sterling, he described history as something complex that goes beyond a "how-to manual filled with analogies" (p. 31). Schama, like Mallon, expressed a sense of "the study of the past in all its splendid messiness" (p. 31). Understanding the similarities and differences in what constituted a workable definition of history for teachers and for historians helped us to form a definition of our own.

> History is a process of constructing, reconstructing, and interpreting past events, ideas, and institutions from surviving or inferential evidence in order to understand and make meaningful who and what we are today. The process involves dialogues with alternative voices from the past itself, with the recorders of the past, and with present interpreters. The process also involves constructing coherent, powerful narratives that describe and interpret the events, as well as skillful analyses of quantitative and qualitative information, from a theoretical perspective. (Leinhardt, Stainton, & Virji, in press, p. 18)

We wanted to develop a working definition of history because our program of research takes the stance that teaching and learning are situated in the particular (Schwab, 1978). They are situated in the particular social system and its dialogues and in the particular disciplinary system and its construction. Thus, throughout our research we have been interested in the nature of mindful dialogue and the process of meaningful construction present in the practice of students, teachers, and historians.

History is layered, and the teaching of it, like other subjects, involves not only a process of acquiring the stuff of the discipline but acquiring a particular rhetorical stance toward it. The artifacts of any given course (multiple texts, documents, discussions, and required essays) and the roles of the teachers and students are unique. Even if it were in an incomprehensible language, one could stumble into a history class and not confuse it with a physics class or a foreign language class, because these artifacts and roles tend to inscribe and define the school-based discipline of history. That uniqueness and generality (the specific history class and the universal class) is established and negotiated in the first few days of school. The first few days of school make explicit, for a moment, the social and intellectual rules that will be tacit for the rest of the year, rules scarcely visible to the observer of the seamless discussions and reports that will take place as the year advances. We chose to examine these first few days for just that reason.[2]

---

[2]This section is drawn from Stainton and Leinhardt (1992).

BEGINNINGS

School years in general and individual classes in particular engage in nuanced balancing acts at the beginning of every school year. Students and teachers together balance what is explicit and stated as required sets of actions and expectations with what is implicit and understood because of the shared culture of the particular school and class. They also balance the actions of the class with the expectations of what is to be accomplished by the class. In AP American History classes the teacher has the privilege, and to some extent the honor, of teaching the equivalent of a college-level course in high school. However, the AP courses have a second attribute: They are designed to prepare students to pass an exam that serves as proof that the students know as much about particular subjects as a particular college hopes that its own students taking its own courses know upon completion. So, although at one level the courses are supposed to be an early experience in college-level thinking and reasoning, on another level they are intensive exam preparation courses.

These AP exams have both powerful symbolic stature and very real financial implications. A strong and highly motivated student can place out of as much as an entire year of college work by receiving college-level credit for it while in high school. This achievement could save the student and family as much as $20,000. Few other high school courses carry that kind of an incentive structure behind them. Because of this financial and academic importance, the relationship between student and teacher in these AP classes is somewhat different. The students look to the teacher as their ally in preparing for an experience that is framed and specified by outside forces. This scenario is in contrast to the more usual situation where the teacher is the power figure to be struggled with and/or placated. Both of the teachers, Sterling and Peterbene, capitalized on this changed relationship.

In the first five of their classes, Sterling and Peterbene both set the goal of achieving good scores on the exam as being one that was reachable for the students; the teachers also set themselves up as being part of the team that could help achieve that goal. In analyzing the features of these first five classes, we made use of two metaphors for teaching: the coach and the artistic director. These metaphors help to evoke the nature and level of discussions that we witnessed as the school year got underway.

Current discussions of school reform rely heavily on the metaphor of teacher as coach in order to contrast it with teacher as dictator (benevolent or not) and teacher as omniscient being (Brown, 1992). Coaches lead, design, cajole, motivate, and organize. But they also specify the nature of the opposition of the other team as they prepare the team members for a game with score cards, winners, and losers. In these history class settings, of course, there is no other team and no score card (we resist the "test grade as score card" analogy), so the sports metaphor is only partially useful here. We also invoked the metaphor of artistic director for the teacher: Artistic directors have the personal history of expert performance because they have actually been there and succeeded. Artistic directors first and foremost love the enterprise (e.g., ballet or music); they select target pieces both for utility and for inherent beauty as exemplars for their students. So, too, with our teachers. They had been successful history students themselves, they both had knowledge and love of the subject, and they chose examples for elaborated discussions both because of the specific knowledge that would be useful and for the importance that the examples had for them personally.

The "stuff" of the first few days of AP history included having the students deal with forms and a large amount of paperwork; it also included exposing them to the massive and intimidating syllabi and texts. The coach had to guide the students through the maze. As artistic director, the teacher had to inspire them to value as well as to reach the goals. The two classes had differing syllabi and texts, but the quantity of material was equally daunting for both groups. Both teachers negotiated a careful line between the school-level requirements (administrative busywork) and the course-level requirements (superficially trivial but ultimately useful). For example, both teachers made jokes or apologies about the petty, school-required forms but went into extensive and specific details about notetaking and notebook management.

Sterling and Peterbene viewed the mechanics of organizing the discourses and written material of the course to be both symbolic of a systematic approach to the volume of material to be learned and an actual device for building that approach. These assumptions did not go unchallenged by the students. Several students tried to negotiate a less burdensome role for themselves as notetakers and notebook keepers. The coaches ordered even more practice and the artistic directors tried to show even stronger connections between the actions of intellectual record keeping and intellectual performance. As Stainton and Leinhardt (1992) pointed out, the seemingly mundane issue of notetaking reflected central concerns these teachers had for their students coming to grips with the content of history. Students would need to learn history well, and doing so would in turn require that the students be able to access their own knowledge in unfamiliar intellectual settings. The specifics of the exams would be unknown in advance, but the knowledge needed would have been "covered." To score high on the exam, students would have to access their knowledge and rearrange it in a meaningful way. Keeping notes that were complete, meaningful, and structurally well organized would, the teachers felt, help in preparing for that rearranging process, both by making the material more accessible and by setting up a device for self-monitoring by the students. In addition, both teachers felt that taking thoughtful notes from texts and class discussions was a college-level activity. Given that the course experience was supposed to be more than just exam preparation, the students were thus encouraged to rehearse "playing college."

When observing teachers having students engage in experiencing history as a process of constructing the past, it may seem somewhat trivial and distancing to consider the more mechanical aspects of being a student, such as notetaking. However, these activities serve to expose students to one of the difficult aspects of history. Because history is largely a discipline of the printed word and of many competing ideas, keeping track of those ideas and being able to readily access them is no small matter. Developing ways of taking useful notes from text and oral discussions that would permit efficient access was one way of dealing with the task.

If the beginning of the year sets up an expectation of the roles of teachers and students and a kind of tension between the mechanical or structural aspects of a course, the rest of the year constitutes a development and continuous elaboration of the meanings of history and its content. Two features dominate the evolution of instruction in history: explanations of historical phenomena, and the development of cases as locations for reasoning. Over the course of the school year teachers and students slowly shifted their stances so that students gained more and more of the intellectual and temporal space of the class. Where teachers led the dialogues by modeling and questioning in the beginning, students modeled and questioned as the year progressed.

EXPLAINING

Instructional explanations within a particular subject matter serve the dual functions of making explicit statements of and about ideas in a field and serving as implicit models for reasoning and thinking in that field. Instructional explanations also highlight what it is that constitutes a question within a discipline. The role and task of the teacher are to query, explicate, and model, whereas the role of the students is to participate by learning both to query and to generate new ideas and answers.

Instructional explanations, as distinct from discipline-based explanations and self-explanations, are designed to teach, regardless of whether the explanation is given by a teacher or a student (Leinhardt, 1990). However, the particular form and impact of an instructional explanation are dependent on the subject matter and classroom within which it is situated. Instructional explanations serve to clarify concepts and procedures, events and ideas, and rhetorical forms and values in ways that help students to understand, learn, and use knowledge in flexible ways. Instructional explanations are required to be complete, but completion does not require the teacher to complete all aspects in one episode. Throughout the course of discussion the aspects must eventually be made explicit by one or more of the participants. Therefore, instructional explanations do not tend to be parsimonious in the way that disciplinary explanations are; they tend to be redundant and exhaustive.

Forms and Occasions

In history, the implicit and explicit queries that stimulate explanations are quite different from those in mathematics. The forms of explanations are quite different form those in mathematics. The forms of explanations that answer queries are also unique.[3] Because the nature of our database in history classes is so extensive, we have been able to trace explanations (and case development) that occur within a single class as well as those that extend over many months (Leinhardt, 1993b). From these traces, we detected two different forms of explanation: *blocked* and *ikat*.[4] Blocked explanations are cohesive, take place in a single unit of time, and they tend not to be interrupted by other topics. Blocked explanations stand alone, and although they may be repeated, or elaborated upon, they are, in general, comprehensively presented on the first occasion. Blocked explanations are especially likely to occur in history discussions about specific events and their causes and consequences.

In contrast, ikat explanations are extended and, as their name suggests, woven over time and intertwined with other ideas. Ideas that are presented in an ikat form of explanation are incomplete and incoherent at first; they may appear as fleeting mentions or asides initially, and only gradually gain in visibility and importance weeks later. Ikat explanations tend to evolve as layers of meaning and

---

[3]This section is drawn from Leinhardt (1993b).

[4]Ikat is a method of weaving cloth in which the overall design emerges from repeating patterns and shapes formed by different colors in the warp and weft.

examples are deliberately added to the sketch that introduces the pattern. This form is in contrast to a blocked "design" that is complete at its first occasion. In a way that is similar to Van Fraasen's (1988) description of the role of a theory in science explanations, historical themes emerge as a prime focus for ikat forms of explanations (Leinhardt, 1993b).

Four occasions in history classes prompted these two forms of instructional explanations, blocked and ikat: events, structures, themes, and metasystems. *Events* are the short narrative nuggets of history, including heroes and villains, critical problems, and causes and consequences. *Structures* are the social/political systems of societies, such as economic systems, governmental systems, religious institutions, and social class organization, that act as long-term backdrops as well as stimuli for the events. *Themes* are the long-term interpretive constructs of history and are both devices for explaining and the objects of explanations. Themes help to frame events and explain the long-term changes in structures, for example, the tensions between mercantile and agrarian interests in the early American colonial period. Finally, the *metasystems* of history are also occasions for instructional explanations. Metasystems include the tools and dispositions of history, for example, analysis, synthesis, hypothesis generation, perspective taking, and interpretation.

In theory, all four kinds of occasions for explanations could be presented in either blocked or ikat explanational form. However, in the classes we observed, some occasions were more likely to be explained using one form rather than the other. Blocked explanations were most likely to be the explanation of choice for events, such as the Constitutional Convention or the elections of 1820 and 1824. Blocked explanations were often used to present specific structures within a domain, such as the system of checks and balances in the Constitution. Blocked explanations were less frequently used to explain themes or tensions (e.g., local versus national control), because the very nature of themes is that they gain and lose prominence. Because themes rarely disappear from view, the themes of an era lend themselves especially well to an ikat form of explanation. Blocked explanations sometimes found their way into metasystem explanations in the form of constraints or definitions of what constituted legitimate evidence or how one was to approach an analysis.

Ikat explanational forms could be used for all four occasions as well. Events were most naturally portrayed in blocked form; some events, such as the ending of slavery, could have had an ikat form. Slavery ends and does not end many times, as when the sale of slaves was ended, when slavery was outlawed in the Northwest Territories, after the

Emancipation Proclamation, when the doctrine of separate but equal was struck down, or when the Voting Rights Act was passed. If the event of ending slavery had been presented with nuances of meaning attached to the economic, political, and social institution of slavery in a particular pattern over time, then the single "event" of ending slavery could have been "explained" as the theme of freedom or of governmental change and growth in an ikat form. The Constitution's elastic clause (a structure) (Article 1, Section 8, Clause 18) is very specific and was presented during the discussion in Sterling's class that dealt with sections of the Constitution, but its significance was not made clear in a blocked way. The implications of the elastic clause were woven through the discussions in many lessons before finally being fully discussed in the context of the early years of the FDR administration. Students learned the metasystems from both blocked and ikat explanations.

Metasystems. The four occasions for explanations in history classes were connected to and influenced by one another. For example, Sterling, as a part of her coaching role, explained how students should generate and develop a hypothesis as part of learning the metasystems of history. In one particular case, the explanation was started with general information. Sterling then added constraints by indicating what topics students should avoid, and finally used an example to demonstrate the power and functional utility of carefully worded hypothesis statements. Sterling explained hypothesis from the base of a specific example: "The American Revolution, once started, could not be confined to political matters, but loosened social and economic constraints that had impeded the emergence of an egalitarian society." She explained that there were constraints on hypothesis selection—a hypothesis should be interesting, neither too old nor too recent, and have properties that permitted further analysis. In modeling the example, she flagged the use of rich, specific, and "historical" vocabulary. Sterling explained the evolution of hypotheses by identifying guides for their selection and by demonstrating the role of the hypothesis statement in writing an historical essay. Metasystem explanations are different from other history explanations because of their coaching quality. In class, Sterling and Peterbene tended to "own" most metasystem explanations—that is, students did not generally take the role of specifying features for metasystem constructs in the way they did for events or interpretations of events.

On the other hand, students did engage in actual perspective taking and subtext interpretations, both of which were instances of metasystem occasions. The distinction here is subtle and points to the layered nature of teaching history and of practicing history. The teachers owned the discourse about perspective taking, but students dominated the activity of perspective taking and interpretation. For example, in discussions of the various interpretations of the Constitutional Convention, Sterling asked students both to describe the particular aspect under discussion and to identify historians who made one or another interpretation. The students engaged in explaining the interpretational debates. Figure 7.4, adapted from Leinhardt (1993b), shows the discussion among students over interpretations of the ratification agreements.

The top node in the figure shows the Constitution. The Constitution was being discussed with respect to the possible arguments in favor of ratification and with respect to the interpretations of those ratification arguments. The three reasons for support of ratification put forth as potential arguments by the students included the threat of political anarchy, the need for economic stability, and the threat of foreign invasion if the new government appeared weak. Economic stability as an issue was discussed from two different perspectives – the self-interest of the writers (of the Federalist papers) and the need for general economic stability that could benefit all. According to the students, the first of these economic interpretations was held by Beard – the Constitution was not a selfless, inspired document but a mechanism for protecting the property of the framers. The second of these positions, the need for economic stability, was held by Commager and Hofstadter.

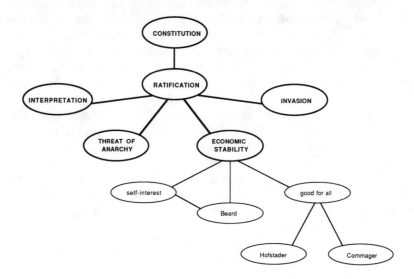

FIG. 7.4. Interpretation and perspectives of the Constitution.

Students, in working with Sterling, thus "explained" an event using two different pieces of metasystem knowledge: perspectives of different arguers, and interpretations of different authors.

In the series of exchanges that formed the explanation, Sterling and the students together wove the students' comments on the ratification process, their arguments for why the Constitution should be ratified, and the positions of the historians the students were reading. Sterling engaged them in analyzing layers of interpretation and perspective taking. This explanation was the beginning of a process of showing students the different positions of authors when describing and analyzing particular events. It also helped demonstrate that a part of history was understanding a sense of how history interpreted itself (Collingwood, 1946). This class dialogue set up the conditions for students to recognize that their role made them responsible for understanding both the specifics of a time and place and the interpretations of those specifics.

Events. Another example of a blocked explanation is for an event. In this case, we consider a narrative telling of the story of a particular event. Blocked event narrative explanations are the lay person's view of history—the farmers at Concord Bridge, the ride of Paul Revere. At the college and advanced high school levels, these events are small pebbles, bearing a relationship to the overall enterprise of history that is similar to the relationship of number facts to mathematics. Events are necessary and valued as knowledge units, but the real work of history goes on beyond them. They are, for the most part, interpreted in light of their cause-and-effect-like roles with respect to structures. For example, of the two blocked event explanations in Sterling's class given during the discussion of the Constitutional Convention, one, the impeachment of President Andrew Johnson, was in response to a query.

The overarching issue under discussion was checks and balances as a part of the Constitution. The class discussion focussed on the provision in the Constitution for removing presidents from office. Figure 7.5 is a net representation of part of the discussion. Bills of impeachment were explained as being a part of checks and balances. In that context, the students wanted to know who among the past presidents had been impeached. (For a while, this was a subdialogue that broke into an argument over Lyndon Johnson and Richard Nixon as impeached presidents.) Sterling answered the question by discussing the case of Andrew Johnson. She walked students through the Johnson case, showing justifiable and nonjustifiable reasons for his impeachment in the Bill of Indictment.

The event flavor of the blocked explanation was captured by the

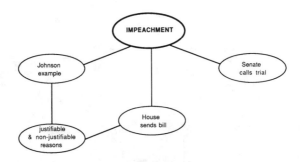

FIG. 7.5. Impeachment.

vividness of the narrative details that Sterling provided—Johnson was fishing when Congress voted; he was an obstinate person; his congressional enemies almost got him but they failed by one vote. Although the event was never referred to again during the year, the theme embedded in the event was one that recurred, namely, the way that political motives influence enactment of law. What was particularly interesting about this explanation of an event was that it showed how the structural knowledge about the process of impeachment was incorporated into the event-based explanation. It was also one of the earliest occasions in which students initiated the query that started the explanational dialogue.

Structures.   In considering an occasion for blocked structural explanations, a distinction needs to be made between structural elements in the analysis of an event, such as the one just discussed, and the structures of society that explanations focus on. In the analysis of an event, structural elements include consideration of political, social, and economic forces and conflicts as motives or pressures that determine the course of an event or, at least, the interpretation of such an event. Structures of society are the organizing elements, frameworks, or representative institutions that support the society, such as the Congress, the Constitution, the economic system, and the power enfranchisement system. The excerpt described next deals with the structures of the colonial governments and their relationship to the structure of the government of the mother country, England. In the net in Fig. 7.6, only a small part of the entire explanation, that focusing on structure, is analyzed.

As Fig. 7.6 shows, the colonial governments were presented as being analogous to the government of the mother country. The position of the king was parallel to that of the governor. Both executives had divine appointments, the king's from God and the governor's from the king

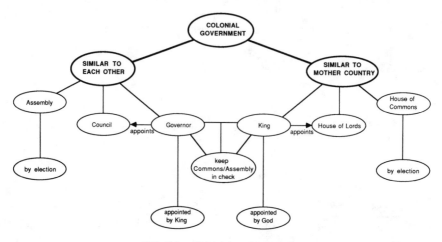

FIG. 7.6.   Colonial government.

and, by inference, from God. The king appointed members of the House of Lords and the governor appointed his council—both of these were the upper houses of the legislature. Both governments had an elected house as well, the Assembly and the House of Commons. The political task for the king was to keep power in the upper houses and the executive branch (king and governor), and to be wary of growth of power in the Commons or in the assemblies. This particular explanation of the structure of the colonial government was given almost totally by Sterling. She used references to political theory, governmental limitations, and unifying social features between England and the colonies to show connections that existed by analogy as well as by law. These ties based on similarity (along with a common language and general Anglo dominance) would later be used as arguments against separation from England by America in the explanation of the event of the Declaration of Independence. The dialogue in this explanation helped to construct some of the threads needed for the ikat explanation of the theme of power and struggles for power that went on throughout the year.

Themes.   Finally, we consider a blocked explanation of a theme. Because of their nature, themes in history classes are usually woven into the rest of the material and their explanations tend to be more ikat than blocked in texture. However, in this rather unusual instance, some thematic elements of a blocked explanation of a theme were presented in separable pieces. The example in Fig. 7.7 is an explanation that included four of the major course themes: slavery, North/South tension, agrarian/mercantile tension, and compromise. Slavery was discussed as the main tension between the North and the South, but the North/South tension

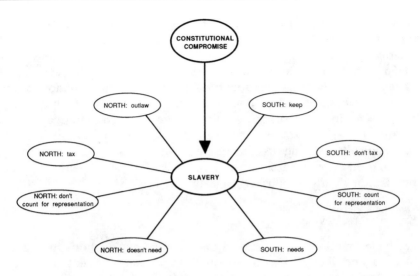

FIG. 7.7. North/South positions and compromise on slavery.

was also seen as a type of tension between different economies. During the construction of the government, these tensions were addressed through the long series of compromises reached between different power brokers. By the time of the Civil War, these tensions were no longer sites for compromise. The compromise by the writers of the Constitution on the treatment of slaves was used by Sterling as an example on multiple levels. The segment shown in Fig. 7.7 dealt both with the specifics of the Constitutional compromise on slavery (blocked theme) and with the more complex theme of compromise and debate that concerned the Constitution as well as the entire period up through the Jacksonian democracy (ikat theme). The explanation began with the query: "What are the compromises that were made by the framers of the Constitution, and how did they foreshadow the events to come during the first 100 years of the new Republic?"

Figure 7.7 shows the four points of the compromise that emerged from the dialogue that followed. On the left-hand side, all of the North's main arguments are displayed: outlaw slavery as morally reprehensible; if slaves are present, tax them per capita; do not count slaves for representation as their interests are not being represented; and the slaves are not or should not be needed. On the right-hand side of Fig. 7.7 are the South's counterarguments. In this blocked theme explanation, Sterling used several rhetorical devices. One device was the use of positional voices ("a lot of Northerners said") as a means to orient the student to the sides of the debate. Another orienting device was the use of references to previous explanations such as, "in that first one." The "first" referred to the first in a list of four areas of disagreement, or areas for compromise that were being discussed. A third device was the use of a series of partial and complete if/then statements. Students were slow to master these three techniques in their own dialogues. However, these devices certainly helped students keep track of the situation under discussion. Long after the students showed a good sense of what should be present in an explanation, they were still exhibiting a certain awkwardness with some features of the explanation genre. Students had difficulty making use of orienting information and integrating points from prior discussions. In their discussions, they neither aligned points, nor clearly established causality.

Explanatory Devices

We have identified two forms of instructional explanations in history, blocked and ikat. These occur on four occasions: event, structure, metasystem, and theme. Explanations, whether teacher-given, student-given, or shared, are intended to teach and respond to an explicit or implicit query. Teachers use explanatory devices in the service of instructional explanation that include representations, examples, and analogies. These devices can both enhance and detract from an explanation. At times an explanation may get lost in the "entailments" of an explanatory device; at other times these devices can be powerful tools for explaining particularly problematic concepts in a domain. We have gone underneath the structure of explanation to look at two devices for enhancing explanations in history: analogy and narratives. In this section, we explore one, analogy.

One way for a teacher to explain, and for students to link the unfamiliar to the familiar, is to use analogies (McCarthy & Leinhardt, 1993). The use of analogy involves accessing a familiar base, and then mapping it to a less familiar target (Gentner & Gentner, 1983). The mapping sets up a framework that can support understanding, reasoning, and problem solving. With very complex domains, the need for multiple analogies, with bridges, arises. The bulk of the research on analogy use has been done in the normative domains of science, and on individuals in the context of problem solving. We wanted to see how analogy functioned in a less normative domain, history, for instructional explanations.

We sampled 10 lessons each from Sterling, Peterbene, and Pine, coding for analogy by occasion (event, structure, theme, metasystem), and author (teacher, student, text). From these extracted analogies, we developed a model of the process of analogy use, its function (purpose), and its functionality (how well it achieved that purpose). In general, analogy was used during instructional explanations in history in ways similar to those sketched in the psychological literature (Gentner & Gentner, 1983; Spiro, Feltovich, Coulson, & Anderson, 1989). For example, we have seen Sterling access a base and target, and check for student familiarity with the base. Then the objects, attributes, and interrelationships of the base are introduced and mapped to those of the target; the particular feature of the target is made salient. This is the full process, but there are also many partial instances. Both full and partial analogies may meet with success or failure. At times, students and teacher become lost in discussion of the more salient base, whereas at other times, when familiarity with the base is falsely assumed, conversation proceeds to the target, and it is never clear in what way the two are similar.

Analogies occurred for each of the four historical occasions. As one might expect, more analogies were used to explain events and structures than metasystems and themes. Event and structure analogies tended to be blocked, whereas metasystem and theme analogies tended to be ikat. All event analogies mapped event to event, and all structure analogies mapped structure to structure; however, there were two different functions—one literal and one contextual. Literal analogies were restricted, equating specific features of events or structures: the Gulf of Sidra to the Gulf of Tonkin, *Plessy v. Ferguson* to *William v. Mississippi*, Great Society to New Deal. Contextual analogies were more broad, and were used to show the context, importance, or impact of an event or structure. King George's reaction to the Declaration of Independence was likened to the spinning of the ghost's head in the film *Beetlejuice*; Watergate was compared to using steroids; Communist Party support of Wallace was like the kiss of death; Roosevelt Corollary was like Monday morning quarterbacking.

Themes often linked various contextual analogies through ikat explanation. These were instances where the same theme was referred to with different analogies—the power theme linked "Congress was in the driver's seat" to "the Republicans were in the harness and were pulling in the reins." The theme of progression or development appeared as "laying the groundwork," "they were on the road to," and "served as an anchor for the future." Sometimes a theme was presented as an analogy, as in "playing the game" for the varied forms of political, diplomatic, and wartime maneuvering. When these analogies are repeated, as in the use of the swinging pendulum to characterize policy change, not only within a class over time, but across teachers and in popular history, the student is given a useful lens to aid in recognizing patterns in varied eras and circumstances.

Analogies used to explain metasystems were also woven together in ikat fashion over time. In explaining how to apply subtext interpretation to an analysis of the Constitution, Pine referred to learning a foreign language, learning the vocabulary, the need for continued practice, playing the game by the rules, and establishing a road map. Sterling, in pointing out the need for careful and critical analysis, warned students, "there may be more meat on those bones [of that subject]," not to judge a book by its cover, and that they must try to shoot holes through an author's thesis. Peterbene reminded students that in history, two plus two doesn't always equal four, and therein is the need for analysis.

Analogies were introduced and owned by either teacher or students, or were shared between them. Student-posed analogies offered a window into their reasoning about an historical event, structure, and so forth. Teachers either picked up and extended student analogies or explicitly corrected faulty ones. Because one way present-minded students make sense of the past is to compare its events to those in the present, the correction of false mappings is very important lest students apply analogy mindlessly.

Failure of analogy to function in bringing about understanding could result from mindless use by the teacher. An instance of analogy as both friend and foe to understanding happened to Peterbene's class. He referred to Nixon's foreign policy as containment in sheep's clothing, and later in the period described Nixon as a dyed-in-the-wool Republican. After class, a student commented that Peterbene had been talking a lot about sheep that day. Although this may have been the joke of a very bright student, it may also have been the result of analogies that failed, either because of student unfamiliarity with, or the overvividness of, the bases. Another reason for analogy breakdown may be the failure of students to follow subtle feature mappings. In one instance, Pine contrasted perennials and wildflowers, noting the extreme care needed for cultivation of the first versus the stubborn resiliency of the second. In an extremely long and entwined discussion, he began by mapping democracy to wildflowers and ended by mapping it to perennials. Although he had indicated that democracy has features of both, one might assume that some students may have been left wondering which was the case.

Analogy is influenced by the domain and context of its use. History is more interpretive than science. When multiple analogies are used to explain the struggle for power in the Colonial period, they are intended to explain multiple perspectives on a historical event or theme, not to unpack various aspects of a single phenomenon, such as electricity. In history, analogies appear in the course of a dialogue with 30 participants. The possibilities for both reasoned extension and diverse breakdowns both exist. Analogy in the history classroom is a device in the service of explanation intended to increase student understanding of, and ability to reason in, history. As such, analogies can be used mindfully to bring about these goals, or used mindlessly as novel ends in themselves.

Explanations in Context

We have given specific examples of types of blocked explanations and discussed devices that were used to accomplish them (analogies and narratives). Explanations take up approximately 78% of an average, 1058-line class protocol in Sterling's class. In a sample of 10 randomly selected lessons, 25% of the explanations were of themes, 22% were event/theme combinations, 20% were of events, 5% were metasystems, 4% were structures, and 2% were event structures. All of the explanations were at least partially shared between the teacher and the students, who were active participants. Generally, Sterling started discussions with a broad, global question and then asked a series of supporting questions. Under this didactic structure, there was room for both the students and the teacher to move and change directions or roles. When the students could answer, they did so, and Sterling either modified, expanded, or summarized their response. If they could not answer, then Sterling either built a more elaborate presentation of context or answered herself. The format permitted major interruptions in the flow and queries from the students. The task for the student was to gradually develop the ability to reason in history. The kinds of questions and answers students provided as the course progressed were indicative of that growth.

Over the course of the year, students gradually assumed more and more of the intellectual responsibility and did more of the talking. The nature of students' talk in the classroom was investigated further by examining two of Sterling's class days—one early in October, the other late in November. Two analyses were performed on this subset of data. The first analysis compared the structural role played by the teacher with the role played by the students in the dialogue on both days. The second analysis compared explanations given by one student on each of those two days, to examine the development of student explanations.

The October class had less class dialogue than the November class (841 vs. 1135 lines of protocol). There were, however, approximately the same number of exchanges (changes of speaker), 221 versus 231. The modest increase in exchanges was probably insignificant given the increase in the number of lines of protocol. Within reason, the more exchanges there are, the more there is a sense of conversation rather than lecture. The number of student-to-student moves is also indicative of conversation, but one that is more or less centered around the teacher. In this situation, one student speaks, followed by another; in these cases, control did not return to the teacher after each student statement. Over the 2 months, student centering grew from 108 to 133 student moves. One might also consider the length of a speech segment, because as the length of the segment increases, so does that speaker's control increase. There was a dramatic decrease (by half) in the number of lines of uninterrupted teacher talk (from 104 to 46 lines), with a comparable increase in the number of lines of uninterrupted student talk, three times as much (from 12 to 39). This indicates an increase in student control. Another way to illustrate the growth in student control was to calculate the number of "control switches," meaning the number of times the topic was changed regardless of who initiated the change. In general, the more topic changes there were, the more the students were actively participating in the class. The number of changes increased from 15 to 38 over the 2 months. Finally, we coded control of topic. We noted whether teacher or student initiated a topic or issue, regardless of who was actually speaking particular lines. For example, when a student asked who had been impeached and the teacher responded, the student "controlled" the teacher's lines of protocol. Conversely, when a student responded to a teacher query, the teacher controlled the lines of protocol. Student control of the dialogue rose from 86 to 453 lines of protocol.

Student Example of Explaining

Line counts and control switches are structural descriptors of explanations. A more substantive issue addresses the degree to which students were learning explanations as a form of reasoning. The following excerpt imparts the flavor of early answers students gave before they learned to construct reasoned, well-grounded explanations. The example is an exchange between Sterling and a student, Paul, in early October. Sterling asked, "Under this framework of government, under this Continental Congress, what were men able to do? And they were men." Paul interpreted the question as being one that asked about pioneers and answered: "Uh, I think one of the biggest things that they did, that we talked about yesterday, was the establishment of the first settlement in the Northwest area [−] states." He used his vague knowledge of the Westward movement and pioneers. His authority for this reasoning was the previous day's class discussion. What Sterling was trying to start was a discussion about the set of powers and political structure put into place by the Continental Congress. She was looking for statements that addressed the relationship between the new government and foreign powers, not a discussion of the pioneer spirit; however, it was too early in the term for students to have learned either the rhetorical style of the class or the nature of historical questions. Therefore, neither Paul nor any other student formulated a historical explanation as an answer to the question they could not yet interpret.

Two months later, Paul provided a lengthy and detailed explanation of the issues surrounding the South's decision to secede. Sterling said, "Okay Paul, let's get started with the collapse of King Cotton because that diplomatically fits in." Figure 7.8 shows the concepts included in Paul's response.

In his long and detailed reply, Paul covered almost all of the salient points of diplomacy between the South and England from an economic perspective. His reply was both an explanation and an instance of historical reasoning. He had facts at his fingertips to show that England was oversupplied with cotton, not only from the South but also from its eastern sources (Egypt and India). Paul indicated that England's need for grain from the North contradicted the South's belief that England's cotton dependence would lead to an alliance with them. Paul continued to detail the military and economic ties between England and the South and, finally, analyzed the social connections between abolitionists in the North and in England. He built complexity and tension into his explanation. He did not simply list the events of the matter but developed a

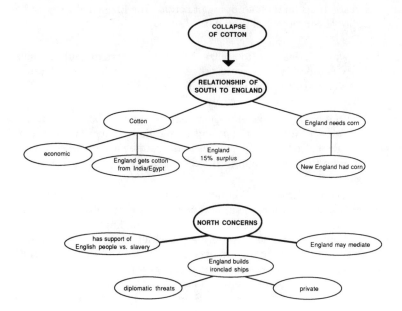

FIG. 7.8. Paul's later explanation: Collapse of King Cotton.

blocked explanation of diplomacy during the Civil War, into which the themes of economic diversity and slavery were woven.

As Fig. 7.8 shows, Paul structured his reply to the query in two parts (eventually he added a third part, not discussed here). His explanation dealt first with the role of the South and England, then with the role of the North and England, and finally, the other diplomatic ties. Paul began his response by backing up to the contextual issue of the South's relationship to England, which was built upon England's presumed need of cotton. He answered an implicit question of why cotton was significant to the South's estimate of support. The South's assumption, according to Paul, was wrong:

Paul: Well, the biggest thing in the South is first of all, they wanted a quick war due to the fact that they thought that England would rush right in and support them in the war against the North due to the fact that they perceive that England needed their cotton so badly that England would have to come in on their part or otherwise they'd cut off their cotton shipments. In fact it also stood to reason that to show them the effect, they actually cut down on cotton production for the first year, the first two years of the war to show the British how much it would mean. Three factors ended up nullifying this though and that was due to the fact that England first of all at the outset of the war had a 15% oversupply of cotton coming from the South so that England and the South put cutbacks on the, for restrictions on their shipping of cotton. The English already had a vast supply of cotton. What they did . . .

T: By the way, uh, leads us to realize that in those days they didn't have economists worldwide who were not . . . you're just in dream land to think that you have this kind of [−] with the English.

Paul: And not only that, we already mentioned English beginning to get their cotton from India and Egypt and in addition we mentioned before that the English also found themselves in desperate need of the corn with corn and grain that was coming from the North.

Paul: The problem with the South was the fact that the South could not really stir up any widespread support at any one given time in England. Although when the cotton burden finally did hit England for a small period of time as I said before these are basically people who are little people, little men who are unemployed [−] [cotton] and they don't have any voice in the government at all and it really didn't make too much of a difference, uh, to the government at hand. Now the biggest thing that the North had to worry about with the South and their cotton was not so much the influence of cotton now, it became two other factors. It became the factor of the British coming in and mediating the dispute between the two which would end up with the South would get recognized as an official state probably. And also second of all the intervention of the English navy of the English ability to build ships. The first of the two as far as mediation was concerned was basically eliminated by the Emancipation Proclamation. After the battle of Antietam originally the English were thinking of coming in and mediating due to the fact that so many lives had been lost and it was basically a bloody struggle, bloody war but once like you said before [−] slavery the aim of abolitioning the war got widespread support from the people of England. Ah, and thus, basically kept the British out of mediation between the two. And like I say had they come into mediation the South probably would have ended up being recognized as a, as a formal state.

T: And that's what the Union [−] said before.

Paul: [−] the Union . . . exactly . . . did not want it all. The Union would much rather of course get them back from secession. And the British have [−] secession would be acknowledged and the [−].

[Sterling, 11/29/88, 1. 1031–1110]

Paul had a substantial command of some parts of an explanation and less of others. He had a solid collection of appropriate facts. He gave causal motivation for the South's position and for the position of England. However, there was a lack of defined scope in the explanation, which left it a bit ragged and unfinished. There was an interesting awkwardness associated with Paul's causal connections between ideas. These connections perform the function of linking strings of ideas together that would otherwise stand in an ambiguous relationship to each other. Paul used the phrase "due to the fact" as his main connective (three times in his first 15 lines of protocol). What the listener (or reader) expected to hear was a premise followed by a fact that supported the premise. Paul did not manage that. Throughout, Paul used "due to the fact," "it stood to reason," and "although" in disconcerting ways. He appeared able in his speech to join lists but not to clearly establish causality. As causal completion is one way of ending an explanation, this absence of causal connection contributed to the lack of a clean end to the statements. What was present was his sense of history and his self-confidence to talk through Sterling. What was emerging was his capacity to use parts of the general language system to support his historical knowledge.

Students like Paul study history not only to learn a specific and detailed corpus of knowledge, but also to learn how to engage in a particular kind of reasoning. The reasoning is primarily inductive, not falling out from first principles. The reasoning requires mastery of complex systems of knowledge and the generation of causally structured cases in response to specific issues. The second example indicates that Paul had begun that process of mastery.

Paul learned to build explanations and to reason by observing the modeled instances in Sterling's class, and by participating in the dialogues of the class. We turn now to examine more systematically how historians think about one type of reasoning, developing a case. Then we turn to the development of a class discussion of a central historical theme as a way of seeing how students other than Paul learn to analyze particular events and structures and how they learn to synthesize relevant information in constructing a case.

REASONING

Historians

Just as we looked to the way historians discuss definitions of history, we turn to examine how they discuss reasoning in history order to lay out a framework for what is meant by reasoning in history. The interviews with practicing historians included discussions of the nature of reasoning in and with history. From coding the interviews, five clusters of ideas emerged in the context of many examples. The clusters were the features of historical thinking and reasoning, not a step-by-step process by which one might construct a case, use it to explain data, and defend it from criticism.[5]

The doing of history implies a *purpose*. One purpose mentioned by historians was that because we as people become and evolve, rather than appear fully formed, history then documents that path. This was stated humorously by one historian as "you are what you eat . . . you are what you were" (Leinhardt, Stainton, & Virji, in press, p. 13). Historians assumed that a historical case existed to help us understand both what was and also what is. For some historians, this understanding was expressed as a notion of honoring the realities of what was, whereas for others, it was a source of finding liberation by recognizing historical communities and fellowship.

All of the historians agreed that the construction of a *compelling narrative* with internal coherence was a major requirement for case construction. The design and development of narrative was not simply a means of conveying a case in a storylike manner but was itself a part of the case. Narrative alone was not sufficient. "Historians actually write

---

[5]This section is drawn from Leinhardt, Stainton, Virji, and Odoroff (in press).

in different modes, and the simplest historians write in a narrative mode, they tell stories. And stories carry an implicit line of argumentation" (Leinhardt, Stainton, & Virji, in press, p. 13). Narrative was seen as encompassing considerably more than a string of interesting chronological tidbits. Narrative skill was a fundamental component in case development, as it was for the historians whose writings were examined. Narrative skill included, in addition to internal coherence, mystery, discovery, evidential exhaustivity, chronology, and causality. The last three of these components are instrumental in the process of transforming narrative into cases.

Historians mentioned *evidential exhaustivity* as a fundamental property of any historical narrative. Exhaustivity meant considering all evidence that could be found to support or to contradict the case. Evidence included written/spoken records, social/cultural artifacts, and even strong inferences about what must have been in place for the surviving piece to have been present. The sense of exhaustivity and narrative together help to form a construct of synthesis. The idea of synthesis as an exhaustive activity as well as a collecting activity is one of the elements that makes historical research quite laborious.

Given large quantities of information, historians used devices to impose organization. One device for organizing information was the establishment of chronology for ordering and framing events. However, chronology was always mentioned in the interviews in an off-handed, almost dismissive manner, as if, "Of course you get that right and then proceed." Another organizing device they mentioned was historical theory of perspective.

Establishing "plausible" causality was another device for organizing information. Historians made the distinction between plausibility that was closely related to narrative coherence and exhaustivity, and lawyerly causality that was rule-bound. (One historian downgraded the value of hypothesis proof; such use is like "devising tests that will confirm or falsify a hypothesis, which is the standard, and most banal, positivistic technique in the social sciences" [Leinhardt, Stainton, Virji, & Odoroff, in press, p. 14]). Uncovering internal causal links within a narrative is one important form of analysis or pulling apart of ideas. A compelling narrative, then, is a weaving of the exhaustive evidence using time and causality as a framework for the story. The selection of the critical questions, the answer to which is the causal narrative, involves the use of theory or hypothesis development.

The use of evidence in a case is more than a listing and yet less structured than a formal, causal, "lawyerlike" case. What is a historical case, then? A case involves building the narrative around a *central hypothesis*. Historians develop hypotheses and support them in their own cases. Hypothesis generation is an outcome of evidential collection and organization; it is also a guide for its collection. Hypotheses are dynamic, having the property of growth and change within a demarcated framework. Further, the theoretical frame one operates within is the filter for interpretation and the means of imposing meaning on the data.

Case construction also required that the evidential list be interpreted in terms of the *context* of the original times, the context of the present time seeking to look at that evidence, and the implications of evidential survival. The survival record was clearly not neutral; victors not only tell the tales but preserve or destroy the evidence. The contextual interpretation of events both past and present formed another basis for analysis as a particular form of historical reasoning.

In Classrooms

Having examined one of Sterling's students as he gained the powers of explanation and reasoning and explored some of the central ideas historians refer to in reasoning, we turn now to two examples of the class as a whole as they acquire some of the tools of reasoning in history. We explore this process in three ways: First, we identify tools used in one form of reasoning—case construction; second, we discuss a central theme used by Sterling around which multiple cases were constructed over several weeks in class; and third, we examine three separate passages from class discussions to see how the group as a whole slowly moved toward more coherent reasoned discussions.

In terms of instructional explanations given to and by students, reasoning emerges from explanations about the metasystems of history and in explanations of the events, structures, and themes in history. Reasoning in history is the process by which central facts (about events and structures) and concepts (themes) are arranged to build interpretive historical cases. Building a case, whether written or spoken, requires analysis, synthesis, hypothesis generation, and contextual interpretation.

Students need to understand the nature of historical ambiguity, follow convergences and diversions, and understand the limitations on perspective that the present imposes upon us. This is what Schama was talking about; such understanding represents mindful engagement with the content. Such thinking requires fluid access to the content and structure of history. Building on the ideas that emerged from our discussions with historians and from our observations of Sterling as she helped her students to produce reasoned cases that made use of analysis and synthesis, we constructed a framework for examining reasoning that focussed on analysis and synthesis.

Analysis of an event or theme in history requires that the *frame* for the event to be clearly established. The subject for an analysis has to be well demarcated. But the frame is arbitrary and amorphous in history—just when does the Revolutionary Period begin or end? What sphere of knowledge encompasses government formation and reformation in the early colonial period? Dates and chronology in general help with this demarcation as far as time is concerned; critical events and people also help for defining scope; and thematic regularity over time helps specify fruitful lines of inquiry into complex historical phenomena. But these frames are critical and ubiquitous; again, Schama played with the time frames described at the beginning of this chapter.

Using the demarcation of an event as a base, an analysis of key forces or moves can be sketched. One way to do this is to systematically inspect aspects of a particular constellation of events from the point of view of the political, social, scientific, and economic conditions prior to, during, and after their occurrence. Focusing on these analytic aspects permits the thinker to step back from and partition the established intellectual space. This partitioning and internal rearrangement of topic space can be considered a form of analysis, a prerequisite to interpretation.

Figure 7.9 schematizes an analysis of a particular event or constellation of events such as the writing of the Constitution, of the Civil War. After specifying what to include or exclude from the scope of that particular event (what might belong in the inner rectangle), the event itself can be analyzed and the topic space rearranged. Strands of issues

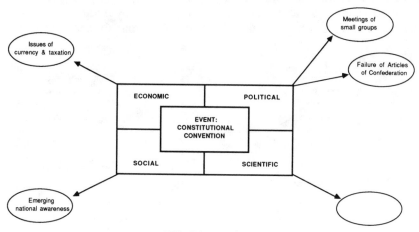

FIG. 7.9. Analysis.

that impacted on and were impacted by the event can be pulled out. Sterling guided students in analyzing the strands of the economic status of the writers of the Constitution, the economic conditions prior to the framing process of the Constitution, and the alteration of those conditions during the period between the Articles of Confederation and the ratification. Later, she had the students analyze economic conditions prior to the Civil War and the alteration of those conditions between the settling of Kansas and the end of Andrew Johnson's presidency. Each of the economic strands could in turn be considered to elaborate a portrait of a time and of currents surrounding notable actions. This kind of analysis, then, takes a whole and pulls apart the issue in order to reveal it.

Synthesis, in contrast to analysis, is a process that forms an idea by weaving together strands from separate sources (Fig. 7.10). This gives form and substance to an event. In their interviews, the historians identified narrative and theory as ways of synthesizing the many elements of a case. In examining the Civil War, Sterling asked students to synthesize governmental compromises across time and events by studying the Three-fifths Compromise, the Missouri Compromise of 1820, and the Compromise of 1850. The examples of compromise could then be contrasted with examples of controversy (such as growing vocalizations around moral issues), which in turn were contrasted with emerging distinctions between economic bases in the North and those in the South. In the discussion, as each of these strands was traced along its chronological path, students came to see that many tensions gave rise to the Civil War, not just one. The firing on Fort Sumter thus became a moment that was indicative of rising tensions, but not a cause or even a start of the Civil War.

Analysis and synthesis were actually used by students as they constructed historical cases in their class discussions. One way of seeing

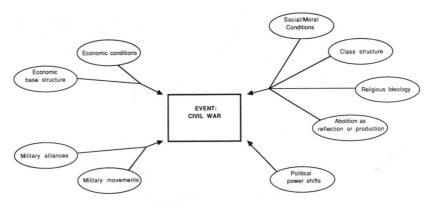

FIG. 7.10. Synthesis.

how students develop these capabilities is to trace a particular case in the context of queries set in classroom discourse. The case, as a form of classroom discourse, is often a hypothesis supported by specific evidence. At first, however, the evidence given in the classroom tended to be little more than a rather compelling list. In learning how to develop a case further, students need to be able to access the kind of detailed information given in readings and formal presentations. Sterling guided the students toward facility at moving between specific evidence and general theories.

Examples of Reasoning

Teaching the period between the Revolution and the Civil War is problematic because many of the changes that occurred during these 100 years had no immediately critical consequences when they occurred. The lack of immediate consequences stemmed in part from the fact that regional expansion acted as a kind of social shock absorber. The emerging interests of the Western pioneers were vastly different from those of the Eastern businessmen, which were, in turn, different from the Southern plantation owners. The manifestations of these differences were not immediately obvious to history students, even though the differences had laid seeds for problems and tensions that would be highly salient later in the course. Until the Civil War, people with dramatically different interests were generally located in separated geographical spaces.

In teaching this segment, Sterling drew upon a number of themes: the role of political compromise, the changing composition of the electorate, the function and symbolism of the elastic clause in the Constitution. The discussion of the themes started well before the discourse on the Revolutionary period and extended into the modern period. One tension that pervaded the discussion of this period was agrarian expansionist interests versus commercial, international trade interests. The thematic tension formed a loosely connected set of ideas that were referred to in class over several weeks as the discussion developed.

Figure 7.11 shows the net representation of the thematic tension between agrarian and mercantile concerns. On the left, the concept node *agrarian* has many attributes: Jefferson, the South, minimalist government or states' rights (which in turn relates to anti-Federalist), Western expansionism, slave holding, and Jeffersonian/Jacksonian democracy. The concept node *mercantile* is connected to commerce, international trade, federalism, Hamilton, and the North.

Each of the nodal concepts was addressed by extended minicases and narratives. These cases were flagged throughout the first 4 months of instruction that covered the 100-year span of history. They became

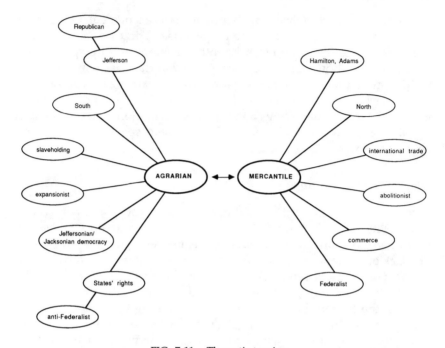

FIG. 7.11. Thematic tension.

familiar exemplars for the teacher to use to bring the students to see particular positions, and they provided a set of concepts that empowered students as reasoners and constructors of history. The power came from the fact that as soon as students identified one part of the net, they had rapid access to the rest of it. Sterling revealed the complexity and "messiness" of history while providing students with the tools to handle that complexity. Sterling moved her students carefully beyond historical narrative into analytic abstractions for understanding history.

To demonstrate this movement toward constructing understanding, in this section we examine a second kind of episode that is revealed through selections of lines of dialogue extracted from three separate lessons. It is important to see how the recurring themes develop from early October to mid-November and to notice the teacher's modeling and students' eventual, if primitive, construction of a dialogue that would lead to jointly designed reasoning efforts. This first selection from October has been divided into lettered segments for ease of discussion, as shown in Fig. 7.12.[6]

The quotes in Fig. 7.12 are from a lesson on the Constitutional

---

[6]The stars between the segments of dialogue indicate breaks.

Convention. In the Segment marked A, Sterling posed questions and sought short answers to develop the agrarian/mercantile themes. At this point in the year students were still slow to risk talking and trying out ideas. The richness of this segment was in the questions asked, not in the answers sought or provided. Students in October were still grappling with the issue of, what is a question in history? The first question sought the distinction between regional and national; the second sought the distinction between local and federal. Each answer was followed by the traditional teacher elaboration. The elaboration on the location of sovereignty extended the students' comments and modeled a more elaborate answer. As usual, the answer led into another question (B): Sterling asked students to elaborate by giving evidence and extending the answer. "Who thinks like this?" As soon as Jefferson was mentioned, Sterling worked the other side of the tension and simultaneously extended the set to include Adams, Washington, and Franklin. These were not just "names"; they were symbols for positions.

A superficial inspection could lead one to conclude that this was a "traditional" teacher-led segment. Had the rest of the lessons looked the same as this, then it might well be argued that students were "learning" to be quiet and get the facts from their elders or to spit them out on command. However, a complex piece of weaving was going on. Sterling was both identifying and elaborating the scene at the Convention—who the players were, what their backgrounds were—and building the subdivisions of interpretations that she would need later in the lesson.

In Segment C, Sterling re-asked a prior question. How is it that all these men with different viewpoints have agreed to come together? What galvanizes them into action? The instructional move was strategic. Sterling could have focused on the divisiveness of the Convention, but then the reason for the Convention's existence would be hard to fathom. In this segment, we see the student's elaboration on the importance of Shays' rebellion for the development of national leadership. Building from that elaboration, Sterling led into another set of questions (Segment D): What do the 55 delegates at the Convention agree on? What do they disagree on? The dialogue produced a workable list, a list that was the beginning of the reasoning about an event. It was also a rhetorical model of what questions would look like and a disciplinary scaffold for what features answers would require.

In Segment D, Sterling elicited from the students the ideas that the framers agreed on a republican form of government, with power residing with the people, and the need for central, as opposed to more dispersed, government. The list of agreements acted as an obvious dialogue prompt for the list of disagreements. Students provided explicit information about one of the disagreements—who was against whom.

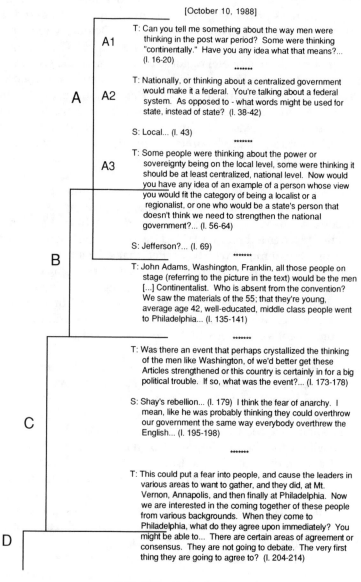

[October 10, 1988]

A1   T: Can you tell me something about the way men were thinking in the post war period? Some were thinking "continentally." Have you any idea what that means?... (l. 16-20)

****

A2   T: Nationally, or thinking about a centralized government would make it a federal. You're talking about a federal system. As opposed to - what words might be used for state, instead of state? (l. 38-42)

S: Local... (l. 43)

****

A3   T: Some people were thinking about the power or sovereignty being on the local level, some were thinking it should be at least centralized, national level. Now would you have any idea of an example of a person whose view you would fit the category of being a localist or a regionalist, or one who would be a state's person that doesn't think we need to strengthen the national government?... (l. 56-64)

S: Jefferson?... (l. 69)

****

T: John Adams, Washington, Franklin, all those people on stage (referring to the picture in the text) would be the men [...] Continentalist. Who is absent from the convention? We saw the materials of the 55; that they're young, average age 42, well-educated, middle class people went to Philadelphia... (l. 135-141)

****

T: Was there an event that perhaps crystallized the thinking of the men like Washington, of we'd better get these Articles strengthened or this country is certainly in for a big political trouble. If so, what was the event?... (l. 173-178)

S: Shay's rebellion... (l. 179) I think the fear of anarchy. I mean, like he was probably thinking they could overthrow our government the same way everybody overthrew the English... (l. 195-198)

****

T: This could put a fear into people, and cause the leaders in various areas to want to gather, and they did, at Mt. Vernon, Annapolis, and then finally at Philadelphia. Now we are interested in the coming together of these people from various backgrounds. When they come to Philadelphia, what do they agree upon immediately? You might be able to... There are certain areas of agreement or consensus. They are not going to debate. The very first thing they are going to agree to? (l. 204-214)

A, B, C, D

FIG. 7.12. First selection.

S: A representative government... (l. 215)

T: What is the name of a representative government that they all agreed upon? (l. 216)

S: A Republic... (l. 227)

D1

T: All agreed on popular sovereignty. Power rests with people, not with the state, in context with the states' rights. Something else they all agreed upon? (l. 246-250)

S: They believe in the power of central government to enforce laws... (l. 251-252)

D2

T: Okay, all agreed that the Articles of Confederation were to be strengthened, that they are too weak, and they need a more centralized federal system... (l. 253-255) [Teacher then reviews power structure within the 55 and need for secrecy and compromises.] As you look at the issues, you see the 4 issues of areas of disagreement. [1] How congress should be organized, [2] how congress ought to be regulated, and [3] how slaves are to be represented, and [4] how presidents are to be elected... (l. 417-421) What were the opposing interest? (l. 430-431)

S: Large states or small states... (l. 432)

D

S: State or federal tax or tariffs...(l. 440)

T: How about [...] group of people by occupation. Not by the interest. (l. 442-443)

S: Wealthy and wealthier... (l. 444)

T: Break it down [...] wealthy and less wealthy; anything else? (l. 445-446)

S: Vendors and merchants versus farmers... (l. 447)

T: Farmers, agrarian or farmers merchants commercial that would include your bankers... (l. 458-459) How about the third opposing interest group here at the convention. People have different opinions?... (l. 463-465)

S: North versus South... (l. 467)

T: How shall the congress be organized?... (l. 487) All right, the Great Compromise. Now sometimes you'll see this by the name of the man from Connecticut who hammered out the final compromise. It didn't come as easily as many were writing that day. Because there were two interest groups [...], the big states and the small versus... (l. 498-504) But it was a great compromise for the Connecticut compromise. And this came as the result of the two plans. Now how did it take place?... (l. 508-511) [Answers are generated correctly. Teacher goes on to interstate commerce.]

FIG. 7.12. *(Continued)*

The class constructed an aside together—a short essay—on the background of the Constitutional Convention. The activity was shared but directed; precise terms were used, meanings were attached to them, and complex ideas were elaborated and exemplified. At this point in the lesson, students were in a position to demonstrate both the facts and spirit of the great compromises that were made by a rather select set of young men in developing the Constitution.

By the end of the lesson, the elements of the tensions had been sketched. What was especially important about this segment was that the information established would be the basis for extending the students' reasoning as they worked on subsequent material. The episode did not close or end; it became a basis for further work. The agrarian and mercantile themes, once developed with names, regional distinctions, and political envisioning, would be repeatedly accessed.

A continuation of this theme occurred 2 weeks after the first and dealt with the emergence of a new political alignment and the political parties that reflected it (Fig. 7.13). Jacksonian democracy was presented as an elaboration and realignment of Jeffersonian positions. The class was laying further groundwork for understanding the Civil War. The discussion was threefold: to discuss Jacksonian democracy, to elaborate thematic tensions leading to the Civil War, and to learn how to analyze and synthesize historical events and structures. Sterling started by asking for a recounting of what happened in the 1824 election with its multiple candidates. In Segment A of the second October selection, a student provided a fairly elaborate answer. The student also cut off and talked over the teacher, in marked contrast to the talking patterns of the early lessons, which were characterized by lengthy teacher segments punctuated by single words or phrases from the students. Not only were the specifics easily available to sketch the event, but also there was a richness of detail.

In Segment B, notice again the student's first and then second extended answer in response to Sterling's request for discussion on the nature of the changes emerging within the executive branch at that time. In Section C we see a student reasoning, indirectly contrasting Jackson to Adams and tying the position of the Indian negotiations back to the tensions between the agrarian Jeffersonians and the mercantile federalist position of John Adams. The dialogue cast a broad net to pull in a wide array of materials and synthesized them into a discussion, if not quite a case. In reading these dialogues, it is important to remember that they are spoken rapidly, not in elegant, developed ways. Nevertheless, the selections show the students' emerging competencies in building a coherent case.

In the third selection (Fig. 7.14), taken from a lesson in mid-

A

T: Maybe we learned a very, very valuable lesson about having too many candidates in a campaign at this point?... (l. 101-103)

S: Well, [assuming] the candidates running remembering the Constitution, ahh, the person named as the president and the second person, the vice president, both those people have to maintain majorities at the electoral level. And what happened with this election was Andrew Jackson won, or... (l. 111-117)

T: Yes, yes. (l. 118)

S: ...won the votes, the most votes, electoral votes, however, no candidate received a majority and thus it just [pushed] the House of Representatives where they debated between the top three. And the top three were Crawford, Adams and Jackson... (l. 119-124) Henry Clay and what happening was Henry Clay transferred after consulting with Jackson and later with Adams; Clay found Adams more to his liking because Adams favored the American system a little bit more than Jackson. Jackson despised it. And what had happened was they gave them the electoral votes - the support he needed in the House of Representatives to win the election of 1824 ... and this would later bring about Adam's demise in the election of 1828... (l. 130-140)

B

T: But how about the role now of the executive? How is it changing? (l. 317-318)

S: The role [--]. They don't have as much power, they don't have as much prestige. It wasn't like Washington's. (l. 319-321)

T: How, how do the roles differ though? [--] get down right to the basics, not to how the [--] are? (l. 322-323)

S: I'm going to try to generalize this way. Ahh, in the 1700's while the country was forming its government and establishing itself as a, as a power to be dealt with so to speak, it was more or less a president leading the people, the president the leader and the people the followers. Any more with the factions and Congress and the beginning of sectionalism in the country, it is more or less the social sweeps in the country are leading the President and finally the [President --]... (l. 324-334)

C

S: He was, he was, he was completely against the Indians. He was in favor of settling in western lands for a cheaper rate, not selling the land for the profit for the federal government but just to sell them for people moving into the western lands. That was definitely a the fact in, back when John Quincy Adams mentioned that Adams wanted to negotiate, renegotiate a treaty between Georgia and the Creek Indians and Jackson chastised him for that. Jackson by no means supported the Indians... (l. 607-618)

FIG. 7.13. Second selection.

[November 15, 1988]

S: Well, I said economic sectionalism because, um, I, I feel that it was really lack of understanding by each, the different sections as to how important slaves were and weren't at the time. In the North slavery [--] wasn't morally acceptable. The South at that time couldn't survive without slaves. So I, I don't feel that, uh, that [--] economic sectionalism really was the dividing factor. There's sort of a lack of understanding... (l. 583-593)

S: Well I put economic sectionalism [--] Well I put it [is that] because the, uh, the Southerners depended on the slaves. And I think because they were so caught up in their slave ways that they didn't adapt to the new, the new ways of the North and the new economic will, will isolate the Industrials from the North. And in the way this causes the South to depend on the North for lots of goods... (l. 598-606)

A

S: Because that, because the South depended, they depended on the North because the North is growing and had all the new railroads and all the new [--]. The South depended on the North and it created lots of problems... (l. 617-622)

S: I did [--], except that, you know, [--] Civil War, it would have been avoided. But, uh [gee, I point back]. To go a step further back in that, in then, derivation of that, I don't think that uh, there would have been that digression had there been not so much sectionalism. And that falls under the category of state sovereignty and uh, economic sectionalism. (l. 1058-1065)

FIG. 7.14.   Third selection.

November, the class was devoted to a discussion of the underlying causes of the Civil War. The task was for each student to select from among six primary positions as the "explanation" for the cause of the Civil War; they then had to defend their choices in class. We examined a portion of the classroom discourse in which several students elaborated on economic sectionalism as an underlying cause of the Civil War. The statements by the students showed them moving toward a more complex case construction. These dialogues began to weave a web of causes by taking economic sectionalism "back to state sovereignty." In other comments during this class, students revisited ideas that they had developed earlier, such as other tensions between agrarian and commercial interests.

As these vignettes show, in each of the lessons the knowledge base grew and became more interconnected. The knowledge base grew from the discussions as well as from the very enriched and extensive reading in texts and source materials that the students were engaged in. They were learning to build up more elaborate and intricate explanations and supports for hypotheses formed around events and conditions. As the semester progressed, the teacher turned more and more of the class time and action over to the students' control (Leinhardt, 1993b).

In these lessons, there were, then, some thoughtful, reasoned discussions. But some of the critical elements of case building that we have found from our discussions with historians were missing. The most notable was interpretive layering. Although two class days during this time period were devoted to contrasting different historians (Hofstadter, Schlesinger, and Beard) and different perspectives (those of people in western Pennsylvania, the South, and New England), these appeared as separated topics rather than as integral parts of the discussion of tensions leading up to the Civil War.

CONCLUSIONS

We defined history as

> a process of constructing, reconstructing, and interpreting past events, ideas, and institutions from surviving or inferential evidence in order to understand and make meaningful who and what we are today. The process involves dialogues with alternative voices from the past itself, with the recorders of the past, and with present interpreters. The process also involves constructing coherent, powerful narratives that describe and interpret the events, as well as, skillful analyses of quantitative and qualitative information, from a theoretical perspective. (Leinhardt, Stainton, & Virji, in press, p. 18)

We also share the stance of Schwab (1978) and Collingwood (1946) that the teaching and learning of history are situated in the particular social system and its dialogues, and in the particular disciplinary system and its construction. Thus, throughout this chapter, we have chronicled the nature of mindful dialogue and the process of meaningful construction in the practice of students, teachers, and historians.

We defined history, in part, as a dialogue between the past, the alternate voices of the past, and recorders of the present. To come to understand history as dialogue, students must engage in historical dialogue that is not aimless rambling, but that is focused through explanations and cases. Students familiar with conversation have to be taught historical dialogue. A meaningful dialogue requires the speakers to be both subject and socially appropriate. Far more difficult than understanding who may speak when are the rules for historical dialogue; these require an understanding of what is worth talking about, and exactly how that talking will proceed. As dialogue is both dynamic and social, so too are the rules and roles that support it. These were carefully negotiated at the beginning of the year, and changed over the course of it. There are indicators that the formal rules and roles facilitated this learning.

As the year progressed, students in our teachers' classes were coached in the uncovering of varied historical perspectives and interpretations. The coaching was done, in part, through the use of multiple documents describing a single event, thematic discussion of opposing perspectives, and the study of varied historical traditions. Students increased their ability to identify the varied voices in an historical dialogue and eventually developed interpretations of their own. As shown in the instances of shared explanation in Sterling's class of the mercantile/agrarian theme, students built narratives and cases and linked them together. All three aspects of dialogue were present: merchants and agriculturists as voices of the past, varied sources as recorders of the past, and the students themselves as interpreters in the present. The students came to dominate the dialogue with extended arguments for their own historical perspective or interpretation. Whereas in the beginning of the year the dialogue was structured and the voices surface name taking, by the end of the year, the dialogues were dynamic and the voices subtly reasoned.

These dialogues are more than exercises in role playing. They are intended to help the student learn to reason about and with history. The dialogues both model and contain aspects of the discipline itself. For the historians, any dialogue between points of view or interpretations required reasoning about change, an activity central to historical understanding. Furthermore, that dialogue is to be, in Mallon's words, both "principled and humanistic." These criteria mirror our stance that history learning and teaching (of which dialogue is a part) is situated both in the particular social system and in the particular disciplinary system. Just talking because students find it engaging, without attention to a query, is as faulty as the endless analysis of an arcane query of no social significance. This tension is not unique to the teaching/learning of history. Historians also experience this tension in the doing of history because history is a discipline both in the social sciences and in the humanities.

We also defined history not only as dialogue, but also as construction, reconstruction, and interpretation. History involves the construction of "past events, ideas, and institutions in order to understand and make meaningful who and what we are today" as well as creating "coherent, powerful narratives that describe and interpret the events, as well as skillful analyses of quantitative and qualitative information from a theoretical perspective." In these classrooms, we saw students constructing meaning of historical events, structures, and themes to learn. This is more than mere semantics: Students must learn hypothesis generation, analysis, and synthesis in order to construct viable historical cases; but it is also true that reasoning emerges from constructing cases.

Mindfulness in teaching and learning is an important goal of education in the United States. It should be the goal of history education as well. However, the movement to teach more than rote memorization to everyone, not just the elite, is a relatively new concept, dating from around 1900, when educators turned their attention from the goals of teaching basic facts to goals of reasoning with facts. Mindfulness suggests reasoning in a thoughtful way about something. It suggests, in the case of history, reasoning with more than an assortment of techniques or just the facts.

Our program of research is in part aimed at helping to make mindfulness integral to history teaching. The investigations first shift the location of mindlessness (or mindfulness) from the subject matter that is learned to the minds of the students and teachers involved in the learning/teaching process. Specifically, mindfulness is present when students and teachers engage deeply in what is being learned and what is being taught. Second, this research differentiates between teaching content, and modeling, enacting, and demonstrating use of content. For example, there is a difference between the student's one-word factual answer, "Jefferson," and the discussion of causes of the Civil War in a later lesson. Finally, there is the difference between simple stories and the intricate, ambiguous ones of history. A simple story about the Civil War might hold that differences over slavery and the firing on Fort Sumter started the Civil War; a more complex story includes social, political, and economic tensions that can be traced back to the Revolutionary Period. Students who have been guided through analysis, synthesis, and construction of cases are mindful; they understand the differences between learning content and learning to reason with content and to construct rich, intricate cases. They learn to construct a historical stance that is evolutionary rather than absolute.

Mindfulness requires that we reconsider how we think students learn to think about history. We need to challenge ourselves and see that students do not need to learn the facts first and then start to do the interesting "good stuff." As Mallon said when discussing these issues, "A crucial part of pedagogy is not to hide what's inside. Not to cloak it, and pretend, and give them only the outside, but to show them, allow them a view all the way in. Even if it's only partial" (Leinhardt, Stainton, Virji, & Odoroff, in press, p. 26). Students certainly can begin the process of reasoning in history from the beginning.

We think that students who have engaged in an experience such as the elaborated explanations and case constructions described here will have a mindful response to dates such as 1776 and 1865, not a mindless response based on rote memorization. The elaborated meaning of the Civil War, which included the sense of tension between agrarian and commercial interests, was used by Sterling as a cohesive force that bound the students' understanding of the issues of Reconstruction after the Civil War to the issues that were first visible in Philadelphia during the Constitutional Convention.

History is a discipline that is framed by chronology and geography but it is not constrained or limited by them. It is not a collection of reminiscences or anecdotal chit-chat any more than it is a list of vacuous dates. Thinking in history means being literate within these frames and being capable of analysis, synthesis, and case building. To achieve these goals, students need to have both opportunities to reason in history and guidance from history teachers who are able to think flexibly, dynamically, and powerfully within their discipline.

In our work we have described the roles of teacher as coach and artistic director, and the metasystems for historical reasoning. We discussed how an explanation is first modeled by the teacher, then shared, then constructed by students, and we discussed what historical occasions warrant explanation. Most importantly, we pushed to examine points of interaction between the varied features of the social and disciplinary systems. We analyzed how the teacher roles support the development of the metasystem skills, and why certain historical occasions are more difficult than others for the student to explain alone.

Successful teaching and learning in a history classroom requires both teacher and students to balance and integrate social and disciplinary goals, attending to the constraints of both systems. A thoughtful analysis of what does go on in the history classroom, much less any prescription about what ought to go on there, must do the same. For its teachers, students, and researchers, history is a time to be mindful.

ACKNOWLEDGMENTS

The research reported in this chapter was supported by a grant from the Office of Educational Research and Improvement (OERI), United States Department of Education, to the Center for Study of Learning, Learning Research and Development Center. The opinions expressed do not necessarily reflect the position or policy of OERI, and no official endorsement should be inferred. The author would like to thank the teachers and students who participated in these studies; Joan Amory, Judith McQuaide, and Elizabeth Odoroff for invaluable assistance in data collection; the transcription staff; and Kathleen McCarthy for her insightful responses to drafts.

REFERENCES

Brown, A. (1992, April). *The cognitive basis of school restructuring*. Paper presented at the annual meeting of the American Educational Research Association, San Francisco.

Collingwood, R. G. (1946). *The idea of history*. London: Oxford University Press.

Gentner, D., & Gentner, D. R. (1983). Flowing waters or teeming crowds: Mental models of electricity. In D. Gentner & A. L. Stevens (Eds.), *Mental models* (pp. 99–130). Hillsdale, NJ: Lawrence Erlbaum Associates.

Leinhardt, G. (1990). *Towards understanding instructional explanations* (Tech. Rep. No. CLIP-90-03). Pittsburgh: University of Pittsburgh, Learning Research and Development Center.

Leinhardt, G. (1993a, January). *Two texts, three readers: Issues of distance and expertise*. Paper presented at the Fourth Annual Winter Text Conference, Jackson Hole, WY.

Leinhardt, G. (1993b). Weaving instructional explanations in history. *British Journal of Educational Psychology, 63*, 46–74.

Leinhardt, G., Stainton, C., & Virji, S. M. (in press). A sense of history. *Educational Psychologist*.

Leinhardt, G., Stainton, C., Virji, S. M., & Odoroff, E. (in press). Learning to reason in history: Mindlessness to mindfulness. In J. Voss (Ed.), *Cognitive and instructional processes in history and the social sciences*. Hillsdale, NJ: Lawrence Erlbaum Associates.

McCarthy, K., & Leinhardt, G. (1993, April). *Wildflowers, sheep, and democracy: The role of analogy in the teaching of history*. Paper presented at the annual meeting of the American Educational Research Association, Atlanta, GA.

Perry, M., Davis, D. F., Harris, J. G., von Laue, T., & Warren, D., Jr. (1985). *History of the world*. Boston: Houghton Mifflin.

Schama, S. (1989). *Citizens: A chronicle of the French Revolution*. New York: Knopf.

Schama, S. (1991, September 8). Clio has a problem. *New York Times Magazine*, pp. 29–33.

Schwab, J. J. (1978). Education and the structure of the disciplines. In I. Westbury & N. J. Wilkof (Eds.), *Science, curriculum, and liberal education* (pp. 229–272). Chicago: University of Chicago Press.

Spiro, R. J., Feltovich, P. J., Coulson, R. L., & Anderson, D. K. (1989). Multiple analogies for complex concepts: Antidotes for analogy-induced misconception in advanced knowledge acquisition. In S. Vosniadou & A. Ortony (Eds.), *Similarity and analogical reasoning* (pp. 498–531). New York: Cambridge University Press.

Stainton, C., & Leinhardt, G. (1992, April). *On a role: Beginning and ending the year in history* (Tech. Rep. No. CLIP-92-05). Pittsburgh, PA: University of Pittsburgh, Learning Research and Development Center. Paper presented at the annual meeting of the American Educational Research Association, San Francisco.

Van Fraassen, B. C. (1988). The pragmatic theory of explanation. In J. C. Pitt (Ed.), *Theories of explanation* (pp. 136–155). New York: Oxford University Press.

Author Index

Note: Page numbers in *italics* denote complete bibliographical references.

Subject Index

A

Active processing (*see also* Engagement), 15, 18, 22
Advanced Placement exams, 219
Alternative frameworks, 27–30, 36, 41–42
  at a metalevel, 43
Analogy, 230–233
Argument
  arguments, 72
  evidence, 72, 138
  evaluating, 143–148
  global, 72, 74–75, 77–79, 82
  local, 73, 80, 82
  model, 48, 49, 71–72, 81–82
  multiple sources, 82
Audience, 156–157
Authority, 147–148
  appeals to, 167, 162–164
  citations, 162
  rhetorical moves, 147, 163
Authorship, 138
  individual contribution, 152, 155, 166

B

Background knowledge (*see also* Prior knowledge), 4

C

Causality
  causal sequence, 10
Causal-temporal model, 47–50, 51–52, 55–57, 60, 71, 73
  core/noncore information, 67–68, 70
  supporting information, 69
Classroom, 28, 29, 218, 240, 250, 252
  beginning of the year, 219, 221, 252
Classroom conversation (*see also* Discourse), 28, 31
Cognitive
  processing and structure, 34, 86
  representation (*see also* interpretation of task), 89–90, 127
    of event, 92, 98–102, 109–111, 113
    of subtext, 92, 118
    of text, 87, 89, 92–94
  theory and research, 2, 44
Coherence, 5, 11, 15, 18
  of recall, 9
  of text, 3, 10, 14–15, 17–18
Conception, 29
  of cause, 33, 36
  of history, 35, 36, 38
  naive, 27